From Holes In My Hose To Rocks In My Socks

A Memoir

DOROTHY STILLMAN

Library of Congress Control Number: 2007905991
ISBN: Hardcover   978-1-4257-6843-0
                   Softcover   978-1-4257-6827-0

This book was printed in the United States of America.

To order additional copies of this book, contact:
Xlibris Corporation
1-888-795-4274
www.Xlibris.com
Orders@Xlibris.com
36390

Acknowledgements

This book was written because Ann and Bunny kept pressuring me about it until I really had no choice. They insisted that my life was at the very least unusual, not to say "far out", that my children, grandchildren and great grandchildren would enjoy reading about it, and would love the adventures of Gramma Dot and Aunt Pete.

Bunny suggested the title. I sent her the rough manuscript and her friend, Janice Gale, an author, edited it and gave me many helpful suggestions. Another of Bunny's friends, Hanora Bishop, typed it and put it on a computer. Ann and Bunny selected most of the pictures. Dick had the first edition of the book published. All I did was write it, which was the easy part!

The poems from "Seeds" were written by my friend Marguerite "Pete" Williams.

I wish to express my thanks and appreciation to all for the help and encouragement they gave me.

(This second edition was re-edited by Ann and Bunny and published by Xlibris Press in 2007)

SEEDS

DOROTHY'S MUSIC
by Marguerite "Pete" Williams

It is music that the world will never hear
A secret thing that's softly played alone.
I drop a halting, hesitating tear
For one who never had the chance to
    make it known.

It's the muted sound of birds, the hum of bees.
It calms the spirit's struggle, stress and strife.
It's Dorothy's gentle touch upon the keys,
And belies the stress and struggle of her life.

Chapter 1

"I'm fixin' to butcher the hogs today so I'd better get at it," Papa said, as he finished his coffee and pushed his chair back from the big kitchen table. "I'll need both tubs filled with hot water, Alice", he told Mama, as he went out the back door and strode off toward the pigpens. This was my signal to disappear, as I always did on hog-killing days, because I could not bear to be within sight or sound of the activities. I continued to sit at the table, pretending to finish my breakfast, until Mama had gone into the backyard to build fires for the tubs of water. When Grandma and the other five children left, I made a sandwich, grabbed an apple and a book and took off through the cornfield where I was hidden from view. Then I crossed the little creek on stepping-stones and climbed to the top of the hill back of the farm and sat under a tree reading till late afternoon, when I knew it was all over and it would be safe to go home.

As usual, I apparently had not been missed. Mama did not glare at me and ask, "Dorothy, where have you been all day?" Perhaps she had known all along and had no objection; to her it would have meant only one child less to cope with on a busy day. No doubt the other children knew what I was doing, but they never mentioned it, not even to me. They had learned the hard way to speak to Mama only when absolutely necessary.

When I was born in Shawnee in 1907 Oklahoma had not yet become a state; it was still Indian Territory. There were no large cities, only small towns connected to each other by dirt roads, and even the small towns were few and far between. Automobiles were unheard of, at least in that area. When people needed to travel they hitched the horse to the buggy, the women tied protective scarves over their heads, stored box lunches under the seats and off they went, amid clouds of dust.

My father, Oliver Ramsey, was from Indiana and my mother, Alice Clark, was born in Michigan. How they happened to meet and why they settled in Oklahoma none of us ever knew, for conversation in our family was limited mainly to reprimands and Bible reading. Papa was twenty years older than Mama and had been married twice before. Both wives had died, leaving him with eleven children; most of whom had grown up and left home by the time I came along. Mama bore eleven children also, so it could truthfully be said that Papa did more than his share toward furthering the population explosion.

When I was a year old we moved to a farm on the outskirts of a little village called Keifer. At that time I had two sisters, Vera and Orva, aged nine and three. Two children had died in infancy. About a year later Morris was born, then the twins, Pansy and Pearl arrived and finally the triplets, two boys and a girl who were stillborn.

Sisters: Orva, Vera, Dorothy (Circa 1912)

There was no birth control then. Babies came along like clockwork roughly every two years and there was nothing a woman could do about it. Most families had eight to ten children. In those days women actually were kept, if not barefoot, pregnant most of the time.

Kiefer was a typical turn of the century small town. Scattered along the unpaved main street there was a livery stable, a lumberyard, a blacksmith shop, two saloons, one small cafe, the Post Office and the Sheriffs office, which contained two seldom used jail cells. There was also a drugstore that sold only drugs and a general store that sold everything else—meat, groceries, notions and yard goods, clothing, furniture, hardware and farm implements. In front of each place of business was the usual hitching post.

The largest building in town was the two-story brick schoolhouse, attended by children of all grades from the first to twelfth. Adjoining the school was a large vacant lot where we often played baseball on summer evenings. Although I was only a girl, I was sometimes allowed to play because I was a good batter and could outrun most of the boys.

There were two regular churches in Kiefer, the Baptist and the First Christian, which we attended. There was also a group of worshipers who held meetings in a dilapidated storefront building. They must have thought God was a bit hard of hearing because their praying could be heard on the next street. They shouted, spoke in tongues and rolled on the floor in religious ecstasy. Sometimes, in their exuberance, they ran outside and rolled on the ground. I don't remember the proper name of this sect but we called them "Holy Rollers" and they were looked down upon by the more sedate churchgoers.

At the far end of Main Street was the depot, where every afternoon a train came chugging in on the single track, belching smoke and steam and frightening the cows and horses in the adjacent fields. There was a baggage car carrying mail sacks, plus crates and boxes containing supplies for the local merchants. There was one passenger car carrying an occasional passenger, and a caboose.

A sign on the side of the depot proclaimed, "NIGGER, DON'T LET THE SUN GO DOWN ON YOUR HEAD." In those days, Oklahoma was a hotbed of prejudice. Negroes were not allowed to live in Kiefer and I never saw a black person until I was in my teens. I grew up believing they were strange creatures about half way between human and animal.

For several years Papa was Postmaster in Kiefer. Then he lost that job, no doubt for political reasons, because at that time Postmasters came and went depending on who got to be President. He then became Sheriff and was thereafter known as Hawk Shaw because of his startling resemblance to a character in a comic strip called, "Hawk Shaw, the Detective." Papa was thin and quite tall, well over six feet. He had a long bony face, a high forehead and prominent chin. He wore a long droopy red mustache that tended to distract attention from his somewhat thinning red hair. In his cowboy shirt and boots, wearing a gun that I doubt he ever had occasion to use, he was the typical western lawman.

He had one deputy, a young man named Hank, and together they kept the peace, which was seldom broken except on those rare occasions when someone drank too much, started a fist fight and was put in jail overnight to sober up. There was no crime in Kiefer. Doors were seldom locked, except on Halloween, when boys raced through town writing on windows with soap, uprooting picket fences and overturning privies. Some of the privies were deposited in front yards, others hoisted to the roofs of buildings. And since there was no stealing or bloodletting, Papa, unable to cope with the situation in any case, took a somewhat philosophical view, "Boys will be boys," he said. "They're only doing what boys are supposed to do on Halloween."

The greatest source of aggravation for Papa was an automobile. It was the only one in town and it belonged to a young man who painted it bright red. He drove it around town at the blistering speed of twenty miles an hour. The 10 miles per hour speed limit signs that Papa put up just for his benefit were blithely ignored. In Papa's estimation anyone who went faster than that had to be crazy. "One of these day," he swore, "I'm going to catch that red devil and throw him in jail for speeding." Papa never did catch the red devil; his horse wasn't fast enough.

In looking back on my childhood I have always regretted that I never got acquainted with Papa. I don't remember ever talking to him, and the only close contact I had with him was once when I was four or five years old and he carried me on his shoulders while we watched a parade. He was seldom home and when he was there he was usually out in the fields plowing or planting. He spent the evenings downtown, probably discussing politics while having a beer and smoking his pipe. Mama wouldn't allow him to smoke his pipe in the house as she considered it not only smelly but downright sinful.

Chapter 2

Our house was shaped like an inverted L, with a wide front porch running along both sides. There was a long swing seat suspended from the porch roof by heavy chains and flanked by two rocking chairs. The usual picket fence separated the big front yard from the public road. Eventually, that dirt road was paved with some sort of blacktop that tended to turn a bit soft on hot summer days.

The living room, or front room as it was called, was furnished with a dark green over-stuffed couch, two rocking chairs and a pot-bellied stove. A rug patterned with pink flowers covered the floor, except for a two-foot border of varnished wood, and green vines. Under one of the windows was a long narrow table on which reposed the family Bible. This book was never opened except to record marriages, births and deaths, and we children were not permitted to touch it, lest we do it some damage.

A door, which was always kept closed except at Christmas or when we had company, led into the dining room where there was a large oblong dining table and a sideboard in which the "good" dishes and silverware were kept. In one corner there was an old pump organ, which must have been given to us since no one in the family knew how to play. When I was about eight years old I became fascinated with it and spent hours learning to play by ear most of the religious hymns, the only music I had ever heard.

The kitchen was the largest and most lived in room in the house. A huge wood stove with a reservoir on one side for heating water occupied at least half of one wall. Next to it was a worktable, and on the opposite side of the room was a kitchen cabinet with a built-in flour sifter and drawers for silverware. Shelves above and below held dishes and pots and pans. Since there was no running water, there was no sink. Used water was carried outside and dumped into a downhill ditch, dug for that purpose. In the center of the kitchen was a round table surrounded by nine chairs. There we ate all our meals, except on Sunday when we honored God's Holy Day by having dinner in the dining room.

We had four bedrooms—one for Papa and Mama, a tiny room for Morris, the only boy, and a large one with two double beds that was shared by us five girls with two in one bed and three in the other. The fourth bedroom was occupied by our maternal grandmother. She was a tall, thin, grim-faced old lady who seldom spoke to us and whose room was strictly off-limits. We never knew her first name. All of us were grown up and married before we learned that our grandfather, Mama's father, was descended from William Clark of the Lewis and Clark expedition. Grandmother Clark lived with us for several years until one day she was killed by a train at the railroad crossing. Vera, being the oldest child, inherited her room.

Mama did not at all resemble Grandmother Clark. Mama was of medium height, and although she was not actually fat, she did tend to be somewhat overweight. Yet she wasn't bad looking and was friendly and outgoing without a trace of self-consciousness. She was President of the Ladies Aid Society, helped organize bazaars and cake sales at the church, and taught a Sunday school class. She was very popular and everyone seemed to like her—except her children.

We were afraid of Mama, not physically for she never abused us in that way, but mentally which was much worse. We learned to "walk on eggshells" to avoid incurring her wrath, but no matter how careful we were she was usually mad at one of us. Instead of spanking or scolding, she would silently impale the current culprit with a baleful, spine-chilling glare. For several days thereafter that child would be treated as a "non-person", receiving from Mama only an occasional nerve-shattering glare. Since there were six of us, the proverbial "doghouse" was seldom unoccupied. To make matters worse, Mama had a persecution complex. Although she never showed this aspect of her character to outsiders, she was convinced that every member of the family, including her only sister, the cousins in Kansas City, her seldom-seen stepchildren and even her own children were out to get her. And like the God she worshipped, she neither forgave nor forgot.

Several weeks after I had accidentally broken a glass, we were setting the table in the dining room when Mama reminded me of my "sin" by saying to Vera, "We seem to be running short on glasses, and it's no wonder the way Dorothy breaks them. She's so careless." One day when we were getting ready for church Mama came out of her room wearing a white blouse and said, "I wanted to wear the blue blouse today but I couldn't because you scorched it, Orva. I really think you did it on purpose because you knew it was my favorite."

I believe that Pansy suffered more than any of us from the slings and arrows of Mama's outrageous disposition, mainly because she was constantly being compared, to her discredit, with her twin sister. The twins were not at all alike. Pansy, like Orva, resembled Mama, a fact that she hated, while Pearl, being short, thin and red-haired was a small replica of Papa. Pearl always got better grades and when they brought their report cards home Mama would look them over, then stab Pansy with one of those awful glares, and say, "What makes you so dumb, Pansy? Why aren't you smart like Pearl?" This refrain repeated constantly over the years was enough to play havoc with the child's self-image, but she also had to live with that horrible name, Pansy Ramsey, and suffer the taunts of the other children because it rhymed. When she entered the second grade she tried to change her name to Alice, her second name, but Mama would not allow it. "The only reason you don't like that name," she said, "is because I chose it."

We were not a demonstrative family and that is an understatement of the first kind. There was no hugging or kissing, no intimate conversation or any close communion between any two members. Each of us was an island unto herself. Although John Donne asserted that "No man is an island," we came pretty close. For us, touching another person with any show of love or affection would have been highly embarrassing. Once I was forced to kiss Mama for the first and only time in my life and it practically ruined my day. I was going to spend the weekend with a girl friend and Mama and I were waiting on the porch for her parents to pick me up. When they arrived I ran down the path and was about to climb into the buggy when Mama called out, "Dorothy, you forgot to kiss me goodbye." I froze, panic-stricken, not knowing what to do. I realized that Mama was putting on an act to impress these people, but having no choice except to go along with it, I went back to the porch and kissed her on the cheek. It was easily the most embarrassing moment of my life.

Chapter 3

Every summer long rows of corn and potatoes ripened in the fields, along with tomatoes, sweet potatoes, cantaloupe (which we called musk melons) and watermelons. These were later sold to the general store or to people who came out to the farm looking for bargains.

There were a few apple and peach trees, and Mama had a kitchen garden where she raised all kinds of vegetables. She canned the surplus in glass jars, which were stored in the cellar in the backyard. The only "store-bought" items were staples such as flour, sugar, salt and cornmeal. We even made our own butter. The top milk was poured into a wooden churn and we children took turns plunging the dasher up and down until eventually the milk turned to butter.

We had two cows, several pigs, lots of chickens, a few ducks and turkeys, two cats that lived mostly on mice, one dog and a sway-backed horse that Papa used for plowing. One year we had a nest of copperhead snakes under the barn and we were afraid to go outside until Papa had gotten rid of them.

One thing that did come from the store was a horrible concoction called Black Draught. It was supposed to cure whatever ailed us, and in case nothing did, it was guaranteed to prevent anything from ailing us. Several times a year we were forced to swallow a tablespoon of the vile stuff, and I developed such an aversion to medicine in any form that for many years I was unable to swallow even an aspirin tablet without gagging. Now at age 83, I have never had a serious illness and I often wonder if perhaps my body would simply not allow itself to get sick knowing that the end result would be taking medicine.

I have often wondered how Mama endured her miserable life yet remained always cheerful and happy, at least toward outsiders. She worked from dawn to dark, under the most primitive conditions, cooking, washing, ironing, scrubbing, gardening, sewing and having babies, more than half of whom she buried along the way. After I grew up and was no longer afraid of her, I felt sorry for her.

Every Monday morning Mama did the laundry in two washtubs set over open fires in the backyard, scrubbing the clothes on a washboard and then hanging them on the clothesline. Sometimes in the winter there would come a sudden cold spell, the clothes would freeze solid and some items would be brought in and hung on a line over the stove. They would create a terrific racket of hissing and crackling as they thawed and dripped. Almost everything had to be ironed since all clothing then was made of cotton. (Nylon had not yet been invented and drip-dry was far in the future.) This feat was accomplished by the use of three appropriately named sadirons that were made of solid iron and had to be handled with potholders. While one iron was being used the other two were heating on the stove.

We had no electricity, of course; for light we used coal-oil lamps. These required a lot of maintenance, for every day the wicks had to be trimmed, the fuel replenished and the glass chimneys washed. No matter how careful we were they still got smoky. Doing our homework by the light of these flickering lamps apparently did our eyes no harm for none of us had to wear glasses.

Far in the backyard was a two-hole privy, where a Montgomery Ward catalog hanging from a nail served as toilet paper. When the weather was warm it was no problem, but during the cold winter months we had to wear coats and caps when we went to the bathroom. Often the snow was three or four feet deep and Papa would dig a path from the back door to the privy.

Once a week, on Saturday nights, we took baths in the kitchen, taking turns in a washtub filled with hot water. We washed with bars of harsh yellow soap that Mama made with lye and ashes. No doubt this soap was hard on our skins but I'm sure it was strong enough to kill any germs that might have been lurking about.

There was plenty of water, but not a drop was ever wasted because it was not easy to come by. It was not far from the house to a well that never ran dry, but getting the water out of the well was a job that required much patience and a strong back. Attached to the well on pulleys was the proverbial old oaken bucket. By turning a handle the bucket could be lowered into the well and brought up full of water, which was poured into pails and carried into the house. By the time I was eleven I had become quite proficient at operating the well. I was tall and strong for my age and it was a job I enjoyed far more than I did washing dishes, ironing or making beds. One day the rope broke and the bucket plunged to the bottom of the well. Mama glared at me accusingly, and since by now I had acquired the habit of blaming myself for practically everything that happened, I became obsessed with the desire to make amends by retrieving that bucket. I spent hours leaning over the well, grappling with a hook attached to a long pole. Finally, I snagged the bucket, brought it to the top and Papa attached a new rope. During most of this time Morris stayed beside me giving me encouragement and moral support. And that is the last thing I remember about Morris, for a short time later, when he was not quite nine he died of diphtheria. I remember the trip to the cemetery in the buggy, with Mama dressed in black, crying, and Papa looking solemn.

Chapter 4

Religion played a big part in our lives. We seemed to spend almost as much time at the church as we did at home. Every Sunday morning we put on our best clothes and went to Sunday school and church, then Sunday night there was church again. On Wednesday evenings we attended prayer meeting and often there were special Bible study classes for the older children. Each of us had a New Testament, a reward for perfect attendance at Sunday school, so the house was overflowing with Bibles.

Papa never went to church with us. He spent Sundays either at the Sheriff's office or working in the fields and, although it was never mentioned, I suspect that he was an early-day atheist.

Sunday was considered a Holy Day and was, undoubtedly, the longest, dullest day in the week. We had to remain dressed up. We were not permitted to play outdoors and could read only our Bibles or the religious papers brought home by Vera from the Epworth League. Indoor games of all kinds were strictly forbidden and I was not allowed to play the organ. (No doubt because I enjoyed it and enjoyment would have been considered a sin.) The only break in the monotony was the three o'clock dinner and we always enjoyed that for eating was not classed as a sin. I can say one nice thing about Mama; she was a good cook. We usually had fried chicken, mashed potatoes with thick white gravy and hot biscuits, with homemade pie and ice cream for dessert.

Christmas was an important event. A tree was set up in the front room and decorated with tinsel, strings of popcorn and cranberries and real candles. We hung up our stockings and when we discovered, one by one, that there was really no Santa Claus, we kept up the pretense for the sake of the younger children. On Christmas morning Papa built a fire in the stove and we gathered around the tree to open our presents.

On Christmas Eve we were always at the church watching the young people put on a pageant depicting the baby Jesus, the star, the wise men and the shepherds. It was much the same every year but we children were quite impressed and never tired of watching it. At the conclusion each child received a stocking filled with hard candy, an apple and that once a year treat, an orange.

Every year, a week or two before Christmas, Mama took us to Sapulpa, the nearest town of any size, and gave each of us fifty cents to buy gifts. It was like visiting Fairyland. The streets were bedecked with tinsel and bells. Each store had a Christmas tree with electric candles and the counters were loaded with interesting items, many of which could be purchased for five or ten cents. People loaded with packages dashed in and out of the stores. In the street automobiles and buggies vied with each other for the right of way and on one corner a man dressed as Santa Claus stood beside a huge iron pot ringing a bell. It was at once confusing, frightening and utterly fascinating.

Our pleasure on these trips was always tempered by our fear of doing or saying something to incur Mama's wrath. Once I dropped one of my packages and broke the pitcher I had bought for her. She acted as if I had committed the crime of the century and during the entire holiday season she never let me forget the terrible thing I had done. That Christmas was ruined for me; I didn't even enjoy my orange. No wonder I acquired the lifelong habit of believing that whenever anything bad happened it was bound, somehow, to be my fault.

Yet we enjoyed our life on the farm when we could be outdoors away from Mama. In the winter we coasted down the hill on a home-made sled, made snow men, constructed forts, engaged in snow-ball fights and made pretend ice cream by adding cream and sugar to bowls of snow.

Summertime was even more fun. Then we could go barefoot all day. An occasional stubbed toe was a small price to pay for that delicious, never to be forgotten experience of walking across newly plowed ground in our bare feet. We slid down the barn roof, landing in the haystack with much yelling and screaming, played "Go Sheepy Go" with the neighbor kids, and climbed trees and hiked in the woods to gather hickory nuts and blackberries. Sometimes we would go into the fields, select a ripe watermelon via the thumping method, break it open and eat it right there sitting on the ground. No watermelon since has ever tasted so good.

One summer Papa built a merry-go-round with four seats made of apple boxes. It was crude looking and had to be pushed by hand, of course, but we thought it was wonderful. For a couple of years our front yard was the most popular place in town as kids gathered from all over to take turns pushing and riding.

Much of our time was spent helping with the chores. We washed dishes, made beds, gathered eggs, fed the pigs and chickens and helped with the washing and ironing. Yet in spite of being raised on a farm I never learned to cook, sew, milk a cow or ride a horse, and I never killed a chicken. By the time I was eleven, however, I was very good at splitting wood and drawing water from the well, both being jobs that I liked.

We loved wading in the shallow creek that meandered across the farm, and spent hours playing with the strange creatures that lived there. They looked like miniature lobsters but we called them crawdads, and we would lure them with bits of bacon tied on a string. When one of them grabbed the bait we could, if we were fast enough, yank him onto the bank before he let go. Then we watched, entranced, as he scuttled back to the water. Once we took two of the crawdads home and made a swimming pool for them in the backyard but they refused to eat and were so obviously unhappy that we took them back to the creek. As I watched them swim away I imagined them telling their friends about their strange experience.

The sandy banks of that creek were streaked with purple, red and green, a sure sign that there was oil down there. No one realized until it was too late, that our farm was on a lake of black gold that would some day be worth millions.

Every summer Mama and we younger children went to Kansas City to visit the cousins, while Vera stayed at home to keep house for Papa and attend to the chores. (When Vera graduated from high school and got a summer job in Shawnee to help pay her way through college, Orva took her place.) I hated those trips to Kansas City. They were a real drag as we were under Mama's eagle-eye most of the time, and they usually ended in a fight between Mama and one or more of the cousins and she would be mad all the way home. I looked forward to the time when I would be considered old enough to stay with Papa. Finally, the summer I was twelve, Orva, who was secretly making plans to leave home, wanted to visit Kansas City and she talked Mama into letting me take her place.

It was the happiest two weeks of my entire childhood. Every morning after Papa left I quickly did the chores, then spent the rest of the day in the house reading or playing the organ. It was nice not to hear Mama's constant reminders that, "if you don't stop reading so much and go out and play you'll get T.B.", or, "quit playing that organ and go outside or you'll get T.B.", or "eat your vegetables or you'll get T.B." Because I was thin she seemed to consider me a likely candidate for that disease and I developed a phobia about it. Convinced that T.B. was my disease, I knew that sooner or later it was bound to get me, yet I continued to read, play the organ and avoid vegetables whenever possible.

One day I decided to read the forbidden doctor book that Mama kept on the shelf in her closet. Although I felt a twinge of guilt as I climbed on a chair and hauled down the big book, curiosity won out over conscience and I sat on the side of the bed and began turning the pages. Interspersed with hundreds of home remedies for various ailments there were many full-page pictures in vivid color of the human body, both male and female. I learned a lot of things that apparently I was not supposed to know but had often wondered about. It was both enlightening and frightening. When I closed the book and put it back on the shelf I was careful to place it in the exact spot where I had found it.

Several days later I went into the front room, and with that old adage ringing in my ears, "You may as well be killed for a sheep as for a lamb," I carried the Old Testament over to the couch and began reading it. In the first chapters of Genesis I discovered to my surprise that God was very absent minded. After creating two people and a lot of animals he forgot all about them and created Adam and Eve and some more animals, this time in reverse. I read the entire Old Testament and by the time I had finished it I was convinced that God really didn't like the people he had created. Once, deciding to start over, he drowned all but eight of them, along with most of the animals. Obviously he wasn't too crazy either about his Chosen People, whom he selected later on to be the cream of the crop, since he often killed thousands of them for what seemed to me to be no valid reason.

Now I understood what people meant when they spoke of the wrath of God. According to the Bible he was a vicious, cruel warmonger who went about brandishing a bloody sword, and who, instead of getting rid of Satan, which he surely could have done, encouraged him to do his worst. From that time on, until I eventually realized that the whole thing was only a fairy tale, I was almost afraid to breathe for fear God would get mad and strike me dead.

Chapter 5

During the war in 1918 there had been many changes in Kiefer. There were now several automobiles in town, all of them black touring cars with isinglass windows to keep out some of the dust that rose in billows from the dirt roads. Those unfortunates whose cars broke down were taunted by passersby in buggies with shouts of, "Get a horse."

All of the business places and some of the private homes now had telephones and one family had something they called a phonograph. It was a square wooden box from which sprouted a large horn shaped like an overgrown morning glory. On the horn was a picture of a white dog and underneath the dog the words, "His Master's Voice." An oblong cylinder was placed in the box, a handle on the side was turned and out of the horn came Caruso's voice, sounding as if he were right there in the room. It was the talk of the town!

It was during the war that I first saw an airplane. It flew right over the town and hundreds of people stood in the streets gazing skyward at this seemingly impossible miracle.

The little town of Kiefer was growing fast. There was a filling station where they sold gasoline and repaired tires. Two women from Sapulpa opened a beauty shop where those who could afford two dollars could get a permanent wave. The drugstore branched out and began selling boxes of candy, greeting cards and magazines, and installed a soda fountain. I remember the first time I tasted Coca Cola. I didn't like it, but in later years it was to become my favorite drink.

Looking back on my childhood, I have often wondered why Mama seemed to single me out to wear outlandish clothes to school. After we grew up I discussed it with the twins and neither of them could remember suffering such indignities. I can only conclude that, although I didn't know it at the time, I was the only child who could even remotely be called pretty, the only one with naturally curly hair, and that Mama resented it and went out of her way to make me look ugly.

My dresses were always too long or too short; whichever was the opposite of the current style. One year I had to wear grown-up shoes with high heels and pointed toes, when the other little girls were wearing flat Mary Jane slippers. I tried to flatten the toes by pounding them against the desk in front of me until the teacher objected to the noise and I had to stop. The only way I could get rid of those shoes was by outgrowing them, which I eventually did.

Once Mama made me wear rayon stockings with openwork clocks up the sides, monstrosities that no little girl would care to be caught dead in. Every day on the way to school I took them off, hid them in a hedge and went barelegged, which was simply not done but was the lesser of two evils. When the bell rang I was always the last one in, remained at my desk during recess pretending to be engrossed in a book, and was always the last one out. On the way home from school I dug out the stockings and put them on. Mama never found out. The twins knew, but we had an unspoken agreement that it was us against Mama and we never told on each other.

I was in the eighth grade when Orva, who at fourteen was quite a grown-up young lady, quit school and with the money she had saved by baby-sitting, went to Kansas City and lived with one of the cousins. Declaring herself to be eighteen, she went to work for the telephone company. In those days it was easy to lie about your age for people were not ticketed and numbered as they are today. All you had to do was to look the part.

During my final year of grade school I was relatively happy. For the first time since I could remember Mama did not make me wear clothes I was ashamed of and it was pleasant to go to school dressed like the other children. I won a story-writing contest, which gave a much-need boost to my morale. Although I had always done well in school and had even skipped a grade, I had a poor opinion of myself and thought everyone else was smarter. I decided then that I would become a writer. "How nice it would be," I thought, "to just sit in a corner someplace all by myself and write, and not have to deal with people."

That year I had a crush on a boy named Raymond. He seemed to like me too, until I won a nail-driving contest in which I beat him and several other boys. After that he went out of his way to avoid me. I really didn't know why he was giving me the brush-off. I had never heard of the male ego and had yet to learn that no boy can endure being beaten by a mere girl.

I was looking forward to graduating from elementary school in May, and when Mama took me to Sapulpa to buy a special dress for the occasion I was thrilled and happy. During the thirty-minute ride on the trolley car I thought about what a good year it had been. Not once had Mama forced me to wear anything ridiculous to school, and with the optimism of youth I thought she had changed. I almost liked her.

When we arrived at the store I immediately selected a white frilly dress with ruffles because I knew that was the kind the other girls would be wearing.

"Oh, I don't like that one at all." Mama said. She held up a horrible blue serge dressed trimmed with red braid. "I think this one is a lot prettier and far more appropriate."

I should have agreed with her, whereupon she would probably have put the awful thing back on the rack. Instead I insisted that I liked the white one better, because I knew that all of the other girls would be wearing white dresses.

She paid no attention. "The only reason you don't like the blue dress is because I picked it out."

She glared at me and as usual my blood ran cold and my bones turned to jelly. We took home the blue serge. Now since Mama was far from being stupid she must have known that the dress was not suitable for such an occasion, so why did she do it? I don't know. And although I have forgiven her for many things, I was never able to forgive her for ruining my graduation day.

During the final two weeks of school I felt as a rat in a trap must feel as he searches hopelessly for a way out. I thought seriously of running away, but my fear of the unknown held me back. I was barely thirteen, looked even younger and had no money. Where would I go and how would I live? No doubt I would just be picked up and returned home. I could take to the hills on the big day, as I had always done during the hog killing, but sooner or later I would have to go home and face Mama's wrath, a decidedly unpleasant prospect. Besides I thought that unless I put in an appearance I would not graduate and would thus not be eligible to enter high school in the fall. I really had no choice; I would have to go and somehow suffer through it.

So I went, and suffered the agonies of the damned. I was the only girl not wearing a white dress, and when we marched across the stage to receive our diplomas I felt like an ugly worm surrounded by beautiful butterflies. My self-image took another blow from which it has never fully recovered.

That night I lay awake for hours re-living those awful moments and hating Mama for forcing me to endure such embarrassment. "Some day," I thought, "I'll be old enough to get away from her. Some day I might get married and have children, and if I do they will never have to wear clothes they are ashamed of. And never, no matter what they do, will I ever, ever, get mad at them."

Chapter 6

That summer Papa sold the farm. He and Mama and we three girls, the only children still living at home, moved to Shawnee. I never knew the reason for this move and can only assume that Papa lost his job as Sheriff because of his advanced age. He was then 68 years old and hoping to find work in a larger town. Since there was no Social Security then and no unemployment insurance, each person was responsible for his own survival, and it was either "root hog or die," as the saying went.

Suddenly we were transported from primitive living to comparative luxury. The house in Shawnee had electric lights, running water, a flush toilet and even a bathtub. There were no chickens or pigs to be fed and wood chopping was a thing of the past for we now had gas for cooking and heating. On the screened-in back porch there were two laundry tubs so we no longer had to do the washing in the backyard. It was exciting and quite wonderful, for a brief time.

To us, Shawnee was a big city. We were awed by the tall buildings, some of them four or five stories high. All of the streets were paved; there were no horses and buggies. Everyone traveled either by automobile or on the streetcars, which you could ride all the way across town for a nickel.

Apparently Papa was unable to get regular work, but he did some odd-job carpentry in the backyard making doors and windows. I remember Pansy and Pearl gathering the long, curly wood shavings that fell from his plane and pinning them to their hair pretending they were curls. Mama did some practical nursing and baby-sitting, but mainly, I suppose, we were living on the money Papa got for the farm in Kiefer.

Vera came home for summer vacation and went to work in an office. She was twenty-one now, had completed three years of college and would graduate next year and become a teacher. We were somewhat in awe of her because she was so grownup and so smart, but she was always nice to us and talked to us as if we were people and never got mad. She gave each of us a necklace made of coral beads. This made a lasting impression on me, because it was the first jewelry I had ever owned.

Once when Mama was away on a nursing job, we spent the evening in Vera's room and it is my most vivid memory of her. She was leaning back on the bed, dressed in her nightgown, and we sat on the floor at her feet listening, entranced, as she told us about her experiences at college. She described the friends she had made and told us about the fun things they did when they were not studying. We could have listened to her all night but, unfortunately, Mama came home around midnight and made us go to bed.

Cousin Hazel, who lived on a farm near a small town in Kansas, came for a visit bringing her two children Tommy and Dora, aged eleven and nine. She was a fat, jolly woman, and a great storyteller. We liked her immediately, even though we were highly embarrassed when she hugged and kissed us because we were not used to such behavior.

One day we fixed a picnic lunch and went on the streetcar to a large park where there was a playground, picnic tables and a lake. In an open booth a man was selling ice cream and soft drinks. We spent the entire day there swinging, sliding, eating ice cream cones and throwing breadcrumbs to the ducks that were swimming around on the lake. It was a memorable day.

When cousin Hazel went home, it was decided for some reason, that I should go along and spend the rest of the summer with her. I managed to hide my elation for fear Mama would change her mind if she discovered how delighted I was at the prospect of being away from home for several weeks. On the way to Kansas, Hazel expressed some concern over the fact that I would be coming back alone. I assured her that I would be all right. Actually, I was looking forward to that long train ride all by myself, with no one along who had to be talked to. It promised to be the best part of the entire trip, I thought, the only trouble being that eventually and irrevocably I would arrive home.

The farm was less than a mile from the village and was surrounded by low, tree-covered hills. There was a windmill, which I believe furnished electricity besides pumping water from the well into the house. Compared to our farm in Kiefer it was quite modern.

Hazel's husband was exactly her opposite. He was a tall, thin and somewhat taciturn man, who nevertheless appeared to be friendly, and I soon overcame my fear of him. Tommy and Dora were fun to play with, and since Hazel never got mad at me, I began to relax and enjoy myself. I almost learned to ride Tommy's bicycle but on the third try I fell off, skinned my knee and said, "darn it." Having learned all about the unchanging God by reading the Bible, I knew that he never forgave anybody anything. All that sweetness and light stuff in the New Testament was only a come-on, and I was convinced that He was not about to forgive me for having said a bad word. I could only wait in fear and trembling for the blow to fall. I never got on a bicycle again.

One day while Tommy and Dora were out in the fields helping their father, I offered to run an errand for Hazel who was cooking dinner and had discovered that there were a couple of things she needed from the store. Tucking the list in my pocket, I set off along the path that led through the woods, over the hill and down into town. It was a pleasant, sunny day and I failed to notice the dark clouds that were gathering in the west. I stopped and picked some wild flowers, found some interesting stones and stood very still for awhile watching a squirrel that sat on a rock and stared at me. The moment I moved he instantly scampered away.

By the time I reached the store I realized that a storm was brewing. I started home carrying the bag of groceries. Then the sun disappeared behind the clouds and I could hear thunder in the distance. I decided to take the shorter way along the two-lane road and was about half way home when the first drops of rain began to fall. I began to run and was making good time when I saw, of all things, a Bible. It was lying in a shallow ditch by the side of the road half hidden by grass and weeds and I saw that some of the pages were torn out and scattered around. For a few seconds I hesitated. "That's God's Book," I thought. "If I don't gather it up and take it home, He will be mad at me." I was torn between my urge to protect the groceries and my moral obligation to save the book, but the groceries won out. Deciding to come back later when the storm was over, I kept right on running and arrived home just ahead of the downpour.

The rain continued to come down in torrents all-night and part of the next day. When it finally stopped that afternoon and I was ready to go and rescue what was left of the book, it was too late.

A telegram arrived saying that Vera had drowned that morning while swimming in a lake, and that I was to come home at once. I knew instantly that it was all my fault. According to the Bible, God often punished people by killing their relatives and there was no doubt in my mind that He had killed Vera in order to punish me.

All the way home on the train I stared miserably out the window, sunk in a morass of self-blame, barely aware of the landscape flashing by. I knew that this was a secret I would have to carry alone, for there was no one at home with whom I could share it. The twins were too young, and I could expect no sympathy from Mama, for I felt sure that she would only get mad and glare at me. I realize now that I should have talked to Papa. No doubt he would have convinced me that I was laboring under an illusion; that no act of mine could possibly have caused Vera's death, but there had never been any communication between us and it would have been like talking to a stranger. I never even considered it.

I arrived home to find that while I was gone we had moved to a much smaller house in a poorer neighborhood. Apparently Papa and Mama, realizing that the money from the farm was not going to last forever and that Papa, because of his age, was not going to find work, were trying to conserve. Finally, realizing he could do nothing to help and that he was only an added burden, Papa went to Los Angeles to live with Alvis, one of my half-brothers. I don't remember his leaving, but I do remember that he sent us a card from California, something about a pelican.

The next thing I remember, we were living in a little shack near the edge of town. We had now come full circle. We were back to using kerosene lamps and a wood stove, in which we burned mostly coal because we could pick it up free along the nearby railroad track.

One night a cyclone came howling through Shawnee and our little shack trembled and shook until we thought it would surely collapse and that we would all die. Mama made us get down on our knees in the dark and pray to God to save us. Suddenly it seemed to me a waste of time because if God had decided to kill us He was not about to change his mind just because we asked Him to. Besides, we had been taught that he was unchangeable. When it was over and we found ourselves still alive we had to pray again to thank God for saving us. I wondered why He sent the cyclone in the first place. What had we done that He should take a fiendish delight in scaring us half to death?

We must have lived there for several months and I suppose we went to school. Pansy and Pearl assured me later that we did, and that I had done some baby-sitting, but I have no memory of it. I have forgotten almost everything that happened during that year after Vera's death, including her funeral, and I believe now that subconsciously I wanted my mind to become a blank, in order to forget that it was my fault she had died.

Chapter 7

Mama suffered a lot with rheumatism and when she heard that the climate in Colorado Springs was famous for improving that condition we packed our few belongings in two old suitcases and set off, like the Israelites toward the Promised Land. It was about a thousand miles and although it didn't take us forty years to get there, we were probably on the road for three or four weeks. Hitchhiking was unpredictable. There were not many cars on the road and often we would walk two or three miles before someone came along, picked us up and took us to the next town.

When a car did show up we were always given a ride because in those days people were not afraid of each other and everyone picked up hitchhikers, especially a woman with three children. The driver was always a man. Driving a car then was a hazardous occupation. To start a car it had to be cranked and many an arm was broken in the process. When a tire went flat it had to be removed from the wheel, repaired, replaced and pumped up with a hand pump. It was no job for a woman.

Sometimes there were trees by the side of the road and we would sit in the shade and wait until a car came into view. Then Mama would stand up and raise her arm, with her thumb pointing in the direction we were going. It always worked, and we were given a ride even it meant much crowding and sitting on each other's laps.

It was on that trip that I first saw a mirage. As we trudged down the highway the road far ahead appeared to be covered with water, yet when we reached that spot the pavement was dry and the water had moved on. No matter how hard we ran we could never catch up with that water. It was fascinating.

We spent the nights in cheap hotels where a room with a public bath down the hall usually cost a dollar, sometimes only fifty cents. We took turns sleeping one in the double bed with Mama and two on the floor. I was always sorry when it was my turn to sleep with Mama, and so was Pansy, although Pearl didn't seem to mind. Both Pansy and I preferred sleeping on the floor, but didn't dare say so.

At one place we stayed, bedbugs appeared in the middle of the night and by morning Mama and I were covered with bites. Before leaving we took baths, washed our hair and shook out our clothes. After that Mama always made certain there were no bedbugs before renting a room.

For me, the most embarrassing part of the trip was the stops we made at various Post Offices along the way. Since we couldn't carry everything with us, Mama always mailed a big package to a town farther down the line. When we arrived in that town she would retrieve the package, open it and the suitcases, spread the contents on the floor of the Post Office and sort out the things she wanted to take along. The rest of the things she would mail to the next town. She seemed to have no self-consciousness whatsoever. She stood in awe of nothing and no one.

On these occasions I always stood off to one side and pretended I wasn't with her, but I doubt if I fooled anyone. I was a bedraggled looking child and it must have been obvious to anyone who took the time to wonder that I belonged with her. However, it made me feel better just being as far away from her as possible during these mortifying episodes.

We spent one night in Pueblo, Colorado, but did not visit Mama's sister, Aunt Inez, whom I had not seen since I was about eight. She and Mama had quarreled several years before and had not been on speaking terms since.

Living on the road had by now become a way of life, but at last, after what seemed forever, we arrived in Colorado Springs. Mama rented a little house in a nearby small town called Manitou Springs, which was at the foot of Pike's Peak. While waiting expectantly for her rheumatism to get better, she got work as a practical nurse. I did light housework and babysitting. The yard was fenced in, so we bought a dozen hens and made a little money selling eggs to the neighbors.

The house was on a slight hill and under the low side there was a crawl space about four feet high. It was supposed to be used for storage, but since we had nothing to store I built roosts with some old lumber that was lying around and we used it as a chicken house. The hens took shelter there at night and during rainstorms.

In early July there was a storm that just wouldn't quit. It rained steadily for three days and three nights. The yard was fast becoming a lake and we knew that the water in the crawl space, because it was lower, must be at least a couple of feet deep and if the rain continued much longer the hens would drown. Wading through waist deep water in the pouring rain, I brought them out two at a time and turned them over to Pansy and Pearl who were waiting on the back porch. Two of the frightened hens drowned before I could rescue them and Mama was quite upset about that. She blamed me for the loss.

Soon after that I got a job in Colorado Springs doing housework for a young couple who were expecting a baby in October. If they were pleased with me I could stay all winter, going to school and doing most of the work on weekends. Fortunately, I wasn't expected to do any cooking, but I was expert at washing dishes and doing laundry.

I had been there several weeks when Mrs. Grant told me that her parents were coming for a visit. She said, "We need your room, could you spend three days at home while they are here?" Of course I agreed and the next morning put a few things in a paper bag and rode the streetcar downtown. I had no idea where I would spend the next three nights, but I certainly could not go home. Our little house was full to overflowing just then with cousins and second cousins from Kansas City and I knew Mama would be furious if I showed up unexpectedly.

I spent some time window shopping, bought a newspaper for a nickel and sat in the park while I read it cover to cover. Then I noticed that there was a Public Library across from the park so I went there and read magazines until it closed at nine o'clock. Putting off the evil moment when I would have to find a place to sleep, I spent a dime and watched a double feature at the only movie house in town. When I left at midnight Mr. and Mrs. Grant and their parents were in the lobby and I ducked back hoping they wouldn't see me.

After they had gone I wandered on up the street wondering what to do. I don't know how many blocks I had walked when I came to the Y.W.C.A. building. A woman was sitting at a desk doing some paper work. I knew they took in homeless girls, but I wasn't exactly homeless and I didn't dare go in and ask for a place to sleep—it would have caused all sorts of complications. I was about to leave when the woman got up and went into another room. Instantly I scooted across the lobby and went up the stairs two at a time. At the top of the stairs there was a lounge with a couch and several big leather upholstered chairs, but I decided to play it safe and went across to the rest room, where I spent the night sitting on the toilet in one of the cubicles. As a place to sleep it left much to be desired. I slept fitfully with my head on my knees. When morning finally came and I heard girls talking outside, I just walked across the lounge, down the stairs and out the front door. No one paid any attention to me.

I stayed in the park all morning, eating rolls and cookies and reading a newspaper that someone had thoughtfully left on a bench. I then went to the library and read until it was time to go to the movies again. This time I slept through most of it because they were the same pictures I had seen the night before. I had no trouble sleeping since there was little noise. The actors' conversation was printed on the screen and the only sound came from the piano player in the pit.

The wait outside the door of the Y.W.C.A. was longer this time, but when the woman finally left I ran quickly up the stairs and into the lounge. Unable to resist the temptation I sank into one of the big chairs. "I'll stay here just a little while," I thought, "then I'll go hide in the rest room." I never made the toilet—the next thing I knew it was daylight and the woman from the lobby was shaking me. She didn't seem at all cross, just puzzled. As I followed her down the stairs I made up a story. If I gave the right answers perhaps she wouldn't call the police, in which case Mama would find out. I was far more afraid of Mama than I was of the police. The worst the police could do was put me in jail and that would be mild punishment compared to Mama's anger.

The lady wrote down the fictitious name and address I gave her and then listened to my story. "I went to the movies last night but stayed too late, and when I came out the last streetcar had gone. We don't have a telephone, it was too far to walk and I couldn't afford to go to a hotel so I thought you wouldn't mind if I spent the night in your lounge."

"Oh, I don't in the least. If I'd known you were there I'd have given you a bed to sleep in. The streetcars are running now so you'd better go home. Your folks will be worried about you." She was so friendly that I felt guilty about lying to her, but it was a matter of self-preservation.

As usual I spent the day in the park and at the Library, then went to the movies again, where fortunately they had changed the billing so at least I wasn't bored. Then I wandered up the street wondering what to do. I passed the Y.W.C.A. building, which was now off limits, and went on for several blocks until I came to a church. The door was locked, but there were steps at the side leading down to the basement. I sat on the bottom step all night and counted the hours as tolled by a big clock somewhere in the neighborhood. Although it was August, it was a bit chilly and I could have done with a jacket. The cement step was hard, but I felt safe and well hidden.

When the sun came up I left my sanctuary and sat in the park for awhile, then rode the streetcar out to the Grant's house. Mrs. Grant met me at the door and handed me my suitcase. Her manner was definitely cold and unfriendly as she gave me the little bit of money she owed me for wages.

"My parents have decided to stay until after the baby comes, so we won't be needing you anymore." I knew then that they had seen me at the movies that night and thought I was some kind of loose character, but I also knew that if I told her the truth she wouldn't believe me, so I said nothing and just got on the streetcar and went home.

Fortunately the cousins, who had been there two weeks, left that day so there was no problem. I gave Mama Mrs. Grant's version of the reason I had lost my job, she accepted it, and no one ever knew about my three days and three nights on the street.

Mama had an indomitable spirit that she must have inherited from her ancestor, William Clark. When she decided to do something she let nothing stand in her way. Had she been a man she might have been a howling success at something or other, but being a woman in the early part of the century she was licked before she started. But she never stopped trying. Now she decided that we should climb Pike's Peak. I believe the general idea was that she would get her name in the papers and become famous for having climbed Pike's Peak with three children. She went to the newspaper office and announced her intention, but when we started off at dawn that morning early in September there were no reporters cheering us on.

We climbed all day and far into the night, following the cog railroad that wound its way through canyons and up steep inclines. By no stretch of the imagination could it have been called a fun trip. Pearl suffered frequent nose-bleeds, Mama's rheumatism plagued her and as we neared the summit Pansy had trouble breathing the rarified air.

Sometime during the night we reached the top of that treeless, snow-covered mountain. It was completely deserted. There was one building, a small shack that served as a waiting room, but since the little train no longer made its daily trips the caretaker had left, leaving the door unlocked. There was nothing worth stealing, and besides no one in his right mind would come up here at this time of year. We built a fire in the wood stove and when we had thawed out we collapsed on the benches to wait for morning.

The only good thing I can say about that mountain climbing trip is that the view from the top of Pike's Peak, with the sun just coming up, was spectacular. It is too bad we were in no condition to appreciate it. Anxious to get home we came down the mountain at a fast clip, like a horse returning to the barn, and since it was all downhill we made good time and got home that evening. The next day Mama went to the newspaper office again, but since our story never appeared in print we must not have been considered newsworthy. All of our suffering was for nothing!

Soon after that school started. I don't remember much about that but I do remember a job I had washing silverware in a restaurant. I was fourteen, but I told the owner I was sixteen. He looked skeptical, but he must have been hard pressed for help because he hired me anyway. I worked there several months after school and on weekends before the authorities made a fuss and he had to let me go.

When we had been in Colorado Springs almost a year and Mama's rheumatism had not improved she decided we would go to Albuquerque, New Mexico, where the climate was hot and dry. So we sold the hens, packed the suitcases and hit the road. We didn't have as far to go this time, and there were more cars on the road now. We made it to Albuquerque in nine days.

Chapter 8

During most of that first summer in Albuquerque we lived in a little house that was shaped like a boxcar. Mama got a job cleaning offices at night and we usually went along and helped her, emptying wastebaskets, cleaning spittoons and dusting. Then she went to work in the diet kitchen at the hospital and we moved to a much nicer house in a somewhat better part of town.

I was well past fifteen now but I didn't look a day over fourteen so I had trouble finding work. No one would believe me when I told them I was sixteen. I did a lot of baby-sitting that summer.

In the fall I got an after-school job mopping floors in a T.B. sanitarium. I held that job for several months until an old man, one of the patients, propositioned me. When I "spurned his advances," as the saying went then, he told lies about me, and because he was a paying customer, they took his word against mine and fired me.

Then for awhile I had a live-in housework job but that didn't last long. The lady was old-fashioned, insisted that I wear a corset and even went out and bought me one. The last thing I needed was a corset since I had a figure like a broomstick. Refusing to wear the thing, I left it on the bed, packed my suitcase and went home. I wonder what she did with it—she was too fat to wear it.

One day a boy at school invited me to a dance. It was my first date, and of course, I would be shy and self-conscious. I had watched couples dancing in the movies so I was eager to find out whether it was as easy and as much fun as it looked. Knowing that Mama considered dancing a mortal sin, I told her I was going to a party at the High School. "There won't be any dancing there," I assured her. This much at least was true, since there would be no party.

The boy was an expert and I soon learned that dancing was both easy and fun, although, "fun" is much too tame a word to describe that experience in ecstasy. I didn't have to learn. I seem to have been born knowing how to dance. As we sailed around the room, dipping and twirling, I felt as if I were floating on a cloud and not until the orchestra played "Good Night Ladies" did I come back to earth. Even after I got home I lay awake for hours dancing in my imagination.

Eventually Mama somehow found out that I had been to a dance (I think Pearl let it slip without meaning to) and all hell broke loose. I had never before seen Mama so angry. She accused me of selling my soul to the Devil, besides setting a bad example for my little sisters. She assured me that I was headed for Hell, that God would never forgive me. She then gave me her old silent treatment, and in this she included Pansy for daring to take my part. Although Mama didn't actually kick me out in so many words, she did give me the impression that if she never saw me again it would be soon enough. I must have been right because when I put my few clothes in one of the suitcases and left she made no objection and didn't even ask where I was going. Pansy wanted to come with me and for that I was thankful. It made the thought of being completely on my own a little less frightening.

Fortunately, we weren't actually broke. We had almost five dollars. For two dollars a week we found a tiny room just big enough for a bed, a dresser and a chair. I started looking for work—it wasn't easy. Although I was well past sixteen now, no one would believe it, and since I had no birth certificate to prove it I was turned down consistently. Finally I got a part-time job running an elevator in a department store for four dollars a week. Either the stress was beginning to age me or the man who hired me needed glasses.

After paying the rent we had two dollars a week for food, and we certainly did not live "high on the hog." We subsisted mostly on bologna sandwiches and milk. Often at night we went out and stole empty milk bottles from front porches and turned them in the next day at various grocery stores for the deposit. We had a choice; we could steal or starve. And as the old saying goes, "do not criticize another person until you have walked in his shoes."

We learned a lot that summer because we spent most of our spare time at the library. We both loved to read and we went through every magazine in the place, plus many books. It cost nothing and we probably enjoyed it far more than we would have the movies, which were, of course, beyond our means.

During this time we had heard nothing from Mama and could only assume that she had lost interest in us. Then one day toward the end of summer she showed up and announced that she was planning to hitchhike to Texas with the twins. Pearl seemed to think it was a great idea but Pansy had no desire to go traipsing off to Texas, or anywhere else with Mama and I certainly did not want her to go. For the first time in my life I had experienced companionship, I didn't want to be left alone. However, since the twins were then barely thirteen neither of us had anything to say about it. Fortunately, Mama did not ask me to go along. To her I was a lost soul unworthy of being saved. One morning in early September, without a hug, a kiss or a backward glance, they set off down the road to Texas. Pansy did turn and wave, and I have always treasured that gesture.

With Pansy to look after I had given up the idea of finishing school but now, feeling that a high school diploma might come in handy, I began looking for work that would include board and room and give me time for classes. I would be entering the tenth grade, although by rights it should have been the eleventh. Somewhere along the way, I have no idea when, I must have lost a grade.

I soon found the perfect spot, waiting on tables in a boarding house. It was a large two-story house in a fairly good neighborhood and was owned by a thin, red-haired, middle-aged widow named Mrs. Prichard. There were usually ten or fifteen boarders. There were two waitresses who served breakfast and dinner. I washed dishes, went to school on weekdays, and changed beds and cleaned house on Saturdays. Besides room and board we were given two dollars a week in wages. Not a bad deal as things went then.

The other waitress, with whom I shared a cabin in the back, was an Indian girl named Hettie. She was tall and slender and wore her straight black hair in two long braids. To me, she was both beautiful and awe-inspiring. At first I was afraid of Hettie. I had never before shared a room with a stranger and I was uncomfortable and ill at ease, but she was so nice to me and so friendly that I soon got over that and we became friends. Often at night we would walk to the edge of town, (it wasn't very far since Albuquerque was a small town then) sit down on one of the bare hills in the moonlight, eat peaches (pilfered from the store room) and talk. She told me about her family, all of whom she seemed to dearly love. She was quite shocked to learn that my mother had gone off and left me to fend for myself. She told me many stories of her life as a child on the reservation. When she graduated in January she planned to go back there and teach school. I dreaded the thought of her leaving and wondered who would take her place.

I enjoyed being at the boarding house, I felt safe and secure. Mrs. Prichard was a pleasant woman to work for and she took a personal interest in "her girls", as she called us. She tolerated no hanky-panky. Any male boarder who dared to get fresh with one of her girls was immediately given his walking papers. She urged us to attend church with her on Sundays, and although by that time I had just about given up on religion, I had no objection to going.

Had it not been for Celia, the girl who took Hettie's place, I might have stayed there and finished high school. Although I made no friends at all, being shy and in awe of the other students, my grades were excellent except in math (I never was any good at figures). I might have stuck it out and graduated, but I was neither mentally nor emotionally equipped to deal with Celia, especially at such close quarters as sharing a cabin.

She was a short, attractive blonde, a year older than I, and from the first she made it plain that to her I was a mere child and as such beneath her notice. She demanded that we switch beds because she wanted the one nearest the bathroom. I complied because I really didn't care. She had a lot of clothes which filled most of the space in our one closet, but that didn't bother me as I had very few clothes anyway. What did bother me was her constant chattering about her many boyfriends. She used me as a sounding board, interrupting my reading, and I lacked the nerve to tell her to shut up. I didn't like her. I endured it for three months hoping she would take a sudden notion to get married and leave.

Then one day Evelyn, one of the boarders, told me that she was going to quit her job and go to Santa Fe to work in a hotel dining room during the two-week Fiesta. She suggested that I go along. "I can get you in," she assured me, "because I know the boss, and it's a chance to make some real money. We'll get our meals and two dollars a day plus tips, which should be at least double that, probably more. And it may turn out to be a permanent job."

It sounded good and I was tempted. It would mean dropping out of school, but actually a high school diploma was of no use to a woman unless she wanted to become a nurse or a teacher and I had no desire to be either. I'd always thought that I would like to be a reporter, maybe work up to become a journalist. Knowing that this was an impossible dream, I had given it no serious thought and since there was no such thing as a woman reporter the very idea was ridiculous. Since I could never hope to do what I really wanted to do I decided to give up the struggle and set about making some money. At least I could buy some clothes that I wouldn't be ashamed of. Mrs. Prichard tried to talk me out of it, but like all young people I thought I knew best. I gave her a week's notice and went to Santa Fe with Evelyn.

Chapter 9

It was an exciting two weeks. The main street in Santa Fe was gaily decorated and the little town, which consisted mainly of adobe buildings, was swarming with tourists. Indians in full regalia danced on a raised platform in the square. Street vendors lined the curbs selling Indian jewelry, moccasins and other Western wear. The carnival did a thriving business. Most of our spare time was spent sight-seeing.

Evelyn and I shared a hotel room, but it cost more than I had expected because rooms were at a premium during the Fiesta. Yet I did make a lot of money. At the end of the two weeks I had saved over thirty dollars, which seemed to me like a small fortune. I had never before had so much money.

I hated waitress work. It was fast-paced, confusing, not at all like working at the boarding house, but it was obviously a way to make money fast and in time I might even learn to like it. However, now I was out of a job because all the temporary girls were laid off after the Fiesta. Feeling that my chances would be better in a big city, I decided to go to Denver. I would hitch-hike, of course. I had been conditioned never to pay train fare when I could ride free, and besides I would need my money to live on until I found a job.

That first day on the road I got several short rides, covered about a hundred miles and spent that night in a hotel room in some small town. The next morning I was out on the highway early hoping for better luck. I hadn't gone far before a man in a shiny new sedan came along and picked me up. When I told him I was on my way to Denver he said he could take me as far as Pueblo.

He looked Jewish and to me he was old, being probably in his middle thirties. The back seat was full of sample cases and when he said he was a traveling salesman I began to feel a little nervous. Having heard several jokes about traveling salesmen I was not inclined to trust them and I began to wonder what I had gotten myself into. He didn't talk much, just kept looking at me in a strange sort of way as if trying to make up his mind about something.

Suddenly he asked, "How old are you?"

"Seventeen."

He shook his head. "You don't look it. Where are your parents? Do they know you're out here being picked up by strangers?"

"My mother is somewhere in Texas, I think. My father is quite old—almost seventy. He lives in California with my half-brother, Alvis." Thinking to assure him that I was not completely homeless and friendless I mentioned that I had an Aunt in Pueblo.

"I don't think you realize how dangerous this is," he said.

"Lots of girls have been raped, beaten up and even murdered when the wrong man picked them up. It's lucky I came along. I'll turn you over to your Aunt and she can take it from there. But please promise me that you won't ever hitchhike again."

"I hadn't planned to stop there and I don't think she will be glad to see me. She and my mother had a quarrel years ago and haven't spoken to each other since. I haven't seen her since I was a child and she won't even recognize me. Why not just let me out downtown? I'll go to a hotel tonight and start looking for a job tomorrow."

But he was not to be swerved from his purpose. He was a nice man, felt responsible for me and was relieved that there was someone, even an estranged Aunt with whom he could leave me. "You'll be better off living with her, at least until you find a job."

He found the address in the phone book and a few minutes later we pulled up in front of an old two-storied house several miles from the center of town. Aunt Inez answered the door, followed closely by Uncle Ben. I had a vague remembrance of them but they didn't seem to know me. Standing farther back in the hallway I could see their two grown sons, Raymond and Norman, whom I remembered as being slightly crippled.

"Are you Inez Gravatt?" the man asked. When assured she was, he introduced himself and said, "I picked up this child, your niece, on the road this morning and I'm turning her over to you because you are her nearest relative. Please look after her until you can get in touch with her father and half-brother in California." Wishing me luck, he waved goodbye, got in his car and drove away.

Aunt Inez looked at me. She recognized me now, but she didn't smile. "Well, Dorothy, come on in." It wasn't exactly an effusive welcome and

I felt sure she was thinking, "as if I didn't have enough troubles already without this."

I followed her into the front room and sat on the horsehair sofa feeling awkward and uncomfortable. Uncle Ben and the two boys tried to make conversation by asking me where I had been and what I had been doing, but Aunt Inez was obviously not interested. She asked me no questions about Mama and the other girls, and she didn't seem all that sorry to learn that Vera had died. That quarrel she and Mama had must have been a real scorcher! Yet she did what she would have called her, "Christian duty." She gave me food and a place to sleep. She asked for Papa's address but I didn't have it and I wouldn't have given it to her anyway. I considered myself grown-up now and I certainly didn't need a guardian.

My heart was set on going to Denver, but I was afraid now to hitch-hike and it seemed sensible to get a job in Pueblo, preferably as a waitress, and work for awhile before spending money for train fare. Two weeks later I had wasted a lot of money on carfare, learned that I didn't like Pueblo (it was an ugly town full of steel mills and freight trains) and had not found a job. Not caring to be beholden to Aunt Inez, I gave her ten dollars for room and board, which she did not hesitate to take, and bought a ticket to Denver. I had no idea what I would do when I arrived there, practically broke, but like Scarlet in "Gone with the Wind," I would worry about that tomorrow.

It was a long, slow trip. The train stopped at several small towns, stopped twice to take on water at tanks alongside the tracks and finally, puffing and snorting arrived in Denver at nine o'clock that night.

I wasn't actually broke; I had fifty cents. Having planned to spend the night in the waiting room, pretending to be waiting for a train, I settled down in an obscure corner and was almost asleep, when I suddenly remembered reading that the Y.W.C.A. took in homeless girls. Well, there was no question about it; I really was homeless so I decided to give it a try.

I found the address in the phone book, got directions from the man at the ticket window and started walking. It was a couple of miles and I was tired when I got there, but the woman who was in charge was very nice. When I explained my situation (truthfully this time) she gave me a cot in a dormitory with five other girls. I fell asleep thinking how lucky I was. Something always came along in the nick of time to save me from total disaster.

A few days later I went to work in a laundry, folding sheets as they came off the mangle. The pay wasn't much but I was able to rent a room and I even managed to save a few dollars. Then I found a waitress job and the money began rolling in. It was in a small "greasy spoon" restaurant run by two Greek brothers. I worked twelve hours a day and received meals and five dollars a week in wages, but it was the tips that made it worthwhile. They amounted to three or four dollars every day. Before many weeks had passed I had sixty dollars stashed away for safekeeping at the bottom of a box of cornflakes.

I still didn't like waitress work, and I was too shy and self-conscious to be really good at it, but given the choice I would have stayed there indefinitely, since that was the only way I had found to make money fast. I believe now that I was hired only because I was young and, although I didn't realize it then, somewhat attractive. Every week I was invited to go along on the regular Saturday night parties with the two brothers and the other waitresses, but I always refused. I really had no desire to go and I was too inexperienced to know that my job was hanging in the balance. The next time Nick asked me to go and I turned him down he said, "Well okay, if you're too good to go out with me, then you're too good to work here. You're fired!"

It was a blow, but I wasn't discouraged. All I had to do, I thought, was to find another waitress job. But although I tramped the streets daily and searched the want ads, I was unable to find one. I took a job clerking in a dime store, where I made a bare living and could add nothing to my savings. I ate the cornflakes and transferred my money to a new box.

Determined to find waitress work I continued to search. One day I found an ad asking for girls eighteen or over to travel with a crew selling magazines on commission in small towns. The company would pay all traveling expenses except for meals. It sounded good and since I didn't see how I could be any worse off, I applied.

When I told the interviewer that I was eighteen she didn't question it. "Thank goodness", I thought, "this rough life must be making me look older." When she asked for my next of kin I gave her Papa's name with an address made up on the spur of the moment. I then signed a paper that I suppose absolved the company of responsibility in case of accidents. She told me to be there at eight o'clock the next morning ready to travel.

I quit my job at the dime store, packed my clothes, hid the money under the lining in my purse, and gave up my room. I could get another when we got back to Denver. I had forgotten to ask the lady when that would be, but it wasn't important.

We traveled in a black sedan with isinglass windows, driven by a young man named Jack. Clarice, the crew leader, a pleasingly plump blonde in her mid-twenties, sat in front and I shared the back seat with Millie and Gertie, both of whom were young, attractive brunettes.

Moving from town to town, we usually spent several days in each area until every residence and place of business had been canvassed. We carried cards containing a list of twenty-five magazines. The customer checked those he wanted to order and gave us a deposit, which was our commission. It was easy work, and although not as profitable as being a waitress it certainly beat working in the dime store.

We stayed in hotels, where Millie and Gertie shared one room, Clarice and I another. Jack, being the only male in the group, had a room by himself. We met for breakfast and dinner at small inexpensive cafes. At these gatherings there was always a lot of laughter, jokes and animated conversation, in which I seldom participated. As usual, I felt self-conscious and inferior, but they were quite friendly toward me and I didn't mind it too much.

Since I was totally unfamiliar with the area I paid little attention to where we were from day to day. Once I remember crossing some high mountains where we saw some spectacular scenery, but I never gave it a second thought. Clarice seemed to know what she was doing.

One evening when we were riding along toward the next town Gertie said, "one of the first things I'm going to do when we get to Los Angeles is to go swimming in the ocean."

"I'll be right there with you," Millie laughed, "that's something I've always wanted to do. California, here we come."

I was shocked and panic-stricken. My first instinct was to get out at the next town and take the train back to Denver. Then I thought, actually what difference does it make where I am? At least it's always warm in Los Angeles and Papa and Alvis are there, so maybe it's all for the best. So I kept quiet, not wanting these folks to know how stupid I had been not to realize that we were going to California.

Clarice had always doubted that I was really eighteen and had asked me about it several times. Finally, (we were somewhere in New Mexico at the time) I admitted that I had lied about my age, but only by a few months I assured her.

"It wouldn't make any difference if it was only a few days," she said. "Jack told me just the other day that there is a law against transporting minors across state lines, so he must be worried about it, too. If you got into any trouble he and I would be held responsible."

After that, when they went out at night to have fun she locked me in the hotel room. I didn't mind being a prisoner as long as I had something to read, and Clarice kept me supplied with magazines. I don't suppose she ever wondered how I would get out in case of fire, and neither did I. Fortunately, that never happened.

We crossed Arizona on Highway "66", which would later become famous in the thirties as the road the "Oakies" traveled in their flight from the dust bowl. In the Mojave Desert we ran into a dust storm and were marooned by the side of the road for some time until it had blown itself out. Those button-down side curtains were very little protection against the blowing sand. When at last it was over we went on across the pass and dropped down into San Bernardino where we spent the night. After working several small towns we arrived in Los Angeles.

It was the first day of December, 1924. In exactly one month I would at last be eighteen. I had decided to follow Orva's example and get a job at the telephone company. The pay would be low at first, but there were raises. At least it would be permanent and I could stop running.

Chapter 10

After telling Clarice and the others goodbye, I found the listing for Alvis Ramsey with no trouble since at that time there was only one phone book for the entire Los Angeles area. I talked to Alvis and his wife, Minnie, neither of whom I had ever met, and they seemed genuinely glad to hear from me. They insisted that I stay with them until I found a job. Alvis told me to wait on a certain corner and he would pick me up. I told him what color dress I was wearing and he said he would recognize me anyway because I would be the only young girl with a suitcase on that corner.

When we arrived at the house my half-sister Ruby and her husband, Will, were there with their son Clifford to greet me, along with Alvis' and Minnie's daughter, Babe. Babe was a tall, buxom woman in her thirties and was a schoolteacher. It was like a family reunion. Although there was no hugging or kissing they certainly made me feel welcome. Papa appeared to be in good health except for some loss of hearing. He said, "Hello Dorothy," and actually put his arm across my shoulders, so I knew he was glad to see me.

That December was a happy month for me. I went to the beach with Clifford and his friends, took my first and last ride on a roller coaster (I just wasn't the dare-devil type) and had my first drink. It was gin mixed with something or other, ginger ale I think, and I didn't like it. I went swimming in the ocean several times, and although I didn't know how to swim, I paddled around and got wet all over, and it was fun. My bathing suit was right in style. It was made of blue serge, had a high neck with a collar, short sleeves, and bloomers, which were hidden by a long full skirt that came to my knees.

I filled out an application at the telephone company, and just in case there was any doubt about my age, I wrote to Oklahoma for my birth certificate and learned that it had been destroyed in a fire, but Papa signed an affidavit stating that I was indeed eighteen. In the middle of January I was hired as a trainee at fourteen dollars a week.

Soon after going to work I rented a room from two old ladies who were sisters. They lived in a private home near Westlake Park, a short streetcar ride from downtown. Most of my spare time I spent in my room reading books that I got free at the library, or sitting in the living room playing records on the old wind-up Victrola. The old ladies were seldom there as they went to bed early, and they said they didn't mind the music. It was soft and beautiful and it put them to sleep. On my days off I walked in the park and sat on a bench watching the swans and ducks on the lake. I even got into conversation now and then with other women, usually those who had brought their children to the park to play. Some evenings I spent a quarter and went to the movies; it was my only extravagance.

The job suited me. Unlike waitress work it was not nerve-wracking or demanding and anyone with half a brain could do it. I sat at one of a long line of switchboards saying, "number please," and plugged in calls, watched over by the ever-present Chief Operator, who paced up and down behind the line of girls ready to take over instantly in case of trouble. She was a friendly person and I liked her. I don't remember her name, but privately I called her "The Ostrich" because she looked like one. She was thin and scrawny, had a long pointed nose, her mouth was a long thin line and her salt and pepper hair was pulled up into a tight knot on top of her head. She wore black pointed-toed shoes and she must have had flat feet, for she walked splayfooted. I often wondered whether the other girls noticed the striking resemblance, but I never said anything because I didn't want to hurt her feelings.

As a matter of fact, during the first three months I worked there I never spoke to the other girls at all, and they pointedly ignored me. I learned later on that they thought I was "stuck-up", that I considered myself superior. Actually I was mentally afraid of them. Several times I even crossed the street in order to avoid passing some of them on the sidewalk and being faced with the terrible dilemma of whether or not to speak to them.

Looking back on it later, I realized that although by nature I was meant to be friendly and outgoing, I was still suffering from the terrible inferiority complex acquired during my unfortunate childhood, and unless people spoke to me first I retreated into my shell and slammed the door, like a hermit crab.

One day I was sitting in the lounge taking my ten-minute break when a girl sat down beside me and introduced herself. Her name was Agnes Bell, she said, but she didn't much like the name Agnes and her friends called her Bell. She told me all about herself. She was nineteen, lived with her parents and had two older brothers and a younger sister. She was a vivacious, attractive girl with a heart-shaped face and straight black hair cut in a pageboy fashion, the latest style. Women had just begun bobbing their hair as a sign of emancipation.

Bell and I became good friends, and since we both worked a split shift we began going to dances every afternoon and every night at Cinderella Roof, a large ballroom just two blocks away. Both of us were good dancers and were soon included in a group of enthusiasts who came there not to meet members of the opposite sex but for the sheer love of dancing. In those days people did not stand in one place, jump up and down and call it dancing. To be a good dancer required talent, expertise and a fine sense of rhythm. It was like floating on clouds in time to music. The best dancer in the place was an old man with white hair who must have been at least sixty. He was an early-day Fred Astair, and I never missed an opportunity to dance with him. He and I won a waltz contest, and it was one of the happiest moments of my life.

There was no dancing in Los Angeles on Sundays, because of the "Blue Law." In fact, the entire town curled up and died on Sunday. All the stores were closed, you couldn't buy so much as a candy bar and the town was like a graveyard. Every Sunday several of us piled into an old open-top jalopy belonging to one of the boys and drove twenty miles to Venice, a beach town where there was a ballroom on the ocean front, and no blue laws.

At that time prohibition was in force and drinking was against the law. Gangsters had come out of the woodwork, had taken over the liquor business and were making millions. A lot of young people, many of whom had never before bothered to imbibe, took to drinking simply because it was against the law and had become the "in" thing to do.

We went to "speak-easies", where you were not admitted unless you knew the password, and where, at exorbitant prices they served what they called "set-ups", which were glasses containing ice cubes and ginger ale. The boys added bootleg whiskey from flasks carried in their hip pockets. There was always a postage stamp-size dance floor, and although space was limited, after a couple of drinks it didn't seem to matter. I had a wonderful time for almost two years.

However, "all good things must end," as they say, and my carefree life came to a screeching halt. After four years of silence I received a letter from Mama. She had finally gotten in touch with Orva, who gave her my address. She said she was glad to hear that I was doing so well. She and the twins, who were now almost sixteen, were in San Antonio, Texas. What with trying to keep the girls in school, she said she was having a tough time making ends meet and that her rheumatism was giving her a lot of trouble. She hoped I could send a little money now and then to help out.

What could I do? Because of my concern for Pansy and Pearl I sent her what little I could spare out of the sixteen a week I was now earning. To make extra money I got a night job, along with Bell, who thought it would be fun, at a dime-a-dance place called Roseland. We were required to dance with any man who gave us a ticket, and since all of them were there looking for dates and most of them were lousy dancers, it wasn't much fun. But I made a couple of dollars every night.

When the place closed at midnight Bell and I walked about six blocks through deserted downtown streets to catch the last street car. It never occurred to us to be afraid because there was very little crime then. Muggers, dope-fiends and rapists were not roaming the streets, and we were quite safe.

When I had been moonlighting for several months a lot of things happened in rapid succession. First, Roseland closed; the place was torn down and replaced by an office building. Second, Bell got married and moved to a small town in Northern California. Third, I received another raise to eighteen dollars a week and then, without any previous warning, Mama and the girls showed up at the telephone office. I was excused from the switchboard and met them in the lounge. We said, "Hello" and sat down on one of the couches. "Why didn't you let me know you were coming?" I asked.

"I thought it would be fun to surprise you," she said. She seemed to take it for granted that I would be glad to see her.

I was certainly surprised. Mama had cut her hair, dyed it red and wore it in tight little curls all over her head. She looked like an overweight, middle-aged floozy. I was thankful that there was no one I knew in the lounge so I wouldn't have to introduce her as my mother. Pearl had changed little. She was still thin and quite short, not much over five feet. Pansy had grown taller, developed a good figure and had turned out to be very attractive.

Mama told me all about the places they had been and the various jobs she had held, but showed little interest in what I had been doing for the past four years. She didn't ask about Papa or about her two stepchildren, Alvis and Ruby. She obviously had no intention of going to see them.

She left the next day for San Diego, taking Pearl with her but leaving Pansy for me to look after. Apparently her sole purpose in coming to Los Angeles had been to get rid of Pansy. She seemed to feel that once a girl had reached the age of sixteen she was grown up and was no longer her responsibility. I have often wondered why she didn't leave both of the twins with me. It must have been because she had always seemed to like Pearl.

Since that summer in Albuquerque, Pansy and I had always been drawn toward each other, and I was glad to have her with me. I rented a housekeeping room with a tiny kitchen. Pansy changed her name to Jean, with my blessing, and began looking for work. Her age and her terrible inferiority complex, which was even worse than mine (if such a thing was possible), hampered her in finding a job. She had to settle for baby-sitting and an occasional job of housecleaning. We went to Cinderella Roof a few times. Jean took to dancing as a duck takes to water, but we had to give it up because we couldn't afford the admission price. No matter how careful we were we never had enough money.

I found an extra job parking cars in an all-night garage from ten p.m. to three a.m. It was really a man's job but because I was young and strong and knew how to drive, but mainly because women always came cheaper, they hired me. After working there a few weeks I knew I would have to quit as I was endangering my job at the telephone company by being late so often. Four or five hours sleep a night really wasn't enough. Another Roseland would have come in handy right about then, but there wasn't one.

Just when I was wondering how we could possibly manage without that extra income, Jean and I saw an advertisement in the paper for girls to tryout for the chorus at Pantages, a big theatre, where before showing the movie they put on a stage show consisting of various vaudeville acts and a chorus. Although we had little hope, we had nothing to lose by trying, and much to our surprise both of us were chosen. The salary would be thirty dollars a week, which to us was a fabulous amount. The temptation was irresistible. Without a backward glance I quit my job at the telephone company. I had worked almost three years and knew I would have to work a lot longer before I could hope to make the money that I would be making at Pantages. No doubt it was not the sensible thing to do but I never regretted it. We had a wonderful time and enjoyed every minute of it—while it lasted. Most of the time we danced in the chorus but sometimes, because we were tall, we became "show girls" parading across the stage in fantastic costumes. Now and then we did "specialties." One week Jean performed an exotic Egyptian dance, and with her straight dark hair and great figure she was perfect for the part. Dressed as a cowboy I did a rope—twirling tap-dancing act. Once I was selected to sit on top of a grand piano pretending to be a statue. I had to be in my place for ten minutes before the curtain went up.

One day, when I was in the middle of an exciting story and anxious to find out what happened next, I took the book along and read while I waited. When the curtain rose I was still reading. Had I been a fast thinker I would have continued to read and perhaps the audience would have thought that's what I was supposed to be doing. Instead, I dropped the book and assumed my pose. It brought down the house (as they say in show business), but I almost lost my job.

We were chorus girls for almost a year and in spite of having to buy cosmetics and have our hair and nails done in a beauty shop, we managed to save quite a bit. Then suddenly the theatres stopped putting on stage shows, switched to double feature movies and we were out of a job.

Dot, the Roaring 20's

Dot, 1927

For a few months we traveled with a road show putting on plays in small towns around Los Angeles. I played the part of an old lady who sat in a rocking chair making caustic remarks, and Jean was the timid wife of an arrogant, over-bearing villain. It was an interesting experience and we made a living, but were unable to save any money since we had to pay hotel bills and eat in restaurants.

Apparently the show was not a howling success. One night the manager took off still owing all of us three weeks pay and left us stranded in San Bernardino. We had dipped into our savings while waiting for those promised paychecks, and when we arrived back in Los Angeles we had only enough money to rent a room and live for a couple of weeks while we looked for work.

Chapter 11

During this time we heard from Pearl occasionally. She and Mama had settled in Escondido, a small town north of San Diego. She had changed her name to Helen, become a waitress and had fallen in love with a 28-year-old fellow named Jess. After warning her not to marry the guy, Mama took off for Alaska. Of course, Helen married Jess. By the time she was eighteen she had two babies and a divorce. Mama showed up again and took care of the children while Helen worked. Several years later, after Helen had married again, had two more children and another divorce, Mama demanded payment for that baby-sitting, but I don't believe she ever collected.

We had gone to see Papa twice while we were dancing in the chorus. He seemed happy to know that we were making money doing something we enjoyed, but the others, being very religious and convinced that dancing in any form was a sin, did not approve. Alvis wrote to Orva warning her that Dorothy and Pansy were "going to Hell in a handcart."

Now as the days passed and we were unable to find jobs, we began to think that perhaps that prediction was coming true. We were literally down to our last nickel and had gone three days without food when we finally went to work teaching dancing in a downtown studio.

There were four sound-proof rooms, each with a phonograph and records, for private lessons and one large room where dances were held every Saturday night free of charge for those pupils who wanted to practice with different partners. It was our first experience at teaching but we loved it, and were so filled with the desire to turn every pupil into a good dancer (even with the hopeless cases we never gave up on) that our appointment books were usually full and we made more than an adequate living.

One of Jean's regular pupils was a young man named Ed Woodward. He was quite thin, had dark straight hair and was of medium height. He was obviously well educated and had a good job with a company that made transformers. He was also a dedicated hypochondriac but neither Jean nor I realized it then. He began asking her out to dinner and to shows, and a few months later they were married.

Several weeks later I went on the bus to San Francisco with Christine, one of the teachers whom I had come to know well. Two years older than me, she was a tall attractive brunette, a good dancer and an excellent teacher with a great deal of experience. She had taught for several years at one of the large studios in San Francisco and had quit to go with her boyfriend to Los Angeles where they had planned to be married. Now they had broken it off and she was anxious to get back up north, where, she said, she could make twice as much money. It did sound promising, and since I no longer had anyone to feel responsible for, I went along.

Christine and I went to work at the same studio where she had earlier taught dancing and I soon found that she was right about the money. They charged more for lessons, hence the commissions were higher and my income was double what it had been in Los Angeles. I opened a checking account (I no longer resorted to the cornflakes box) and bought some new clothes.

Life was fun in San Francisco. I was making good money doing work I loved and I met several interesting men. One of them took me to Seal· Rock, where we watched hundreds of seals cavorting in the water and basking in the sun on the rocks. I saw the famous Golden Gate and it was a breathtaking, awe-inspiring sight. The bridge that would someday span that vast expanse of ocean was still in the future. One day I rode the ferry across the bay to Oakland and spent the day climbing a mountain with a group of outdoor enthusiasts. Several times I had dinner in quaint little cafes at Fisherman's Wharf.

It was during this time that I passed up the only chance I ever had to marry for money. His name was Jay Watt. He was a rich, fifty-one year old banker whose wife had died several years before. Now he lived alone in one of the swank hotels, and he was trying, with little success, to learn to dance. He was short and pudgy and what little hair he had left was more grey than brown, but I liked him very much and enjoyed his company. It was with him that I saw the world's first talking movie, "Sonny Boy." He took me to the best restaurants and to theatres and concerts. He seemed to enjoy listening to music, although he was utterly devoid of a sense of rhythm. I tried my best to teach him to dance, but I had no desire to marry him.

Hoover was elected President for a second term and less than a year later the stock market crashed. Wealthy men, unable to face the horror of being down to their last million, hurled themselves from high windows. Business at the studio fell off alarmingly and several of us were laid off with the promise that we would be called back as soon as business picked up, as everyone seemed to think it was bound to do. Hoover made speeches on the radio promising that soon there would be a "chicken in every pot and two cars in every garage." It wasn't too long before a lot of people didn't even have a pot, much less a chicken.

Since I was out of a job now, and there seemed none to be had, I thought this would be a good time to go to Kansas City to visit Orva, whom I had not seen for twelve years. In a few weeks this economic crisis would be over, as everyone seemed to think, and I could come back and resume teaching.

Orva had been promoted to chief operator. She and her husband, "Judge" Crockett, who also worked for the telephone company, had three children, two boys and a girl, and they enjoyed a happy, stable marriage. Of the four of us who survived, she was the only one who lived a sensible, normal life, possibly because she had been able to get out and live with relatives when she was so young, thus escaping those horrible hitchhiking years.

The news from the dance studio was negative, so there was no point in my going back to San Francisco. Instead of improving, the situation was worsening. All over the country banks were failing and since there was no deposit insurance, many people lost their life savings. The jobless rate zoomed as thousands of workers were laid off. Men sold apples on street corners trying desperately to make a dime to buy a loaf of bread. The Great Depression was on, growing deeper with each passing month.

There was no work of any kind to be found in Kansas City. When I heard that a new show was opening in Fort Wayne, Indiana, I went there, tried out and once again became a chorus girl. The main thing I remember about that show was that the Mills Brothers, four black men who later became famous, sang there twice a day for a week. They were wonderful and I never missed a performance. One of the songs that seemed to have a special appeal for me was called, "Lonesome Road." I never forgot the words or the melody.

One day I was sitting in the hotel lobby reading a newspaper when a young man sat down beside me and introduced himself as Ralph Cramer. He was tall, dark and although not handsome, was not bad looking. He appeared to be in his early thirties. He said he lived with his widowed mother and younger brother, and that he happened to be in the lobby talking to a friend when he noticed me. I felt sure he was handing me a line (I had learned to be wary of men who approached me in hotel lobbies)

55

and tried to ignore him, but he was persistent. He gave me a card bearing the name of a men's clothing store and said he worked there in the credit department.

He was attractive and I really liked him, so when I realized that he wasn't just a guy on the make we became good friends. He often came to the hotel during his lunch hour, which happened to coincide with the time I went to work. We would have lunch together and then he would drive me to the theatre. Sometimes he picked me up at night when the show was over and we would have a midnight snack and talk. Once he took me to a nightclub where I met his brother, Howard, a quiet, soft-spoken young man who played trombone in the orchestra. We didn't do any drinking because Ralph didn't drink, but we had dinner and danced. I found him to be a fairly good dancer with a great sense of rhythm. I learned later that he was an excellent piano player.

When Ralph asked me to marry him, instead of turning him off with the usual "thanks, but no thanks," I told him I would think about it. He took me out to his house to meet his mother, Isabel. She was a thin-featured, austere, no nonsense woman in her late fifties. She wore her long brown hair pulled back severely and twisted into a knot. Although, on the surface she was friendly and polite, I· knew somehow that she did not approve of me, but I didn't know why. Several years later I learned that it was because I was a dancer. Had I been a nurse or a schoolteacher she would no doubt have welcomed me with open arms, but to her anyone in show business was automatically suspect.

The show in Fort Wayne closed because of low attendance, due no doubt to the depression, which was worsening day by day. I went to Indianapolis and tried out for a show there but was turned down because I was too tall. They were hiring only "ponies", girls five feet three or less. After applying, without success, at every dance studio in town, I finally settled for waitress work, the only job available.

Ralph followed me to Indianapolis, still intent on getting married. We set the date for the following week. I wrote to Orva telling her I was getting married and that we would stop and see her on our way to California. Ralph drove to Fort Wayne, told his mother and brother goodbye, collected his clothes and other belongings and was back the next day ready and eager to travel west.

As luck would have it, Mama was at Orva's the day my letter arrived and two days later she showed up at my rooming house. She wanted to attend the wedding. She said her other three girls had married without letting her know, (how could they since most of the time none of us knew where she was). This would be her last chance to see one of her girls married.

This was indeed her last chance, and she blew it by making it obvious from the start that she didn't like Ralph. She criticized him for quitting a good job, and called him a Jew (he wasn't; he was Scotch, German and French). He retaliated by making fun of her hat and suggested that she should go on a diet and lose some weight. They quarreled bitterly over the rules when we played cards one evening and the next day she left in a huff, after warning me not to marry that "opinionated, over-bearing, good for nothing man." I believe she went to New York that time. I should write a book about her and call it, "What Makes Mama Run?"

A few days later Ralph and I were married in a church in Kansas City. Unlike his mother, who was a staunch Episcopalian, he was not very religious but he apparently felt that having a minister perform the ceremony would make it more binding. I really didn't care and would have been quite willing to settle for a Justice of the Peace.

It was not what could be called a big wedding. There were just the two of us, the minister, and the minister's wife who acted as witness. Afterward we stopped to see Orva and Judge, then set out for Los Angeles in Ralph's car, a 1926 black Ford roadster with what was then called a rumble seat.

Ralph Cramer, 1930

Chapter 12

We arrived in Los Angeles to find that there had been some changes since I left. Papa had died at the age of seventy-five and Alvis was dead from a heart attack. Clifford had joined the Navy and was stationed in Florida. My sister Helen had married an Army man, had another baby and was living in Panama.

Ed was still working for the transformer company, but several of his co-workers had been laid off and he was just counting the days until it was his turn. "The handwriting is on the wall," he said. He and Jean often came over in the evenings and played cards with us for pennies.

Ralph got a job selling life insurance and I learned to cook by the trial and error method. I will never forget my first attempt at making a cake. When I removed the two layers from the oven they looked great. I put them together and covered the whole thing with chocolate frosting. No one had ever told me that you were supposed to let the cake cool first. It was beautiful, but it weighed a ton and was practically inedible.

In December I discovered that I was pregnant. Having learned from Orva that Mama was in Gallup, New Mexico, working in the diet kitchen at a hospital, I wrote a long, friendly letter and told her that I was expecting a baby. I should have known better. I received no answer. She immediately wrote to all of the aunts, uncles, cousins and half-brothers and sisters all over the country and told them that Dorothy had gotten into trouble and had had to get married. This was long before the sexual revolution; such a thing was a terrible disgrace and no girl ever lived it down. When Orva found out about it she bought back copies of the newspaper containing the vital statistics of our marriage and mailed them to everyone, along with her comments on the subject. Mama never apologized; she just shrugged it off as being of no importance.

Ann was born on August 10, 1931. Obviously disappointed that she was not a boy, Ralph called his mother and made the statement that she would never forget, one that was destined to have an adverse effect on the childhood of his only son, who was born two years later.

"The baby's here, but it's a girl," he said.

I was not present during this phone call. Not until several years later did I hear about it when Ralph's mother threw it up to him during a quarrel and he admitted it. Not until then did I realize how much he had counted on the baby being a boy. He had never mentioned it to me, and for this forbearance I can only give him credit.

When Ann was three months old Isabel came for a visit, which turned out to be permanent except for one short break. She fell in love with Ann, and assuming that Ralph cared nothing for the baby because it was only a girl, and since her opinion of me was less than zero (she was careful not to make her dislike obvious) she felt she should stick around and protect Ann from being mistreated. I went along with it because she was Ralph's mother and I lacked the nerve to tell her to leave. Besides, to me she was old and needed to be taken care of. Little did I know then that Isabel had a will of iron and was quite capable of taking care of herself.

Ralph lost his job with the insurance company because he failed to pass the physical examination. He had gained a great deal of weight and he was found to have some sort of kidney trouble. We moved to San Bernardino and he went to work in the credit department at a clothing store.

He was lucky to have a job for the depression was growing steadily worse. Ed's company went bankrupt and he and Jean were barely existing on what little he could earn doing odd jobs. There was no unemployment insurance then. Hoover continued to rant about "a chicken in every pot" while doing absolutely nothing to ease the situation.

Prices sank to their lowest point since the turn of the century. Eggs were fifteen cents a dozen. Bacon and hamburger were ten cents per pound. A pound of real butter cost a quarter but oleomargarine was much cheaper. It looked like slabs of white lard, but could be colored by breaking open an enclosed capsule of coloring matter. The big dairy companies made it unlawful to sell it already colored.

One day Mama stopped by for a couple of hours, having gotten my address from Jean. She was on her way to Colorado. She immediately antagonized Isabel by criticizing her hair-do and her lack of make-up. She then made some snide remarks about the fact that we bathed Ann in a small tin washtub (she didn't offer to buy us a baby bath) and went away mad, as always. I feel sure that because of Mama I must have dropped a few more notches on Isabel's popularity chart.

Although there was no love lost between us, Isabel and I never quarreled. She was a strong, silent type of woman, and since I had a thing about anyone getting mad at me (probably a hangover from my childhood) I went out of my way to avoid dissension and we got along all right. Every afternoon she would put Ann in the buggy and take her to the park, while I played baseball with the little boys next door. We could not afford to buy many toys for Ann. We used to give her an old glass sugar bowl filled with buttons of various sizes and colors. She would remove them one at a time and line them up on the floor, then replace them one by one. She never put them in her mouth. She was not yet a year old but she seemed to know instinctively that those buttons were not for eating.

When Ann was a year old we moved to a big old-fashioned house with high ceilings and a fenced-in yard, only a few blocks from the railroad tracks. A lot of men were riding the freight trains from town to town looking for work, and almost every day one or two of them would knock on the back door and ask for a handout. I always gave them a sandwich, a cup of coffee and a couple of cigarettes. It never occurred to me to be afraid of them. Even though many people all over the country were on the verge of starvation, there was very little crime. Times have certainly changed; nowadays I would lock the doors and call the police.

Times were tough and we really didn't plan to have any more children, but birth control methods then left much to be desired and I soon learned that I was pregnant again, or as they called it then, "in the family way." The word "pregnant" was as taboo as the word "sex" and was never spoken, nor did it ever appear in print.

Urged on by Isabel, who was dead set against our having another baby, Ralph brought home some medicine that was supposed to cause a miscarriage, but unable to bear the thought of killing this unborn child I simply could not bring myself to take it. I flushed the medicine down the toilet and told Ralph that it didn't work.

The baby arrived in March 28, 1933, and we called him Richard Allen, a name that was almost immediately shortened to Dick. Almost from the day we took him home trouble began. Isabel disliked Dick and ignored him. She and Ralph had a serious quarrel, and I learned about the remark he had made when Ann was born. She felt that since Ralph now had his longed-for boy, poor little Ann would be pushed aside and neglected. With a deplorable lack of logic she took out her anger on a helpless baby.

Until he was about four months old Dick cried a lot and I was often up with him half the night. Thus I learned that Isabel was giving Ann a bottle

Ralph, Dot, Dick—1933

in the middle of the night. I thought it was ridiculous, told her so and tried to get her to stop. She flatly refused and I then realized that she had come to feel that Ann was her child and that it was none of my business. I lost my temper and we had some hot arguments. Ralph got into the act, took my side and told her that under the circumstances it would probably be best if she left. She went back to Fort Wayne, and peace descended.

Roosevelt was now President. He had ended prohibition, thus cutting off the main source of income for the gangsters who had become rich and powerful selling bootleg whiskey. He straightened out the banks and put many thousands of people to work on W.P.A. and in the C.C.C. camps. Ed had a steady job now on W.P.A. and thought Roosevelt was wonderful. When World War II came along, he made a lot of money with his own transformer company, turned Republican and became a Roosevelt hater, which was a typical reaction at that time.

In 1935 we moved to Bell, a small town near Los Angeles, where Ralph had a much better paying job as credit manager in a clothing store. Except that he was now grossly overweight, he appeared to be in good health and was never sick. We had been married for almost five years now and had never had a quarrel. We were happy, things were looking up and we were planning to buy a house. At that time nice three-bedroom homes in good neighborhoods could be had for two or three thousand dollars.

Then suddenly, without any warning signs, Ralph had what I thought was a nervous breakdown. He quit his job. He became critical and hard to get along with and didn't seem to care that there was no money coming in now to pay the rent and buy food. He wrote his mother a crazy mixed up letter, and she, knowing instantly what was wrong, came out to do what she could to help.

Isabel took care of the children and I went to work on W.P.A. That didn't last long because they put me to work hand sewing. I was inept and awkward; my only experience at sewing had been mending rips on my old treadle sewing machine. I would have done better digging ditches or driving a truck, but being a woman I had to sew or else. When the boss insisted that I use a thimble that really tore it; I opted for the "or else" and quit. I got a job selling a product called "Marvel" house to house. It was a white powder that was supposed to prevent runs in stockings.

Since Ralph refused to let me use the car, I rode the streetcar every morning to Los Angeles, where a couple named Johnson operated the business from their apartment. I was one of six sales ladies. Each day we were driven to our assigned territories where, with a stocking on one hand and a sharp pointed tongue depressor in the other, we demonstrated and sold "Marvel" for fifty cents a package. Each evening we were picked up, returned to the apartment and turned in our unsold packages, keeping half of the day's sales as commission. After the first couple of days I managed to overcome my fright at the thought of ringing a stranger's doorbell and was soon doing quite well making about twice what I had earned on W.P.A.

I had always assumed that the Johnsons ordered the product from some big company, until one evening when I went back to the apartment to retrieve a package I had left there. No one answered my knock, but I knew they were there as I could hear a radio going full blast. I opened the door. There was no one in the living room. They had an assembly line set up in the kitchen. Mr. Johnson, wielding a scoop, was filling the envelopes, his wife was sealing them, one of the girls was squirting perfume on each package and another girl was piling them in stacks of twelve and placing a rubber band around each stack. Without announcing my presence, I left, gently closing the door behind me.

All the way home I thought about my astounding discovery and the more I thought about it the more obsessed I became with the idea of making up the stuff myself, thus reaping a larger share of the profits. It might be an impossible dream, as I had no idea how much it would cost to have envelopes printed or how to go about learning the formula.

The next day while we waited on the corner for Mr. Johnson to pick us up, I told Corrine what I had found out. Over the weeks she and I had become good friends, and I suggested that we pool our resources and go into business together.

"I don't want to get involved," she said, "we might be breaking the law."

I had worried some about that myself but not enough to stop me. After all, Johnson was getting by with it so why couldn't I? Of course, he might have a license to operate a business since he was hiring people to work for him, but somehow I doubted it.

"Do you happen to know what this powder is?" I asked Corrine.

"No, but my boyfriend is a chemist and I'm sure he can easily find out." I gave her a package of Marvel, which I would report as having been sold, and told her that I would certainly appreciate it if she could find out what it was.

A few days later she reported that the powder was aluminum sulphate, a chemical that tended to tighten and strengthen threads. There was also a bit of Epsom salts but that was apparently added in the hope of confusing would-be imitators.

Having decided to call my product "Runproof", I designed an envelope, then spent hours trudging from place to place downtown, only to find that the cost for printing was more than I could afford. I finally found a little "hole in the wall" place on south Los Angeles Street, almost in the slums, called "Levi Printing" I'll always remember Mr. Levi with affection; he made it possible for me to realize my dream.

He was a little old man with grey, bushy hair. He squinted at me over his glasses. "I tell you vat I can do for you," he said. "If I haf only to run these through the press once with mucilage on the sides, you can fold them yourself. It vill take time but it vill safe lots of money." Since I had far more time than I had money I thought it was a wonderful idea. I ordered a thousand envelopes, which would be ready in about a week. While waiting I went back to selling "Marvel".

Early one morning the following week I took the car key from Ralph's pocket while he was still sleeping, drove to Los Angeles, collected the envelopes and picked up a ninety pound sack of aluminum sulphate at a wholesale drug company. I decided to dispense with the Epsom salts; it would just be a lot more trouble and I had no desire to confuse anyone.

When I figured it out later, I found that the packages cost about five cents each, so with each sale I made forty-five cents profit. Besides supporting the family I was able to save a little. The situation at home seemed to be going from bad to worse and thinking that it would be smart to have some "mad" money, as they used to call it, I opened a savings account and kept the bank book carefully hidden in my big "Runproof" purse.

Chapter 13

It was November now and the days were getting shorter and a little chilly. Ralph and I saw very little of each other during these troubled times. He was usually still asleep when I left in the mornings and Isabel told me that often during the day he would take the car and disappear, returning late at night. I knew he was not going to bars because he didn't drink, but I never asked him where he had been. Sometimes he would try to start a fight by making cruel, sadistic remarks, but I managed to ignore it because I knew that basically he was good-natured and easy going and I felt sure he would eventually recover and get back to normal. It turned out that I was whistling in the dark.

One night while I was folding envelopes Ralph and his mother had a terrible argument and during the course of it I learned that he had had several of these attacks before, at long intervals. He claimed that it was temporary insanity, but I didn't believe that. Insane people never realize they are crazy; they think everyone else is. Isabel insisted that the attacks were caused by a football injury. Years later I learned that he was what is now called a manic-depressive, but at that time little was known about the condition and doctors usually diagnosed it as a nervous breakdown.

The fight went on but it was now one-sided. Isabel just stood there tight-lipped and silent, while Ralph continued to hurl insults at her. Finally, he told her to get out of his house. At this point I intervened. I reminded Isabel that this was my house, too, and I didn't want her to leave. I urged her to ignore Ralph and go on to bed. Paying no attention to me, she packed her suitcase and spent the night in a hotel.

I was shocked that Ralph would put his mother out in the middle of the night and made the mistake of telling him so. He gave me a black eye along with various other bruises and then fell into bed. I spent the rest of the night sitting on the couch putting cold cloths on my eye and wondering what to do. Although I didn't realize it then, Ralph had suddenly gone from the depressive to the manic stage. For the first time I was afraid of him and of what he might do to the children, and my only desire now was to get him out of the house. As soon as it was light I went to the neighbor's house, called the police and had him arrested for assault and battery.

Knowing little then of court procedures, I had assumed that Ralph would be held for awhile, but he was released the same day. His trial would be held in two weeks. But at least, being arrested had frightened him into leaving me alone. The next day he gathered up his clothes, got in his car and took off, apparently unconcerned with how I was going to cope with my situation.

I couldn't find a baby-sitter; everyone who needed a job seemed to be on W.P.A. now. The nearest day nursery was ten miles away and I had no car. Jean came out and stayed with the children several days while I sold Runproof and continued to look for a baby sitter.

One evening I came home and found that Ann was gone.

"Ralph came this afternoon and took her away," Jean said. "He told me to tell you that he wants a divorce."

I called the police station and reported that my little girl had been abducted, but when they learned that Ralph was the child's father they said there was nothing they could do, since they had no court order restraining him.

Jean took Dick home with her so he would be out of harm's way in case trouble erupted. I wasn't really worried about Ann, as I felt sure she was with Isabel, who had no doubt talked Ralph into this, but I had no idea where she was living. I spent a lot of nickels in a phone booth calling every hotel and rooming house in Bell asking whether Isabel Cramer was staying there, but the answer was always, no. Finding her seemed to be impossible, and it would do me no good anyway because I could not legally force Ralph to bring her back.

But I did have an ace in the hole. His trial would be coming up soon, and unless I dropped the charges he would probably be spending some time in jail. I would wait, hoping that he would show up and would be in a bargaining mood.

One day when I came home from work the car was parked in the driveway and Ralph was loading Ann's clothes and toys into the back seat.

"Hello, Ralph," I said in a friendly tone, "I'd like to talk to you about this situation." He was in no mood for discussion, friendly or otherwise. Ignoring me, he made another trip into the house. I got into the car, determined to stay there until I had a chance to talk to him. At least if he went to his mother's place I would find out where she lived.

When Ralph came out of the house and saw me in the car he walked around, opened the door and told me to get out. I refused and he began pulling on my arm. "If you try to put me out I'll scream bloody murder and some one will call the cops," I said.

That stopped him. Slamming the door shut, he backed the car out of the driveway, parked it in front of the house and asked the man next door to stand on his front porch and watch. "I'm going to put my wife out of the car and I'd like you to witness that I don't hit her or harm her in any way."

He started toward me, I screamed and he froze with his hand on the car door. Then he smiled, went around the car and got in. Now we can talk about it, I was thinking, when he suddenly started the car, took off, and was soon going fifty miles an hour down the main road that led out of town. Looking at me with a cruel, fiendish grin, he said, "Okay, you asked for it!"

I was really frightened now and regretted staying in the car. I remembered stories I had read about gangsters who took people for rides from which they never returned and wondered it that was to be my fate. When we passed a service station I rolled down my window and shouted for help, but no one heard me.

Ralph drove out into the country and parked on a deserted road. The nearest house was at least a mile away. When I started to get out of the car Ralph said, "It won't do you any good to try running away. I've got a gun and I'll shoot you before you've gone very far."

Although I doubted that he had a gun, I didn't care to find out the hard way. My only chance, I thought, was to sit quietly, not fight back and hope he would come to his senses. For what seemed like hours I silently endured Ralph's verbal and physical abuse. Once a rural mailman came along and in desperation I honked the horn. Thinking that we had car trouble he came over and asked if there was anything he could do.

"No thanks," Ralph told him. "My wife and I are having an argument and you know how women are; they get hysterical."

I begged him to take me back to town, insisting that my life was in danger, but apparently he believed Ralph and didn't care to get involved in a family squabble. He got back in his car and drove away, leaving me there with that maniac.

Ralph seemed to think this episode was amusing. "I sure fooled that guy, because I'm such a good actor," he bragged. He went on talking about himself, "I've got a job playing piano in a bar and I've met some very influential people. Some day I'm going to be famous." The longer he talked the more his mood changed. Now he was affable, even friendly. "Let's go to that little cafe on the highway and have a sandwich," he suggested.

I was in no condition to eat anything, but I was all for getting someplace where there would be other people. I agreed and he drove back to the highway. While he ate and I drank iced tea, I told him that I was two months pregnant. He seemed to take the news in stride and suggested that I have an abortion. He could ask around, he said, and find a doctor who would do it. I refused, not only because I was afraid of back-alley doctors but also because I was against abortion on general principles.

Now that Ralph was in a genial, friendly mood, I brought up the subject uppermost in my mind. "I'll make a deal with you. Bring Ann back and I'll drop the charges so you won't have to worry about going to jail. I'll also file for divorce providing you agree that I'm to have sole custody of the children."

The threat of that pending jail sentence had been hanging over Ralph's head like the sword of Damocles, and he was so relieved to have it removed that he agreed to everything with no argument. He knew I would keep my promise. Actually, I had no desire to see him in jail, but I was glad now that I had had him arrested because it gave me a strong bargaining tool.

The next day Ralph brought Ann home and I dropped the charges. Jean helped me move into a duplex in Southgate, a suburb of Los Angeles. I had met the elderly woman who lived alone in the other half of the duplex. In her late sixties, Mrs. Silverman was a friendly Jewish woman. She liked children and if I lived next door she would be glad to earn a little extra money taking care of Ann and Dick during the day. My problem was solved, at least temporarily.

I was soon able to make a down payment on a used car. Often on Sunday I took the children to see Isabel because, even though I didn't like her, I felt that she had a right to see her grandchildren now and then. She was living in a tiny furnished room, making coffee and heating canned food on a hot plate. Although she never voiced her dislike for me, I could sense it. We were living under what might be called an armed truce. She appeared to be no longer holding a grudge against Dick and always seemed glad to see him.

I was afraid Mrs. Silverman's reaction would be, "no thanks," when she learned there was to be another baby, instead she seemed delighted. She knew all about babies, she said, having raised two of her own and she would be looking forward to it. She became very motherly, worried about my diet and wanted me to go to a doctor, but I could see no point in paying a doctor to tell me I was pregnant when I already knew it. Besides, I had Mrs. Silverman to advise me; who could ask for anything more? By some strange coincidence, these people seemed to come along just when I needed them most.

This peaceful existence ended abruptly in early February when Mrs. Silverman suffered a severe stroke and her children moved her to a nursing home.

I went to see her once, but the stroke had affected her mind and she didn't know who I was. She didn't even recognize the children. I was grief-stricken, not only for her but for myself. I had suddenly lost the only person who ever came close to being the mother I had never had.

Once more I was "up the creek without a paddle." I couldn't work because I couldn't find a baby sitter and even if I could find one I knew it would be only temporary, and that soon I would have to find another, and yet another. In desperation, and on the advice of a friend, I put the children in a Catholic Home, where for a nominal sum they would be cared for but not put up for adoption. A couple of days later, however, I removed them because I could not bear the thought that those "penguins," as I called the nuns, might brainwash them in the Catholic religion. There must be a better way.

As I lay awake that night wondering what to do the solution came to me and it was so simple that I wondered why I had not thought of it before. I would make a deal with Isabel. I knew that in order to have Ann with her she would be willing to do almost anything, even live in the same house with me. Also, she was obviously running out of money. She was sixty-five now, too old to get a job and there was no social security then. She certainly couldn't count on either of her sons to help her. She needed me as much as I needed her. The fact that she didn't like me was not important; she would take good care of the children and nothing else mattered.

The next day I talked it over with Isabel and she agreed, as I had known she would, that it was the only sensible thing to do. I rented a house in Huntington Park, we moved in together and I went back to work. Since Isabel was the strong silent type, a woman of few words, and I had an absolute aversion to quarreling, we got along fine and on the surface all was serene.

My sales increased along with my girth. I'm sure many people bought simply because they felt sorry for me. I didn't like that, but there was nothing I could do about it, and the extra money was welcome.

One day while I was extolling the wonders of Runproof, nature began sending signals. "Make up your mind quickly," I told the woman, "because I have to go and have a baby."

She became quite agitated. I think she was afraid I'd have the baby right there on her front porch. To calm her down I lied and told her that my friend was working on the next street and that she would take over. Then I went back to the car and drove to the hospital in Los Angeles.

The lady in the office told me to follow the ramp up to the next level and she must have notified the nurses in the emergency room that I was on my way. When I parked the car and got out there were two young men with a stretcher waiting for me. The very idea of lying down and being carried in made me feel like a fool.

"Surely you don't expect me to get on that thing" I said, "Don't be ridiculous! I'm able to walk." I strode past them toward the entrance and they followed along behind carrying the empty stretcher, nonplused by this unprecedented breaking of protocol.

Chapter 14

The baby arrived on July 4, 1936. I named her Elaine Martha but before she was a year old we were calling her Bunny and the name stuck. The day after I brought the baby home from the hospital I went back to work selling Runproof. I didn't even look for another job. Although I hated ringing doorbells, I was making more money than I could hope to make in an ordinary job even if I could have found one, which was doubtful.

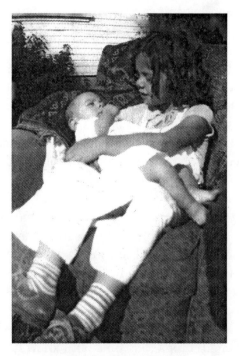

Ann and Bunny—1936

Isabel took good care of the children and they liked her, so I had no worries on that score or so I thought. They called her "Mom" and she taught them to call me "Dot". I often wonder why I didn't insist on being called

"Mother" but at the time, I suppose, it didn't seem important to argue about. And, she had the advantage; she was with them a lot more than I was.

I knew she didn't like me but she was quite adept at hiding her true feelings and I had no idea how deep her hatred for me was. Not until the children had grown up did I learn that during those years she had tried her best, without success, to turn them against me.

She was less successful in hiding her dislike for Dick and I soon realized that she was still holding a grudge against him for being Ralph's longed-for boy. It seemed totally illogical and senseless in an otherwise logical, sensible woman. She never abused him physically for she was essentially a good person, albeit with a hang-up. The cruelty was all in her mental attitude. She treated him the way my mother had treated me. Yet Dick was a well-behaved child; he did nothing to deserve such animosity.

When I tried to talk to her about it she refused to admit she didn't like Dick, insisting that she treated him no differently than she did the girls. Even Ann, who soon became aware of the situation (and whom Isabel practically worshipped), was unable to get through to her. It was like trying to reason with a block of granite.

I lacked the money to send Dick to a boarding school. Once, in desperation, I took him to live with Jean and Ed. Although they were glad to have the extra income, it didn't work out and after a few weeks I brought him home. Because of Ed's hypochondria they had become vegetarians, and Dick was like me—he didn't care much for vegetables. He claimed several years later when we were talking about it, that they even had vegetable ice cream!

My only recourse would have been to get rid of Isabel and face the prospect of hiring baby sitters, probably a succession of them, some of whom would have been unreliable. The lives of all three children would be disrupted with who knows what dire consequences. I chose what seemed to be the lesser of two evils, hoping that Dick would come through it with no permanent psychological damage. At least he knew that I was on his side and that I cared about him.

Ralph had called the hospital when Bunny was born but I didn't talk to him. I hadn't seen him for a long time but I knew he came to the house occasionally to see his mother and the children. Although Isabel never told me, I learned later that he gave her a little money now and then to help out. Having recovered temporarily from his "nervous breakdown" he married an extremely homely but very nice woman named Rose. A few years later he had another attack, divorced Rose and married again. He died when he was in his early fifties. I felt only a deep sorrow for him. Through no fault of his own he had had a miserable life.

One Saturday night, following a sudden impulse to walk down memory lane, I went to Cinderella Roof. Several years had passed but the place was unchanged except that there was now a bar downstairs where drinks were served. I was shocked and also pleased, that for the first time in my life my age was questioned and I had to produce my driver's license to prove that I was over twenty-one. Actually, I was twenty-nine, old enough to be glad that I looked younger. I saw no one I recognized. The original group had dispersed, replaced by others who seemed equally as dedicated to the art of expert dancing. I had such a wonderful time that I went back again every Saturday night just to satisfy my craving for dancing. I wasn't interested in dating anyone; I simply didn't want to get involved.

Then one night I met Herman Nienhuis, a tall thin man in his mid-forties. He resembled Abe Lincoln, except that he was younger and better looking. Born in Holland, he had come to this country when he was a child, had gone to work when he was fourteen and had never attended high school. Yet he was one of the smartest men I have ever known. Being naturally endowed with intelligence, he had educated himself by reading. He worked for the Post Office as a mail carrier and was thus one of the fortunate few who were not adversely affected by the depression. He lived by himself in an apartment and had never been married. He was the perennial bachelor and for that I was thankful, for although I liked him very much I had no desire to get married.

As a dancer Herm was only passable but he enjoyed good music. We went to concerts and movies, mostly musicals, and he introduced me to opera, some of which I liked. But his first love was the great outdoors. During the seven years I knew him I must have climbed every mountain in Southern California with Herm and his two best friends, Harold and Lois. Every year in the spring we made a trip to see the wild flowers bloom on the desert. It was a breathtaking sight; a carpet of color as far as the eye could see. He was good to the children. Although they were too young for hiking he often took us on picnics in the mountains. Once when Dick was about eight, he went with Herm and Harold on a weekend camping trip.

One Sunday Herm took me to Santa Anita. It was my first experience with horse racing and I immediately became obsessed with the idea that perhaps I could make money playing the horses and give up doorbell pushing. Thereafter many of my evenings were spent poring over racing forms looking for a sure-fire method. I didn't go to the track; I wasn't about to risk any money until I had found a way to beat the horses. Needless to say, I did not find it and finally had to give up. Not until many years later did I discover that the answer was not in the racing forms, instead it was at the track on the "tote" board.

Eventually I had to go farther afield to find new territory and to avoid competition so I began working the small towns between Los Angeles and San Francisco. I was usually away from home for two or three weeks at a time. To avoid paying for motel rooms I slept in the back seat of the car in trailer parks, where for twenty-five cents I could park in one of the spaces and use the shower. Every morning I went all out and spent thirty-five cents for a ham and egg breakfast. The rest of the time I lived on sandwiches, cokes and cigarettes. I had given up milk, my favorite drink, when I discovered that it was giving me headaches.

Those little towns were a real bonanza. It was virgin territory, there was no competition and I made a lot more money than I had in the Los Angeles area. My traveling expenses were minimal and for entertainment I bought books at Goodwill stores for three cents each and spent the evenings reading.

On one of my trips home I learned that Mama had died. She had been visiting Jean, and although she wasn't feeling well she refused, as usual, to stay in one place and had started for New Mexico. This time she didn't make it; she had a fatal heart attack in Riverside. She was sixty-five years old and was still running. Although her death saddened me, as anyone's death does, I felt guilty that I was unable to shed any tears for her.

Chapter 15

When Herm told me about an upcoming civil service examination for Postal employees, I thought I had finally hit the jackpot. All I had to do was to pass the test and eventually I would have a lifetime job and could kiss doorbell-pushing goodbye. The passing grade was seventy and I felt sure I could beat that by ten or fifteen points. I boned up on arithmetic, took the test, and much to my surprise and joy I received a ninety-seven. Being so near the top, I was confidant that I would not have long to wait. I even put off ordering supplies for Runproof.

Several months passed during which I heard nothing and I could only conclude that there must have been a great many extra smart people whose grades had beaten mine. Then I learned that two of Herm's men friends, whose grades were in the low eighties, had been called and were working at the Post Office. Thinking that there must be some mistake I checked with the man in the office who did the hiring and discovered that there were two lists, one for men and one for women. Only when all the near-morons on the men's list had been hired would they start calling women. Some day, probably several years down the road, I would possibly get a job at the Post Office.

This was the first time sex discrimination had cost me a job and I was bitter. Being a woman, I thought, was a terrible misfortune; it was almost as bad as being born black in a white society. No wonder the Jew thanked God every day in his prayers for not making him a woman!

A couple of years and several thousand doorbells later the Japanese bombed Pearl Harbor and suddenly we were in the midst of World War. Soon the shipyards and airplane plants were operating twenty-four hours a day and anyone who wanted a job could have one. Cripples on crutches and in wheelchairs, blind people with seeing-eye dogs, even women were put to work building ships and planes. The standard joke then was, "If you're breathing, you're hired."

I went to work at Lockheed operating a drill press, then later became a riveter. It was hard work but I loved it and it was a welcome change from selling Runproof. Of the many kinds of work I had done up to that time, the only three I enjoyed were teaching dancing, being a chorus girl and working at Lockheed. I was blithely ignorant of the fact, as was everyone else, that the constant exposure to noise would eventually have a bad effect on my hearing.

At that time we were living in Montrose, a small town high in the hills north of Los Angeles. We had moved frequently over the years trying to find a place where Ann could be comfortable. A bout with scarlet fever had left her with asthma and hay fever. According to the tests she was allergic to Bermuda grass and it was difficult to find an area where there was none, but we kept trying. Then one day I read an article in which it was stated that people with asthma are sometimes better off if they live near a large body of water. Well, you can't find any body of water larger than the ocean and we had tried everything else, so I moved the family to Laguna Beach. Almost from the day we arrived there Ann began to improve and eventually she outgrew the condition.

Mom on the Beach—1942

We rented a small two-bedroom frame house on a quiet street. The house sat well back on the lot leaving a large front yard where the children could play. The only tree was in the side yard quite close to the house, so close in fact that some of the roots disappeared underneath the house. It wasn't a very big tree but we treasured it because it was the only one we had.

However, our little tree refused to remain little. It grew taller and wider and before long it was pressing against the side of the house. Soon a bulge appeared on the living room wall and as the months passed the bulge grew wider and deeper until the entire wall bowed inward. No doubt it would eventually have collapsed, but a couple of years after the war ended the place was sold and we moved to a large old two story house on High Drive, where we remained until the children had grown up.

Bunny, Dick, Ann (Circa 1945)

Bunny, Mom and Ann—Circa 1947

After I moved the family to Laguna Beach, I lived in a rooming house near Westlake Park. Since it was impossible to buy gasoline without a special permit, I gave up the car and joined a car pool. On weekends I usually rode the bus to Laguna Beach. Since there were more bus riders during the war than there were buses, the lines were long and there was always a two or three hour wait. Some people brought sandwiches and cold drinks and ate right there on the floor of the bus station while holding their places in line. I sat on the floor and read a book. Several times the children came to visit me on the weekends and we went for boat rides on the lake and fed the swans.

Although I had a regular job now, I was no better off financially than I had been pushing doorbells. Prices on everything had gone up because there was a war on, I had to pay room rent (I couldn't live in the car since I no longer owned one) and I had to eat in restaurants. Few items, not even a loaf of bread, could be purchased in a grocery store without food stamps. Groceries were rationed during the war. Everyone received a book of stamps each month and I always turned mine over to Mom so she could buy extra food for the children. Fortunately there was a cafeteria at Lockheed, where prices were reasonable. I was forever counting pennies, trying to make my paycheck last from one week to the next. I even dropped my group insurance at Lockheed. I had never been sick in my life and didn't expect to be, and I felt that the two dollars a week was wasted.

Women were required to wear slacks at Lockheed and I bought mine at the Salvation Army Thrift shop, which I had long ago nicknamed "Sally's" to hide the fact that it was a second-hand store. How times do change! Then it was considered a disgrace to wear second-hand clothes; now well-to-do women brag about the bargains they find at thrift shops.

During the three years I worked at Lockheed I became so used to wearing slacks and found them to be so comfortable and so sensible, that I never again wore a dress except when forced by circumstances to do so. I remember when Ann was married several years later that she and Bunny had me all decked out in a suit, high-heeled shoes, gloves, and even a hat, of all things. The suit had a narrow skirt, and I was so used to wearing slacks that I almost fell on my face getting into the car.

Soon after going to work at Lockheed I learned that those who were willing to work overtime on Saturdays and Sundays were paid time and a half and double time, and I thought my penny-pinching days were over. I was young and strong and could easily work six or even seven days a week without thinking twice about it. However, although I put my name on the list week after week, I was never able to get in on the bonanza. When I inquired about it the man in the office told me that the overtime was offered to men only because they had families to support.

"I'm supporting three children and a mother-in-law," I said, "doesn't that count? I certainly need the extra money."

He shook his head. "I'm very sorry, there's nothing I can do about it. It's Company policy."

Again I was being discriminated against and penalized for being a woman. I was beginning to feel that there was no greater curse and my self-esteem, already low, took another plunge.

One day I received a letter offering me a job at the Post Office and I decided to take it. The pay would be less but it would be permanent for I knew that once on civil service you had to practically commit murder to be fired. I also realized that when the war was over the women and other undesirables would soon be kicked out of Lockheed.

At the Post Office I was interviewed by a pleasant grey-haired man in his mid-fifties. He filled out several forms, recorded my vital statistics, informed me that although the starting pay was somewhat low I would receive periodic raises, and told me to report for work the following Monday. Then, as though it was an afterthought and not very important, he pushed a paper across the desk and asked me to sign it. It was an agreement whereby I would be willing to give up my job if necessary, when the war ended, in order that men who had left to join the service could be rehired. That seemed only fair; those men certainly deserved to get their jobs back. I was willing to gamble on the chance that I wouldn't be asked to quit, and was about to sign when a sudden thought struck me.

"You're probably hiring a lot of men now, 4F's and those who are past the draft age. Are you asking them to sign this agreement?"

"Well, no, we don't expect them to sign it. We figure there will be enough jobs to go around without letting any of the men go."

A hot wave of anger and resentment washed over me and for the first time in my life I really blew my top. Scooping up the papers, I tore them up, threw the pieces on the desk, told the man in very unlady-like terms what he could do with his job and stormed out, slamming the door behind me.

No doubt I should have submitted meekly to the demands of this man's world, as women were supposed to do, and been grateful for the crumbs that were tossed to me, but they had finally pushed me too far, and in one sudden burst of fury I lost all hope of ever working at the Post Office. I never regretted it.

When I had been at Lockheed for about a year I was allowed to work on the graveyard shift, midnight to morning, probably because there were not enough men who were willing to work nights for no extra pay. It suited me fine; my days were free now and I made extra money teaching dancing. I slept on a split shift, three hours in the morning and three in the evening.

I was alone in the studio from noon until 7 p.m., when two other teachers came in and took over. Between pupils I read and sometimes put a record on the phonograph and danced around the room by myself. And that is how I happened to meet Red Stillman. He was a Master Sergeant in the army, and was doing some paper work in an office across the way.

He glanced over, saw me dancing and came up to get acquainted. He was tall, attractive in a rugged sort of way, and he was a good dancer. It was a case of infatuation at first sight.

Soon after we met, Red was sent overseas. Then the war ended and a few weeks after he came home we were married. I was almost forty then, certainly old enough to know better, and besides I had been warned. Red's ex-wife had called and tried to tell me what I was letting myself in for, but I mistakenly thought it was just sour grapes and paid no attention.

During the first year we were reasonably happy. We moved around a lot because Red worked as a mechanic on big construction jobs such as bridges and roads. He seemed to prefer that I do some of the driving, and although I had driven many thousands of miles without an accident, he felt that he had to monitor my every move. He told me when to stop, when to go, warned me constantly about cars ahead and behind and told me how to park. It made me nervous and undermined my self-confidence.

Men are the world's worst backseat drivers when a woman is at the wheel, but while most of them criticize silently, husbands tend to become vocal about it. I suppose they can't help it; it's born and bred in them. Every married woman I ever knew had the same trouble. I solved the problem by simply refusing to drive when Red was in the car. He was angry about it for a few days, then seemed to accept it.

We moved to Crescent City, where we would stay for at least a couple of years and Dick came to live with us. Red was delighted. He had always wanted a son, he said, and Dick was almost thirteen, at that age when he most needed a father. It appeared to be the perfect solution to one problem and possibly two. Dick would be away from Mom, who had always gone out of her way to make him feel unwanted. And if Red had a young boy in whom to take an interest, life with him might be more endurable.

I had learned over the months that living with Red was a bit like living with Mama. I found myself "walking on eggshells" as I had when I was a child in order to avoid trouble. Every now and then Red would get mad for no discernible reason and give me the silent treatment, refusing to speak to me for several days. Then he would suddenly get over it and act as if nothing had happened. When I tried to find out what was bugging him he refused to discuss it. It was frustrating, but I was willing to put up with it because I really thought that Dick would be happier living with us.

He was for awhile. He went on hunting and fishing trips with Red and they seemed to enjoy each other's company. But it was too good to last. Before long Red's true nature took over and he became jealous of Dick, loudly resenting the least thing I did for him. Then he began making fun of Dick, belittling him and putting him down until he was almost afraid to speak for fear of being ridiculed. Dick was fast developing an inferiority complex. That did it for me! One day while Red was at work I left a "goodbye forever" note and we packed our suitcases and went back to Laguna Beach.

There were plenty of jobs now for young people but for women in their forties with no training or experience the outlook was bleak. The only way I could make much money was by doing waitress work, perish the thought, so I went back to selling Runproof. At least I was my own boss.

Dick, wanting to help me, went out one day armed with a stocking and a tongue depressor. He made no sales of course; women just don't buy products like Runproof from a teenage boy. But one of my fondest memories is that he tried.

We left the tree house, as we called it, and moved to the place on High Drive. Red, who had moved back to Los Angeles, called several times begging me to come back. When I refused he showed up at the house one day and made himself obnoxious. Dick went upstairs and came back with the shotgun that Red had given him and taught him how to use. He pointed it at Red and told him to get out and leave me alone. He left in a hurry then, without further argument.

But he didn't leave me alone. He called several times, threatening to kill all of us. I couldn't put a restraining order on him because I didn't know his address, and it wouldn't have stopped him anyway if he really wanted to kill us. Often at night he parked by the house for hours, with a gun, he claimed. We kept the doors locked and never turned on the lights without first pulling the shades. This state of siege continued for several months until he finally gave up, and I learned by calling various construction companies that he was working on a job in Nevada.

Finally, after almost a year, Red was leaving me alone, but was it only a temporary respite? When the job in Nevada was over would he come back and start pestering me again? I had no way of knowing and only time would tell. The women's magazines were full of advice on how to get a man, but for most women, myself included, that was not the problem. What we really needed was some advice on how to get rid of one.

Chapter 16

Because of Mom, Dick had a miserable childhood. I have felt guilty about that, but I actually didn't realize how bad the situation was until he was ten years old. I was seldom at home, and children have a tendency, as I remember from my own childhood, to suffer in silence. She didn't mistreat him physically, but she did not like him, and he knew it, of course. I tried to reason with her and so did Ann, but it was hopeless. If she refused to listen to Ann, certainly no one was going to make a dent in her stubborn Scotch mind.

When Dick was sixteen he and three other boys went out one night, drank some beer, drove to what we called the "Snob Hill" section of town and engaged in a rock throwing contest to see who could break the most street lights. Late that night the phone rang. It was the Laguna Police Department.

You'd better come down right away," the man said.

"We're holding your son and three other boys for disorderly conduct. They got a little high on beer and broke some streetlights."

Thank goodness I was home that night, because Mom acted as if Dick had committed the crime of the century. To me it was just a teen-age prank, serious of course, but hardly earth-shaking. When I arrived at the Police Station, all four boys were sitting in the front office looking guilty and I felt sorry for them. They were old enough to know better, sure, but even grown-ups can make mistakes.

Dick was released in my custody, and the next day we talked to a probation officer and signed some papers. All of the boys were placed on probation until each had paid his share of the damages. Dick had a job that summer setting up pins in a bowling alley, so before too long he was able to pay his share and get off probation.

One day when we were talking about that episode Dick surprised me by saying, "You know, Dot, the main reason I felt guilty about it was because you didn't get mad at me."

After that incident Mom treated Dick as if were a criminal and the situation became so intolerable that as soon as he was off probation he and I moved to an apartment in Los Angeles. It meant that he would have to change schools again, thus adding another to an already long list. No wonder he lost interest. When I mentioned college he just laughed.

"No way!" he said. "I might finish high school, but you could not pay me to go to college!"

Suddenly, near the end of the school year, he decided to join the Navy. I was definitely against it; in just one more year he would graduate and that seemed of the utmost importance. Also, in 1950, the Korean War was going on then, and he would be exposed to danger. I tried to talk him out of it, as did the High School principal, who used the most compelling argument he could come up with.

"Just think how inferior you'll feel when you get married, Dick, if your wife has a High School Diploma and you don't."

Dick was still determined. The final decision was up to me and it was the hardest one I'd ever had to make. Since he was only seventeen, and since everyone now had a number and it was impossible to lie about your age, he could not join the Navy without my consent. I could refuse, but in his present mood he would probably quit school anyway and take off for parts unknown, and that would be worse.

After agonizing over it for several days I finally opted for what seemed to be the lesser of two evils and went with Dick to the recruiting office to sign the papers.

After Dick left I gave up the apartment, moved back to Laguna and resumed working the small towns up north. Ann finished her first year of college and decided that instead of working at the bakery that summer, as usual, she would travel with me and sell Runproof. Bunny would take care of the mail order business.

It was nice to have Ann with me. She was always happy and cheerful, and I really enjoyed just sitting part of the time, while she did the driving. And I'll always remember Ferndale, a small town near the top of the State, as it was there that, thanks to Ann, I pushed my last doorbell.

We were sitting in the car eating lunch and feeling a bit discouraged because of the weather. It was a drizzly, overcast day, threatening to get worse rather than better, in which we would have to quit and go back to the motel.

"One of the women I sold to," I said, "told me that the County Fair started today and suggested that I go out there and rent a booth. Of course I have no intention of doing it. The very idea of talking to more than one person at a time is too frightening. One at a time is all I can handle."

"I didn't even know that people could do that, but it sounds like a great idea." Ann started the car. "Let's go out there and find out about it."

Ignoring my protests, she drove to the Fairgrounds, talked to the manager and learned that he had one vacant booth. He could let us have it for twenty-five dollars, he said, for the remaining four days. That was a lot of money then, and it would take at least two days of doorbell pushing to make it back, but without hesitating Ann gave the man a check.

We now had a booth, but it was totally empty, and somehow we had to furnish it. At a grocery store we bought six wooden orange crates for ten cents each and stacked them across the front to make a counter, then covered them with the cheapest material we could find. Two apple boxes served as seats. Unable to afford drapes, we covered the bare boards at the back with crepe paper. Compared to the other booths, we looked like something out of "Tobacco Road" but when the Fair opened at ten the next morning we were ready for business.

But there was no business. We didn't have a choice location, being in the center of an aisle, flanked by what pitchmen call "dead joints" which are used by local merchants to display stoves and refrigerators. Across from us there were no booths, but there was a new automobile on display and it drew people like a magnet. When they entered our aisle they went directly to that new car, and after admiring it, passed on down the aisle and out. We may as well not have been there.

It is said that when a person is desperate enough he can perform feats that would normally be impossible. After two hours of being ignored, while watching Ann's money disappear with no hope of retrieval, I was desperate. Holding up my stockinged hand and frantically wielding the sharpened stick, I called out in a loud voice, "Have you folks seen this treatment for your nylons?"

Ann was horrified. "You can't do that, Dot. This isn't a carnival, you know."

When I persisted she left, unable to endure the sight of her mother making a spectacle of herself. While she was gone I made a few sales so I was prepared to defend my actions when she came back, but I didn't have to. She had changed her mind.

"When in Rome do as the Romans do," she grinned. "I walked all over the place watching people sell things and a lot of them were doing that, so I guess it's all right."

By the time the fair closed at ten o'clock that night we had taken in fifty-four dollars. We went back to the motel, spread the money out on the bed and counted it several times, unable to believe we had made so much with so little effort. And the next three days would be all gravy. It was like finding a gold mine. That was August 10th, Ann's nineteenth birthday. What a way to celebrate!

The next day I asked a man who was selling Indian jewelry how to find out about other fairs. "Get a copy of the Billboard on the news stand," he said. "That's the Pitchmen's Bible and all of the upcoming fairs will be listed."

We wrote letters, sent deposits to reserve spaces and left Ferndale three days later with more money than we could have made in weeks of doorbell pushing. On the way to the next fair we went to Sally's and bought a folding ironing board, two folding chairs and some drapes. Then we went to a lumberyard where we got a large piece of heavy plywood. Fastened to the ironing board it would serve as a collapsible counter.

For the rest of the summer we worked the fairs. Then it was time for Ann to return to college, and I had to go back and replenish supplies. The ten-day State Fair at Phoenix, the last one of the season on the West Coast, would be opening soon and I intended to be there. The cost for a booth would be two hundred dollars. To make sure of having a spot, I had sent a deposit of fifty dollars several weeks earlier. Bunny and I spent the next two weeks folding and sealing envelopes and I set out for Phoenix with everything I needed to work that fair.

Except for one minor detail—I was almost a hundred dollars short of having enough money to pay the balance on the booth space. But I did have a checking account containing six dollars at a Laguna bank so I gave them a rubber check. I was scared and had visions of being thrown in jail, but again I was desperate. Fortunately sales were good and I was able to get the money to the bank on Monday morning before the check bounced.

It was a good show; my gamble certainly paid off. I went back to Laguna determined to go to Florida, since that was the only place where there were any fairs during the winter.

I sent deposits to several Florida fairs, ordered five thousand envelopes from my friend the Jewish printer and bought three sacks of aluminum sulphate, one of which I would take along for use later on. Bunny and I made up hundreds of packages of Runproof and I had a luggage rack installed on top of the car since I planned to sleep in the back seat at least part of the time. I gave Mom enough money to pay the rent and live for a couple of months and with ten dollars and a tank of gas I set out on my three thousand mile journey.

It took me about two weeks to get to Florida as I did most of my driving at night. Around midnight I would stop in whatever small town I happened to be in, sleep in the car in a trailer park, then work the business district the next day. There was a greater risk now of being picked up for selling without a license but it was a chance I had to take, as it was faster than going door to door. Once in Alabama I was stopped and had to pay a ten-dollar fine, but luckily I had enough gas to get to the next town, and it was the only time I was bothered.

At the first fair in Florida I again had to give the manager a rubber check but it bothered me very little. I was getting to be an old pro at passing bad checks. Also, I realized now that if the check did bounce the manager would be happy to take the cash, which hopefully by then I would have. It did not bounce and after that first fair I was able to pay in advance.

Florida was an interesting place but I had no time for sightseeing. During the five winter months I worked many fairs all over the state and made five thousand dollars, which was a lot of money then in the early fifties. Most of the time I stayed in motels; cheap ones could be had then for a couple of dollars a night. It was a worthwhile trip; it certainly beat selling door to door. I had no car trouble, not even a flat tire, and I arrived back in Laguna in late April.

Bunny was in her second year of high school and Mom, who was now eighty-one, was still going strong. She was quite friendly toward me and was even pleasant to Dick who came home on leave while I was there. Ann came down from college for the weekend and it was like a family reunion. As I watched them talking and laughing together, I thought how lucky I was to have three such nice, attractive children. All were slender, dark haired and tall. Bunny, at 5'8" was the shortest, Ann topped her by an inch and Dick was almost six feet. I had always thought that I was unusually tall for a woman; now for the first time in my life I felt little.

Ann went back to college. I made up Runproof for the summer fairs and Bunny practiced the violin and the piano, which she could play by note and by ear, a talent she had inherited from Ralph. Dick looked up his old Laguna buddies and one day he went to Hollywood Park with one of them and made six hundred dollars playing the horses. He very wisely wired the money to me before going out on the town to celebrate.

Dick had two more years to go in the Navy and with a war going on I knew he was in constant danger. A boy standing right next to him on the ship was killed one day. Yet there was nothing I could do about it but hope. I spent some sleepless nights and had some bad dreams.

While waiting for the fairs to start, I went to see the twins who were both living near Los Angeles. Helen had left her second husband, moved to Glendale with her four children and had gone to work at Lockheed during the war. She was still there, being one of the few women who were not fired when the war ended, probably because she worked in the paint department. I always felt sorry for Helen. She was such a tiny little thing and she had such a miserable life. Those years at Lockheed were probably her happiest. She died of cancer when she was in her early fifties.

Jean and Ed had two children, a girl and a boy, and were living in North Hollywood. Ed had started his own transformer company during the war and was making lots of money, but besides being an incurable hypochondriac he was also quite stingy. He had convinced Jean that they were poor and they lived as if they were just one step removed from going on relief. The only money she ever saw was the stingy amount he doled out to her each week for housekeeping expenses. Once when she happened to see a cancelled income tax check for fifty thousand dollars he told her that was the reason they were so broke, that he had to give most of the money to the government. Knowing nothing of the relationship between taxes and income, she believed it.

One day when I stopped by to see Jean she mentioned her daughter, Lois. "She often spends the night with her girl friends but she never invites any of them here, and I don't understand why."

"If you really want to know, just take a look at her bedroom," I said, "It looks like poverty row. She's ashamed of it. Why don't you fix it up?"

Jean said, "I can't, I don't have any money except the little bit Ed gives me every week.

Like all of us, Jean had started out with a horrible inferiority complex and she had never had a chance to get rid of any of it by knocking around the world as the rest of us had. Yet she was highly intelligent. She read good books, was interested in politics and world affairs and her published "Letters to the Editor" would have made a college graduate proud. But she was afraid of Ed as she was of everyone in the family except me. I felt so sorry for her I could have cried.

"Don't you and Ed have a joint checking account?" I asked her.

"Oh no. He did open an account in my name but I'm not supposed to touch it except in an emergency."

"Well, this is an emergency, so come on, let's go."

We bought curtains, a bedspread, some decorative pillows, a rug and a frilly dressing table with three mirrors. We spent the rest of that day transforming Lois' room into a thing of beauty.

Jean told me later that when Ed came home that night, he took one look at that room, shook his head and said, "I see Dot's been here," and never mentioned it again. When I finally convinced her that Ed had plenty of money, Jean demanded and got new furniture for the entire house. He wasn't really a bad guy; he just needed to be pushed.

In spite of all this Ed did not dislike me and we got along fine. He was one of the few people I ever knew who could argue about a difference of opinion without getting mad, and since we agreed on nothing we had some interesting discussions. And he had a sense of humor. He took it good-naturedly when I kidded him about his many imagined ailments. Once I told him, "Ed, when you die at the age of ninety-five you'll have engraved on your tombstone, "See, I told you I was sick."

Ed is now eighty-six and shows no signs of shoving off.

Chapter 17

The summer of 1952 I worked the California fair circuit, all the way from San Diego to Ferndale and back to Phoenix. I then went again to Florida for the winter fairs. Having now heard about Home Shows, which were much like fairs except that they had no carnivals, I worked three of those on my way home.

I did so well at those shows that I decided to skip California that summer and make the mid-west fairs. Ann went along, and it was a fun trip. We traveled all over the mid-west, and Ann met a lot of people the likes of whom she would never have seen in Laguna or at college. Sometimes she even went out on the carnival lot, watched the "carnies" and made friends with some of them. When she went back to college that fall she told her psychology professor about her experiences. He was quite interested in her description of the various characters she had met. "You probably learned more about human nature during that one summer," he said, "than I could teach you in four years."

After spending the winter in Florida as usual, I went back to California and had another go at the fairs there, and it was during that summer that I met Marguerite Williams. She was selling a rug braider in the booth next to mine at the County Fair in Vallejo. I had never talked to her except to say, "Hi," and I had no idea that she was a Southerner.

This was the third day of the fair, which was easily the worst one I had ever worked. There were plenty of people but they weren't "springing" as the pitchmen say. They would watch my demonstration and listen to my spiel, but few of them bought. At this rate I wouldn't even make the "nut", the cost of the booth space. I wasn't alone; everyone was complaining about poor sales. Only my neighbor seemed to be doing well and I could only conclude that these countrywomen were more interested in turning rags into rugs than they were in preserving their nylons.

The next morning I stopped at a little store to buy cokes. The owner was very friendly and when I left with two six-packs and a bag of potato chips, he said, "Y'all come back now." Then I noticed that most of the streets were named after Southern states. Apparently, Vallejo was a hotbed of misplaced Southerners. I had always found them to be very likeable and I loved their Southern accent, but they were probably the most skeptical people in the country and it was usually a waste of time to try to sell them anything. Once at a Fair in Kentucky a pitchman displayed a perfectly good five-dollar bill and offered it for sale for one dollar. There were no takers.

I put some cokes in the little box under the counter, and then walked over to the divider that separated the booths. "I just found out why this show is no good," I said. "We're trying to sell to a bunch of Southerners, and as you must know that's an exercise in futility."

The lady had a temper. Giving me a look that would have· shriveled an extrovert, she walked over to the divider and pulled herself up to her full five foot three and said, "I'll have you know, you Damn Yankee, that no Southerner wuth his salt would have any truck with that junk you'ah sellin."

"Oh, are you a Southerner?"

"Ah shuah ain't no Damn Yankee!"

"Neither am I," I grinned at her. "I'm one of them there Damn Westerners."

For a few seconds she continued to glare at me, then we both burst out laughing. And thus began a friendship that was to last for more than thirty years.

Marguerite "Pete" Williams

She had worked her way from Virginia to the West Coast selling rug-braiders in department stores, traveling with two friends, Warren and Jessie, in an ancient car that was subject to frequent breakdowns. They had worked the San Diego Fair and were on the way to Vallejo when the car conked out in Santa Rosa. Faced with a two-day delay for repairs, she went on alone on the bus.

"It was awful," she said, "I had to hire a man to haul my stuff to the Fairgrounds and set up my booth."

"Are Warren and Jessie planning to come on here when they get the car fixed?"

"Yes, they should be here today or tomorrow, and I hope they make it or I'll be stranded. There's no way I could travel alone because as you've probably noticed, I'm a little bit crippled. I can't drive a car because I can't lift my feet when I'm sitting down and I can't lift anything that weighs more than a cup of coffee. Otherwise, I'm in pretty good shape."

"It seems to me you had a lot of courage to come all the way out here."

"Well, I always wanted to see the West so when the chance came along I just grabbed it. I had polio when I was twenty-six and my hair turned white almost overnight. The doctors put me in iron braces, told me there was nothing more they could do and that I would have to live with it. But I went to a chiropractor and in less than a year he had me out of braces and walking almost normally. I just list a little to starboard."

We were about the same age; she was forty-five and I was a year older. Her real name was Marguerite but she preferred to be called Pete, a nickname she had acquired when she was a child and pretended that she was Peter Pan. "I just tell people that Pete is short for Marguerite," she said.

One day Pete and I took a walk through the big building and watched the pitchmen as they demonstrated the various items that were designed to separate the customers from their cash. There were vegetable slicers, can openers, blenders, paper towels that would soak up an amazing amount of water, vacuum cleaners guaranteed to out-vacuum all other brands, eyeglass cleaners, magic menders, knife sharpeners and dozens of other items. In a corner booth three young Mormons were giving their all in an effort to save souls, and across from them a man extolled the merits of a liquid that when poured into a carburetor was supposed to miraculously increase gas mileage.

An extremely attractive young man who looked to be in his mid-twenties was showing a group of women how, by using his little gadget, they could embroider monograms using their own sewing machines. With his wavy, dark-blond hair, eyelashes that would make any girl envious, flawless complexion and somewhat long polished fingernails he was indeed, as Pete said, "A thing of beauty and a joy forever." He was wearing a blue silk shirt decorated with a yellow monogram.

Jerry and Pete, 1954

When the women left, without buying, we walked over to his booth and he started to go into his spiel. "Save your breath," I said, "we're with it. We just stopped by to say hello. Are you doing any good?"

"To tell you the truth, Doll, I'm starving to death. These women don't seem to appreciate art. I've been working my fingers to the bone showing them the wonders they can perform with this thing and they are supposed to be so amazed they can't wait to hand me their money, but they aren't cooperating at all. I did fine at the last fair and I just don't understand it."

"Well, join the club," I told him. "Most of these people are Southerners and they don't trust us Damn Yankees, so no one is doing much, except Pete. She's from Virginia."

"Maybe I'd better start practicing. I can say "y'all" and "this heah." Pete shook her head. It won't do you any good. We Southerners can spot a fake accent a mile away."

Two curious women stopped at Jerry's counter, so we left. On the way back, I said, "He's obviously a homosexual, you know."

"I suspected as much, although I've never met one before. He has a great personality and he's fun to talk to. A year ago I'd have been shocked spit-less but now it doesn't seem to matter. I guess, as they say, travel is broadening."

Later he came over, curious to see what we were selling, and stayed quite awhile talking up a storm. His name was Jerry, he said; he was hoping to make the grade in the movies, but so far had had no luck. He told us he could sing and dance, and that all he needed was a lucky break. When the fairs were over he planned to have another go at it.

After that we joined him every day for lunch at the snack bar where we sat at one of the tables and ate hot dogs or hamburgers and drank milk shakes. Jerry was a fun-loving, outgoing person, with a quick wit and a seemingly inexhaustible fund of amusing stories. In spite of his being so young, we enjoyed his company and the three of us became good friends.

One day when we met Jerry at the snack bar he wasn't his usual happy self; something seemed to be bothering him. He fiddled with his glass, moving it aimlessly from spot to spot on the table.

"What's the matter, Jerry," I asked. "You seem to be worried about something."

"Well, I have a confession to make and it will probably mean the end of our friendship, but in all fairness I feel that I have to tell you. The truth is, I'm a —"

"Don't say another word, Jerry." Pete reached across the table and put her hand on his. "We know what you want to say and it doesn't make any difference."

"You mean you've known all along? I didn't realize it was that obvious."

"Oh, it's not," I lied. "Just put it down that Pete and I are a couple of extra-smart cookies. And it doesn't matter, so forget it. We like you right much, as Pete would say, and we figure that your life style is your own business."

Jerry was both surprised and relieved. "I must say it's unusual for straights to be so tolerant. My mother and father both went through hell at first, then finally became reconciled to the fact that they have a gay son and we get along fine. I hope you can meet them sometime. You'd like each other."

Chapter 18

Warren and Jessie, who worked a hamburger joint on the Midway, arrived on the third day of the fair. They were the only carnival people I had met, since the carnies and the pitchmen generally lived in two separate worlds and seldom mingled. Pete traveled with them to the next four fairs and all turned out to be much better than Vallejo had been. I had meanwhile gone north to Ferndale and was loading my car, preparing to head south again, when Pete came by my stall. I knew something was wrong because she wasn't her usual smiling self. She looked worried.

"I'm stranded," she said. "Warren's car broke down again and they have to send to San Francisco for a part. It'll take three or four days to get it fixed."

"That means you'll miss the first few days at the next Fair."

"I could take the bus, but it's an awful drag. I was wondering if you'd take me and my stuff to Stockton. I'll pay the gas."

"Sure, no problem," I said.

Warren and Jessie dismantled Pete's booth, loaded her stuff into my old station wagon and assured us that they would be seeing us within the next three or four days. That same evening we arrived in Stockton where I unloaded everything and set up both booths.

Pete had three colorful rugs for display and as I tacked them up I asked her if she had made them. "Good heavens, no," she laughed, "I never made a rug in my life. I just show other women how to do it."

"That figures," I said, "I don't use Runproof, either. I just show other women how to prevent runs."

Jerry was there too and we all went out to a fast food place for hamburgers and shakes. I don't remember who first suggested it, but we ended up sharing a motel room. We told the owner that Jerry was Pete's nephew, and since he was twenty years younger it was a plausible story. Pete and I shared the double bed, Jerry slept on a cot and we all saved money.

When the fair ended Warren and Jessie had not shown up so I took Pete to the State Fair in Sacramento. Again we shared a motel room with

Dot & Pete on the Road

Jerry. We thought it was a perfect arrangement, a real money saver for all of us, and Jerry was a lot of fun, always joking and laughing.

Then one day, without warning, my sister Orva and her husband Judge arrived from Kansas City. They were on a vacation trip and were planning to spend a week in Sacramento before going on to see the famous Redwoods and other points of interest. I had written Orva and mentioned that Pete and I would be making the Sacramento Fair, never dreaming that she would show up. And there we were, living with a man!

We couldn't tell them the truth about Jerry. They may have heard about "queers" but I'm sure they had never met one, and they would have gone into instant shock, so we introduced him as Pete's nephew. They had rented a two-bedroom motel, expecting me to stay with them, so I had to move out and leave Jerry and Pete alone. But everything was copacetic. Orva and Judge were kept in happy ignorance of the true state of affairs. Jerry took Pete to the Fairgrounds every day in his car.

Then one night Pete received a shock that she said temporarily paralyzed every muscle in her body that wasn't already paralyzed. It was about two a.m. and she was sound asleep when she was suddenly awakened by a loud crash. She sat up in bed and saw Jerry sitting on the floor struggling with his cot. One of the legs had broken and he was trying to fix it.

She watched him for awhile. "Jerry, there's no way you can fix that cot. We'll just have to get another one from the manager tomorrow. In the meantime, come over here and get in bed and let's get some sleep."

Jerry, abandoning the cot, crawled in next to the window. Pete was drifting off to sleep again when she heard tires crunching on gravel, but she paid no attention, as that's a normal sound at motels. A few seconds later she was brought wide awake by the sound of loud knocking. Thinking that it must be me, probably with bad news, she was about to get out of bed and go to the door when Jerry peeked out through the curtains.

"My God, Pete, it's the cops. What'll we do?"

Pete was absolutely terror stricken. This was in the days before gays came out of the closet and they were fair game for the Vice Squad. Being gay was considered a crime and they were constantly being arrested and thrown into jail. Driven by the horrible thought of being arrested for harboring a so-called criminal, Pete got up and started toward the door.

"Quick, Jerry," she whispered, "hide under the bed, and take that broken cot with you. I'll try and convince them they've made a mistake."

Jerry started laughing. "Calm down, Pete. That was me knocking on the wall. I was just playing a practical joke."

At that moment Pete was so furious that she felt like killing Jerry, but by the time she told me about it she had forgiven him and was able to laugh about it. This became one our favorite stories, at least for those who were broad-minded enough to appreciate the humor.

"I'll tell you for sure though, Dot, if I ever were arrested for sleeping with a man I'd prefer that it be a real man."

We expected to see Warren and Jessie at Sacramento but they failed to appear and we heard via the grapevine that they had split up and were no longer working the fairs. Feeling that she was becoming a burden on me, Pete talked about taking the train back to Virginia.

"There are only two more fairs and if you leave now you'll lose your deposits. Why don't you finish out the season, then if you want to you could go along with me and work the Florida Fairs."

"Sounds great, but it means a lot of extra work for you, setting me up and tearing me down at every show."

"Oh well, I'm pretty tough, I can take it. And it will really be a help to me because we can split expenses."

After spending ten days at Pomona we had almost two weeks before going on to Phoenix so we drove to Laguna. Our place, an old two-story house with peeling paint and cheap rent, sat all by itself on a small hill with a nice view overlooking a canyon. We seldom used the front door as there were about fifteen steps leading up to it, so as usual I drove up the side alley and parked in the back.

It was a pleasant surprise to find Ann there, and Bunny had just come home from the beach in a bathing suit and with a gorgeous tan. Mom made coffee and brought out some home-made cookies and we sat on the two big couches in the living room and talked.

Noticing Pete's accent, Ann asked her where she was from. "Ah'm from N'yawk, honey chile, wheah y'all from?" When the laughter had subsided she said, "I'm from Virginia. I was traveling with a couple but they left me stranded in Ferndale and Dot rescued me. I'm going to work the Florida fairs with her on my way home."

"How is the mail order business, Bunny?" I asked.

"Oh, it's moving right along, as usual. But I have to tell you about a boo-boo I pulled. Some guy from San Diego wrote in for a hundred packages so I made them up and shipped them out. A week or so later he wrote back and said that when he soaked some nylons in the stuff they turned white and stiff. At first I had no idea what had happened but I soon found out. You know that sack of Redi-mix cement that you bought to fix the steps? Well, I thought it was Runproof—it looks the same, and I had sent the guy a hundred packages of cement. So I sent him some Runproof explaining what had happened and told him to keep the cement to mend sidewalks or whatever. I must say the fellow had a sense of humor. He wrote back saying he thought it was absolutely hilarious, that it would make a good story to tell his friends."

While we were in Laguna I made up several hundred packages of Runproof, and Pete ordered a supply of rug-braiders to be picked up in Florida. We stashed the counters, folding chairs and other light weight items on the luggage rack and covered them with canvas. Heavy boxes and suitcases filled the tail-end and the rest of the space was taken up by the mattress. It's always handy to have a bed in the car, just in case.

Jerry turned up at the Phoenix show and so the three of us shared a motel room. He had traded in his car on a six-year-old yellow sports car, which he named Tallulah. He planned to spend the winter going to beauty school, as his ambition, in case he didn't make it in the movies, was to have his own beauty shop.

It was a good show, and when it was over we told Jerry goodbye and set off across the desert toward Florida. Since Pete couldn't drive she couldn't offer to "spell" me, and that was fine with me since I had no desire to be "spelled." I loved to drive especially across the wide open spaces with those bare, gaunt mountains, no two of which were alike, and I could easily make five or six hundred miles a day, even more if necessary, without getting tired. That was one of the many reasons I had turned down a couple of chances to team up with other women. I had always tended to be a loner and I didn't want to get involved with sharing driving.

Pete had fallen in love with the West. "The only thing I'm disappointed about is that I haven't seen any cowboys."

"If you want to see cowboys nowadays you have to go to Wyoming or Montana. There are plenty of them up there chasing cows across the plains."

"I'm sure sorry I didn't get a chance to see them, but who knows, maybe I will some day." She gazed across the flat land toward the distant mountains. "Hey, let's pretend we're gypsies and sleep on the desert tonight. It will be my farewell to the West, because I'll probably never get out here again. Besides, it sounds like fun!"

I hadn't even thought of suggesting this, as it never occurred to me that Pete would enjoy "roughing it." Few women would; they tend to like their creature comforts. Apparently, she was a gal after my own heart.

Late that night, somewhere in New Mexico, I turned off on a dirt road, drove a mile or so away from the highway and parked on the desert pavement. We put on our sweaters and walked a little way across the sand.

There is something awesome about the stillness of the desert at night. The only sound was the occasional howling of a coyote. Millions of stars, undimmed by city lights, spread their brilliance from horizon to horizon. It was a new experience for Pete and she was so entranced that sleeping seemed a waste of time. The next morning we watched the sun come up and paint the mountains in various shades of red and purple, then reluctantly drove back to the highway and continued on our way.

Pete was a wonderful story teller. She kept me entertained with tales of her happy childhood in Virginia. Because her mother had T.B., they lived for several years in the mountains where her Dad ran a country store. It was hillbilly country. There were turkey shoots, square dances and bootleggers who had stills hidden in the hills and who sometimes had run-ins with revenuers. It was an interesting, unusual life for a city-bred family.

By the time Pete graduated from high school both her mother and father had died. She and her sister Mary spent two years in nurse's training, but were forced to give it up when a new law was passed to the effect that nurses must be college graduates. Her sister married an alcoholic, had three children in quick succession, then the stock market crashed and the Great Depression was on. During the years when Pete should have been dating and having fun she was living in abject poverty, selling various things "doah to doah," as she called it, to help support Mary's children.

Pete was very enterprising; she had the makings of an entrepreneur. She covered vanilla wafers with chocolate frosting and sold them six to a package. She made up small bags of cedar shavings, meant to discourage moths. She also made bars of soap by boiling up soap flakes and pouring the mixture into trays to harden. The customer had to use this soap within a few days or it would shrink to a sliver. Peanuts were profitable so Pete bought them by the bushel, bagged them and sold them for twenty-five cents a bag.

When she mentioned peanuts Pete started laughing. "Looking back on it now it's really funny. One day I got into a crap game with some guys in a garage and lost all my peanuts."

Pete had been married twice, but she had no children. She spent seven happy years with her first husband, Mark Williams. Then he died during the war, and she went to work in a studio retouching negatives. Several years later she married a man with three children whose wife had died. "I found out later that she had committed suicide and I don't doubt that he drove her to it. He didn't drink but he had every other fault you'd care to mention. He was very dictatorial, a real Hitler type. I got along fine with the children but I couldn't stand him and I left him in less than a year."

She went back to demonstrating in stores, selling vegetable slicers, Bibles, and children's books. She was selling rug braiders when she met Warren and Jessie and decided to go to California.

Chapter 19

By the time the last fair in Florida ended four months later it was just taken for granted that we would continue to travel together, and I no longer considered the possibility of going on without Pete.

We were as different, both in appearance and personality, as any two people could possibly be. I was tall and very thin, with an English reserve and a low self-esteem that made it difficult for me to make friends. Unless I remembered to smile I was often mistakenly thought to be either mad or sad. Actually I was quite attractive but I didn't realize that until many years later. I thought I was ugly.

Pete was short and slender then, and with her pink and white complexion and pug nose she looked decidedly Irish, which she was mostly. She was always happy, always smiling, and she never met a stranger. Everyone loved her. She often joked about being crippled because she couldn't bear to have anyone to feel sorry for her. She always helped me pack the boxes but she couldn't lift them. She would stand there watching me load things on the car, grin and say, "Goody, goody, I'm crippled."

Our likes and dislikes, however, were almost identical. Both of us loved to read and we spent many of our spare hours immersed in books which we bought at Goodwill and Salvation Army stores for ten or fifteen cents each. We enjoyed the same music, mostly semi-classical and Western and we had the same politics. The only subject we didn't agree on was religion. I had been an atheist since I was seventeen and Pete was a Presbyterian turned Catholic. No one is more dedicated to religion than a converted Catholic and I learned early on that Pete was a bit touchy on the subject so we never discussed it. I sat in front of churches all over the country and read while she attended Mass.

We left Florida, drove up the coast to Virginia and stayed a week with Mary, Pete's sister. She seemed pleasant enough but I sensed instantly that she didn't like me, although at the time I had no idea why. Later, I realized that she was jealous. She was overweight and looked about ten years older than Pete, although there was only two years difference in their ages. Pete's niece, Dixie, was slender, blond and very good looking and had a sense of humor that never quit. I met Pete's tall, dark and handsome nephew, Fred, but the other nephew, Bob, was away at sea with the Merchant Marines.

On our way back to California we slept in the car in trailer parks, spent two nights on the desert under a full moon and arrived in San Diego the day before the fair opened. Many of our old friends were there, including Jerry who was now the proud owner of a small travel trailer, which he had named "Hernando's Hideaway."

"Tallulah pulls it along like it was nothing, and I'll save a lot by staying in trailer parks instead of motels."

"We know what you mean, Jerry," I said. "We seldom stay in motels now, and we never pass up the chance to spend a night on the desert whenever there's one handy."

Jerry grinned. "That's just the kind of thing you two oddball characters would do. I think both of you must be part gypsy."

When the fair ended, Pete went with Jerry to work a show at the Cow Palace in San Francisco. On the way they visited a few of the Gay clubs in Santa Monica, and Pete said it was a real education and she wouldn't have missed it. She felt that it was too bad such nice, intelligent people should be so mixed up sexually but she realized that they had no choice in the matter. She was propositioned by a lesbian but was rescued by Jerry, who explained, "She's straight, so leave her alone."

In 1953 I went to Laguna and took Bunny and Mom to see Ann graduate from college. That winter Mom had lost an eye to glaucoma, had put on quite a bit of weight, had let her hair go white and for the first time she seemed old and feeble.

During the past few years Mom's attitude toward me had gradually changed. I first noticed it during the war when she got cigarettes for me now and then at the grocery store, when they were hard to come by. When I mentioned this to Pete, she was as usual quick with the quip. "Well," she said, with a mischievous grin, "she just had to get old and senile before she could like you."

Ann and Bunny worked that summer as maids in a Laguna motel. The car I had given Ann was still clicking along virtually trouble-free, but mine was fast falling apart and I could no longer depend on it to get me from here to there. In a rare moment of optimism I bought a new Pontiac station wagon and drove to Santa Rosa to meet Pete and Jerry.

Several of the fairs had half-mile race tracks, known as bull rings, and that summer, for the first time in my life, I bet on horses. Since that time years ago when I had spent a lot of hours trying to figure out a system, I had never even been tempted. Then Pete got interested in horse racing, decided it was a fun thing to do, so now and then she and I risked a dollar each and split a bet. We lost more often than we won.

One day a pitchman, who was an inveterate horse-player, gave Pete a tip. "He's running in the fourth race and he's sure to win. I know the owner and he said today's the day. You'd better put a saw-buck on him."

Blissfully unaware of the old saying that "tips" usually run last, we each put ten to win on the horse, and so did Jerry when we told him about it. That horse came galloping in at twelve to one and each of us made over a hundred dollars. We celebrated that night by splitting a bottle of champagne with Jerry in Hernando's Hideaway.

As a result of all this activity I came down with horse fever again and spent most of my spare time poring over racing forms, looking for a system. When I came up with a system I felt sure would work, Pete and I, having a few free days between shows, went to a regular race track. We slept in the car on the beach and gave it a tryout. Fortunately, all we lost was the price of admission for three days since we didn't bet, we just checked to find out if it would work. It didn't.

On the way to the next fair we stayed overnight with Jerry's parents, Fern and Ralph, who lived on a small farm near the Sacramento River. About our age, they were warm, friendly people and we were glad to know them. We met Jerry's older brother, Ray, who was married and had three children, and his little sister Bonnie, a beautiful child only five years old.

"She was an afterthought," Jerry said, as he picked her up and hugged her. "And thank God for afterthoughts. Isn't she a living doll?"

Fern was a wonderful cook. For dinner we had fried chicken, mashed potatoes, home grown vegetables (Pete loved those) and pie made with peaches from their own trees. It was a pleasant change from our usual diet of hot dogs, hamburgers and milkshakes. The next morning after a real farm breakfast, including hot biscuits, we thanked them for their hospitality, promised to keep in touch, (which we did), and went on to Ferndale, our next stop.

After setting up our three booths at the Fairgrounds, we set out to look for a trailer park and soon discovered that there was only one in town. It was called, of all things, Fairyland. Jerry was so amused that he laughed and joked about it all the while he was parking his trailer. Then we all got in his car and started toward town to look for a McDonalds or a similar fast food place.

On the way we met Eileen and Bill Talley who sold salt water taffy at the fairs. Since there was no traffic on that country road we stopped to talk a minute, car to car. "We got our joint all set up," Bill said, "and we're on our way now to look for a motel. Did you find a trailer park?"

"We sure did and you'd never guess the name of the place. It's called Fairyland."

Bill burst out laughing while Eileen, with a warning glance at the two children in the back seat, tried to shut him up. Twelve year old Julie, wise beyond her years, smiled knowingly, but as we drove away innocent little ten-year-old Peter stuck his head out the window, waved at Jerry and called, "Goodbye, Fairy." He must have wondered why his father thought it was so funny.

At Ferndale that year a woman named Rosa was telling people all about themselves by looking at their handwriting, and Pete thought it would be interesting to see what she had to say. Most of the things Rosa told her were true, which didn't surprise Pete since she knew that an expert can tell a great deal about people by analyzing their handwriting. But she was surprised when the woman looked at her strangely and said, "Sometime during the next two or three years you're going to cross an ocean and go to a foreign country."

"Do you mean to say you can tell that by my handwriting?"

"No, of course not. It's just a sudden feeling I had. Call it a hunch."

Since at that time neither of us believed it was possible for anyone to see into the future we thought no more about it, but two years later when Pete did cross an ocean and go to a foreign country we remembered it and wondered. Was it coincidence? Perhaps.

When we finished the summer circuit I invited Jerry to stay at Laguna while we waited for the Phoenix Fair. I had told the children all about him so they were forewarned, and I wasn't surprised that everyone liked him. It was impossible not to like Jerry; he was kind, thoughtful and quite entertaining.

Dick had finished his stint in the Navy and was working in a service station in Laguna. He was taking a correspondence course to get his high school diploma as he was now determined to go to college and get an engineering degree. "I'm going to have a million dollars by the time I'm thirty," he declared. (He missed it by one year; he made it when he was thirty-one). Ann was teaching school in a small town near Los Angeles but she came home for the weekends, and Bunny was in her final year of high school.

Mom wasn't feeling well; she was barely able to walk and seemed to be in constant pain. She told us that the day before we arrived she had fallen out of bed and sprained her hip, but insisted that given time it would get well. We took her to the doctor and x-rays confirmed our worst fears. She had broken her hip and would need surgery.

That meant Phoenix was out for me. I had to stay home and look after Mom. Jerry offered to give up his sewing machine gadget, which hadn't been doing so well anyway, and sell Runproof for me on commission. He and Pete went to Phoenix and I took Mom to the hospital.

The night before she was operated on I sat beside her bed all night keeping her leg straight because if she moved it, which she frequently wanted to do, the pain became intense. Would I have done it had I known then that she had tried to turn the children against me? I don't know, but I probably would have, as I was never inclined to hold a grudge, and after all she had spent almost twenty years of her life raising my children. The nurses thought she was my mother and were surprised to learn that she was my mother-in-law. They said I should be called Ruth after the woman in the Bible stories.

Mom was taken home from the hospital in an ambulance and was put to bed, where she remained bedridden, requiring constant care for a couple of months. I slept on the couch just outside her room in case she called during the night.

Pete and Jerry came back from Phoenix and Jerry went on to continue his training at the beauty school. Pete told me an amusing story about an incident that had occurred while they were working the fair. She and Jerry were sitting in a booth in a small cafe across from the fairgrounds. The booth behind Pete was occupied by a young, well dressed woman and Pete was surprised to notice that Jerry was smiling and seemed to be interested.

After awhile, the woman got up and walked over to Jerry and said in a deep masculine voice, "Have you a match?" Only then did Pete realize that this was a man dressed as a woman. After Jerry supplied a light, the "woman", who seemed to be quite at home in high heels, went off down the aisle toward the rest rooms, while Pete watched, fascinated.

"Jerry," she cried, horror struck, "He-she-it, whatever, went into the ladies rest room."

"Well, after all, Pete, you didn't expect her to go into the men's, did you?"

I tried to find someone in Laguna to come in during the day and take care of Mom so that Pete and I could go to Florida, but there was no one available, so we resigned ourselves to waiting it out. The doctor said that Mom would have to stay in bed at least another month.

There was only one Home Show in the area during this time, at San Bernardino. I worked it while Pete took care of Mom who was a model patient except for one frustrating habit. Every morning at five o'clock she would wake the entire household by calling, "Bunny, don't be late for school."

Both Pete and I tried to dissuade her by promising that we would take care of it, but she kept it up and Pete, with her Irish temper, must have spoken sharply to her about it. One day when I brought her a cup of tea she said, "Dot, you should have been a nurse, you have so much patience. Some people don't have so much patience." Meaning Pete, of course.

Finally Dick talked to Mom about it and she never called out again. She thought well of Dick now, often bragged about him and seemed to have forgotten that she had caused him to have an unhappy childhood. He was now a man; as such, his words carried a lot of weight with her.

The new Pontiac was giving me more trouble than had any of the old junk heaps I had driven, so rather than make any more payments I gladly turned it back to the dealer, went from the sublime to the ridiculous and bought a 1941 Chrysler wagon from a friend of Helen's for a hundred dollars. It was a weird looking thing. The wooden body was badly in need of a paint job, which it never got, and the back end was shaped like a bay window. The man had driven it ninety thousand miles, but he assured us that it was in good mechanical condition, and it must have been as I drove it another sixty thousand with no serious trouble. We christened it the "Gremlin".

By Christmas Mom was getting around quite well and could safely be left alone during the day while Bunny was at school, and Ann would come home every weekend. So in early January Pete and I took off for Northern California and Oregon where there were several winter Home Shows. Things went well at home, Bunny was doing a good job looking after Mom, and since Ann would soon be home for summer vacation we decided to stay up North for the summer.

In June I received a letter from Ann with the bad news that Bunny had been in an automobile accident. The car in which she was riding had overturned and pinned her underneath. The boyfriend, who was thrown clear and was uninjured, then performed one of those acts that we've all read about. With a sudden spurt of energy he lifted the car and freed her. Fortunately, there were no broken bones but she had a very bad cut on her leg that was destined to leave a permanent scar.

I called Ann and told her that we were leaving at once and would be home in two days, but she assured me that it wasn't necessary for me to interrupt my work, that Bunny's leg was healing fast and that she had everything under control. Knowing Ann, I didn't doubt it; she was a born manager.

Chapter 20

There was a lot of talk that year about the big uranium run that was sweeping the west, equaling if not surpassing the famous gold rush of 1845. Thousands of optimistic amateurs were out scouring the mountains and canyons looking for instant wealth.

Visualizing the riches that would be ours if we happened to find the right spot, we bought a Geiger counter, collected all the literature we could find on the subject, and whenever we had spare time between fairs, went prospecting. We decided to keep it a secret from our families.

"All of them consider us a little pixilated anyway," I said, "and if they knew about this escapade they'd really think we'd gone off the deep end."

That summer we found a lot of agates, some quartz and amethyst crystals and many apache tears, those small black glass-like stones spewed out by volcanoes in the distant past. We didn't know what any of them were, but we found out by taking them into rock shops. Once we felt sure we had struck it rich when we found tons of what we thought was petrified wood strewn over the hillside, but it turned out to be ordinary water-worn rock.

Since Pete's climbing ability was severely limited, she wore out the seats of innumerable pairs of slacks by bumping on her "whichend", as she called it, from boulder to boulder up the canyons, but since we bought our clothes at thrift shops for practically nothing, we didn't care.

One night we parked in a clearing at the foot of a canyon we planned to explore the next day. It was pitch dark, for there was no moon, and the only sounds were the rustling of the leaves in the trees, a chorus of crickets and the hooting of an owl somewhere in the distance.

We smoked a cigarette, shared a coke and climbed into the back of the car to go to sleep. Suddenly, I heard men's voices and saw a light bobbing up and down. I could barely make out the figures of two men coming up the dirt road toward the clearing.

I grabbed Pete's arm. "Hey, some men are coming up here!"

The Prospectors Looking for Uranium, 1956

We rolled up the windows; I leaped into the front seat and started the car prepared to take off instantly in case they appeared hostile. By that time they had reached the car and we could see that they were boys in their late teens. They were smiling and did not look dangerous, so I turned off the motor and rolled down the windows.

"Well, hello," I greeted them. "What are you kids doing wandering around in the mountains at night?"

"We work for one of the ranchers, looking after his cattle and horses," one of them said. "We thought if you ladies were planning to spend the night here we'd better warn you that it's dangerous."

"What could possibly be dangerous about it?" Pete asked. "There are lots of coyotes around here. They get on that cliff the other side of the creek and howl, and if you get out of the car they'll come at you."

"We love coyotes," Pete said, "and we like to hear them howl. Besides, from what I've read about them they don't bother people anyway."

"Then there's a white puma that wanders around the clearing here at night. He's really dangerous."

"And don't forget the bears," the other boy said. "They're big and vicious, and they'll even try to break the windows to get in the car."

Pete was leaning over the back of the seat and she gave me a nudge. I knew she was thinking the same thing I was. We could not imagine why these boys were telling us all this stuff, but we were not buying it.

"I guess we'll stay, I told them. If you find our bloody, mangled corpses in the morning it won't be on your conscience. You've warned us."

Defeated in whatever their purpose was, they told us goodnight and went back toward the highway. We were laughing about it and trying to guess what their purpose might be, when all of sudden here they came again, running this time. As they dashed past the car one of them shouted, "The coyotes are after the horses!"

They disappeared up the canyon, and we sat there expecting to hear the frantic neighing of horses but there wasn't a sound. A little later they came running back, out of breath and excited. It crossed my mind that if this was an act these boys belonged in Hollywood.

"The coyotes got one of the horses," they told us, "and the rest of them ran away. We'll have to round them up in the morning."

One of the boys had a long scratch across his upper arm, where he said a coyote had clawed him. As I painted it with iodine and applied a band-aid, I was thinking that if a coyote had done it the scratch would be vertical rather than horizontal. It looked suspiciously like a wound inflicted by a sharp branch on a bush.

We did not want to accuse the boys of lying, but we did ask a few discreet questions trying to find out what it was all about. They stuck to their story, however, and presently they left, this time for good. We spent some time trying to solve the puzzle and finally decided that they must have done it just for kicks to see if they could frighten us away. The right answer never occurred to us. We went to bed and slept through the night, sans bears, pumas and coyotes.

After spending most of the next day exploring the canyon with no luck, we drove on down the highway, and had gone only a mile when we saw a rancher working in the field with a tractor. When we stopped and walked over to the fence, he came across the field to meet us.

"We were just wondering," I said, "if you have two boys working for you up in the mountains at night looking after your horses and cows?"

He shook his head. "Gosh, no. I don't keep horses up there and neither does anyone else, and the cows can look after themselves. They don't need baby-sitters."

When we described the strange goings-on in the clearing the night before, he laughed heartily. "You girls were parked in the local lover's lane, and those boys were trying to scare you into leaving so they could bring their girl friends up there."

"Well, for Heaven's sake," Pete said. "I wish we'd known. We never once thought of that."

In another canyon not far from there we got our first high reading on the Geiger counter. The area was strewn with huge boulders, and in the cleft between two of them the needle hit the top of the scale. Convinced that underneath these rocks our fortune awaited us, but having no idea what to do about it, we called Dick, who was, at that time, working his way through college to get an engineering degree. The next day he and a friend arrived, loaded with dynamite.

After blasting several big rocks into little ones, and frightening a lot of cows, they discovered that it was only radon gas, which makes needles on Geiger counters leap wildly, but in which there is no profit. Promising to keep our secret, Dick went back to college, no doubt reflecting that when mothers were handed out he was given the "cream of the crazies."

After making a couple of fairs we stopped to explore the Chuckwalla Mountains, which are located near the highway in the desert country between Blythe and Indio. This area looked more promising than any we had tried. We followed a dirt road across the bare rocky foothills until it suddenly ended, as desert roads have a way of doing. As we walked toward a dry wash and turned on the Geiger counter our hopes soared; the needle zoomed to the top of the scale and stayed there. The trouble was that it stayed there no matter where we went. We covered a lot of territory with the same result, and discovered that the source of the radioactivity was the black sand that was spread liberally over the entire area, all the way down to the highway and beyond.

"There's just too darn much of it," I told Pete. "Whatever it is, it can't have any value or someone would be mining it."

"Wouldn't you know!" Pete laughed. "First we can't find any and now we find too much."

"Well, let's take a sample, anyway. Maybe we can find out what it is."

Pete found an empty jar and filled it with black sand. "Let's go to that little town up north were the fellow at the fair told us someone had found uranium."

The map told us it was only about two hundred miles and off we went. For the last fifty miles the road wound through mountainous country and that slowed us down so it was quite late when we arrived in the little town.

Everything was closed except for one small cafe. We went in and ordered hamburgers and coffee.

There were only three people sitting at the counter—an older couple who looked to be in their late sixties, and a man of about forty, who had a Geiger counter. All of them were discussing uranium, including the young couple who ran the place.

"We heard that someone found uranium around here," Pete said.

"That's just a rumor," said the man with the Geiger counter. "I'm a geologist, and I've been all over this area. There's no uranium anywhere around here."

"We found some stuff down in the Chuckwallas that makes the needle go crazy," I said. "It's not like any uranium we ever saw or read about and we don't think it's worth anything, but we brought along a sample. It's out in the car."

Everyone looked interested. "Bring it in. Let's have a look at it."

When Frank, the geologist, held his counter over the jar and the needle leaped, he got excited. "I don't know what this is, but it looks good. I'd like to see the area where you found it and check out the rock formations."

"Let's all go down there tomorrow," suggested the young man. "We'll close the cafe for one day, okay, Edna?"

Edna wanted no part of it. "If you want to go on a wild goose chase, John, go ahead. I'll stay here and run the cafe."

Everyone else wanted to go, including the older couple, Tim and Millie, and we had no objection to leading the way. Since there was no uranium in that area there was no point in staying. We would have to go back soon anyway, as the family was expecting us in Laguna for Thanksgiving.

We took off at the "bust of dawn," as Pete said, and arrived at the Chuckwallas around noon. Pete and I did no hiking; we had already covered the ground. We just sat in the car and watched the others scrambling over the rocks and up and down the gullies hoping, against better judgment, that Frank would come up with something. He didn't. By late evening we knew no more than we had before, except that Frank was no geologist. Both Pete and I knew more about it than he did.

Tim and Millie had given up long before and had gone home on the bus. The "geologist" and his friend, John, gathered some samples and left for San Bernardino, where they planned to spend the night and have the stuff assayed the next day.

We drove to Laguna, arriving late that night to be greeted by Ann with the news that a woman named Edna had called. "She wanted to know what you and Pete did with her husband. I know you two do some crazy things, but I'm sure you haven't taken up husband stealing, have you?"

"Well, hardly. That's a hobby we can well do without." I assured her. Pete and I exchanged amused glances. "The last we heard he was on his way to San Bernardino."

A few days later we received a note from John telling us that the black sand contained Thorium, and that it was worthless, as no one had yet figured out a way to process it. Again we had found something that turned out to be nothing.

"But just think of all the fun we've had." As usual, Pete looked on the bright side. "Maybe the third time will be the charm."

That fall marked a turning point in all of our lives. Bunny went off to college and Ann quit teaching and married a really great guy named Orris Flatten. His first wife had died in childbirth leaving him with twin boys who were not yet two years old. They were being temporarily cared for by Orris' mother in North Dakota.

Since Mom was no longer able to live alone there was only one way to go. We gave up the house, sold the furniture and put her in a nursing home. At that time Ann and Orris were living in a small apartment. A few months later they bought a house, Ann adopted the twins, and they moved Mom to a nursing home near them.

I have always felt bad about uprooting Bunny at this crucial time in her life. She was only eighteen, in her first year of college, and now she had no place to come home on week-ends or for summer vacations. But I really had no choice. I was past fifty now, with no experience or work record, not exactly in demand for a steady job. Fortunately Ann was nearby, so Bunny was not completely alone.

Dick was now in his last year of college, having put himself through by doing odd jobs. He spent several months wielding a pick and shovel on the roads. Now he was working for Scripps Institute during his spare time. Once, during Christmas vacation, he got the bugs out of one of their new computers and they sent him to Chicago to demonstrate it to some of the businessmen there. No one goes to Chicago during the winter without an overcoat and a hat, and since he had neither, and no money to buy them, he said, "Oh well, like mother like son," went to a Goodwill store and got both for less than ten dollars.

When everything was settled Pete and I hit the road again, heading for Florida. All of our worldly possessions were now either in or on the car, and it became truly our home on wheels.

Chapter 21

As we traveled across the country we attracted a certain amount of attention. Often when we stopped in a small town to do some shopping we would come back to the car to find several curious men looking it over from stem to stern. Once we heard one of them say, "Well, if that ain't a hell of a looking thing!" And we had to admit that with the peeling paint, the canvas-covered load on top and the mattress in the back we did somewhat resemble the Joad family leaving the dust bowl.

On our way to Florida we stopped in Indianapolis to work a Home Show. One day we were driving down the street in near-zero weather when the Gremlin suddenly let loose with a chorus of noises the like of which we had never heard. "Squawk, cackle, squawk." It sounded like a hen house being invaded by a fox. I thought I had heard every sound a car in distress could make, but this was something new and different. After a minute or two the noise stopped, but a few blocks farther on it began again, startling pedestrians with its "cackle, cackle, squawk".

We went into the first garage we came to and the mechanic told us we had a frozen speedometer cable. He could install a new one, he said, for fifteen dollars. I looked at Pete; we gave each other the thumbs down signal and drove away to talk it over.

"No wonder it's frozen," Pete said. "Goodness knows its cold enough here to freeze anything. But why spend money for a new one when we'll be in Florida in a couple of days where it's warm."

"Sure, that makes sense." I really thought it did. "It's bound to thaw out in that hot sun."

When we had been in sunny Florida a week and the car continued it's periodical chicken serenade, we finally gave up and told our story to a mechanic. "—and we've been here quite awhile and it hasn't thawed out worth a darn."

When he was able to stop laughing, the mechanic installed a new cable and we went on our way, embarrassed, amused, and a lot wiser. No doubt the mechanic repeated that story many times, about those two dumb broads and their frozen speedometer cable.

Three months and a lot of fairs later we started West again after a side trip to Virginia to see Pete's folks. On our way West we stopped in St. Louis to make a Home Show and almost got arrested for robbery.

We left the Home Show about eleven o'clock that night and had just pulled into our space in the trailer park on the outskirts of town when a police car drove in and stopped behind us. Expecting to be given a ticket for some traffic violation, we watched the officers get out of their car and walk toward us. Imagine our surprise when we saw that they were carrying guns.

They ordered us to get out of the car and stand off to one side, and while one of them kept his gun pointed at us, the other searched our car. Now, searching that car was not child's play. It took the cop a long time to go through our suitcases and boxes, shake out the bedding, look under the mattress and under the seats, and search the glove compartment. Pete got tired of standing and sat down on the ground.

"What's he looking for?" I asked the cop with the gun.

"He's looking for an orange scarf. Do you have an orange scarf?"

"No, we don't, but we'll be glad to give him the money to buy himself one, if that's what he wants," I said.

"Very funny," the cop replied, but he didn't smile when he said it.

"What's this all about, anyway?" Pete asked.

He didn't answer, just stood there grim-faced, holding the gun. When the other cop finished searching he came over and joined our little group.

"I didn't find the scarf or the money," he said.

"I think we have a right to know what's going on," I insisted.

"Two women held up a theatre tonight and got away in a station wagon with California plates. The driver was wearing a red coat, like yours, and an orange scarf."

"What a horrible combination," Pete interrupted. "I must say she had poor taste."

"You two fit the description, so we followed you. Where were you at eight o'clock tonight?"

"We were at the Home Show. We have a booth there. If you'll promise not to shoot me I'll reach in my pocket, get my wallet and show you our passes to prove it."

They looked at the passes, seemed satisfied, and started toward their car without even an apology.

"Hey," I called. "How about writing a statement saying we're not guilty, sign your names and stick it on our windshield so we won't have to go through this again? It's not exactly our idea of fun and games."

Much to my surprise they complied. "And you might pick her up," I pointed to Pete, "she's crippled and once down can't get up by herself."

I could have picked her up, as I had several times, but with two big strong men there I saw no point in straining my muscles. After they had gone we remade our bed, then sat in the front seat for awhile talking and laughing about the incident, and marveling at the strange coincidence that had brought it about.

From St. Louis we moved on to Home Shows in New Mexico and Colorado, and went back to prospecting for uranium. Our hopes were high now, for we were in the area where most of the big strikes had been made.

By the time we ran out of Home Shows we had hiked a lot of miles, with no luck, and were working our way West in Colorado. We were on our way back to the car one day, after exploring a place called Skull Creek Canyon, when we met a young man with a Geiger counter. He was of medium height, slender and thin-faced, and looked to be about thirty years old.

"My name's Wayne Anderson," he said. "I came out here from Indiana to look for uranium. My trailer's parked down there in the clearing."

We walked back with him and discovered, to our horror, that not only was his trailer parked there, but so were his wife, Susan, and their three babies, aged five, three and one. And we had thought we were crazy!

Susan was a thin, pale blond, two or three years younger than Wayne. They had never been out West before and we soon realized that they knew less than nothing about the hazards of desert travel. We described some of these hazards, and warned them that it was unsafe for them to leave the main highways and go trekking across the wastelands in a trailer, especially with little children. But our hope that they would be frightened into going home was futile. They seemed to think a fortune awaited them around the next bend and they were not about to turn back.

The only thing that we accomplished with our dire warnings was to frighten them into sticking with us. When we pulled out onto the dirt road the next morning they were right behind us and followed us across Southern Colorado and parts of Utah. They seemed to think we were seasoned prospectors and that we knew what we were doing. I know now how Moses must have felt when he led the Israelites across the wasteland. Fortunately, unlike Moses, I didn't have God to contend with; I had enough trouble without that.

Twice the trailer got stuck in the sand and Wayne and I got out the shovels and dug it out. We discovered that they were keeping water in open pans, thus losing a great deal of it. The children were unhappy and wanted to go home, but Pete, who was wonderful with children, kept them entertained with songs and stories while Wayne and I explored dry creek beds and canyons looking for uranium.

Following the road across the valley floor, we passed a small community where there were about a dozen houses, a general store and a gas station. According to our map, and confirmed by the old man who ran the store, there was a paved highway about twenty miles farther on, leading to a small town. This sounded good to us, so we bought some cold drinks and pushed on. We were climbing a steep, narrow mountain road when I glanced back and saw that the Andersons had stopped. Setting the brake, I walked back to find out what was wrong and met Wayne half-way.

"I can't go any farther," he said. "The car doesn't seem to have enough power to pull the trailer up this mountain."

"Well, then we'll just have to go back. Put Susan and the kids in our car and turn the trailer around."

Wayne looked at the thirty-foot drop-off and shuddered. "I just can't do it, Dot. I've never turned a trailer around at all, much less on a narrow road, and I don't know how."

"I've never even pulled one, much less turned one around, but it's got to be done so I'll have a shot at it."

Cautiously I inched the trailer back against the cliff and discovered right off that for this job you have to turn the wheel in what seems to be the wrong direction. Then I carefully pulled forward a few feet, conscious always of that awful drop-off looming ahead. Then back against the cliff again and forward a few feet, always with the panicky feeling that the brakes might not hold and I would go plunging over.

After a dozen or more of these spine-chilling maneuvers the thing was finally facing down hill. I turned off the motor, set the brakes and just sat there for a few minutes recovering. When my knees stopped trembling I walked back to our car.

"Well," I told Pete, "all I can say is that this is a hell of a place to learn to turn a trailer around."

On the way back we stopped and bought gas from the old man and asked about a road that angled off to the left toward a town on the highway. If it was passable we would save about thirty miles.

"Waal," he drawled, "it sure ain't no four lane highway.

Y'all just might make it in the wagon but there ain't no way you're goin' to get that there trailer acrost it."

We took the long way around, arrived in town that evening and spent the night in a trailer park. Early the next morning the Andersons, cured now of uranium fever, and wanting only to get home, headed East. Pete and I started for San Diego.

Chapter 22

"Well, I guess that does it for uranium hunting," Pete said, as we rolled across Arizona. "I'm not sorry we did it, though, even if we didn't find anything we had a lot of fun and met some odd-ball characters."

"That's right. It may not have been profitable but it sure wasn't dull, but now we have to think about the situation that's facing us and try to figure out what to do about it."

For the past year sales at the shows had been steadily declining, not only for us but also for almost everyone in the business. Many pitchmen had given up and had gone on to find other ways of making a living, and most of them blamed it on television, which by the middle '50s had become so widespread that almost everyone in the country had it. The commercials were out-pitching the pitchmen and the public was becoming more amused than amazed at the demonstrations they saw at the Fairs and Home Shows.

Runproof was especially hard hit because a large company, in which Bing Crosby happened to have an interest, had come out with a rival product that was advertised on television and could be purchased in drug and department stores all over the country. With that kind of competition, no wonder sales were falling off.

"You know, Dot, we're going to have to find something else soon or quit working the shows." It was the first time I had ever seen Pete in a pessimistic mood. But, she added, "What else can we do? Can you imagine working for someone else on an eight to five job? The very idea is revolting! Besides, I doubt if anyone would hire us at our age, and with our lack of experience. We'd probably end up scrubbing floors or babysitting, or something equally horrible."

"The San Diego Fair is a really big one," I reminded her. "Maybe we'll see something there that's selling like crazy that we can get into."

"We'd better. Remember, some of the shows we worked lately we didn't even make the nut. Even the Florida shows weren't so hot."

"Cheer up," I said. "We'll find something soon, I feel sure. Anyway, we can always shock people by telling them that Bing Crosby ruined us."

There were plenty of people at the Fair, but business was poor and we spent a lot of time wandering through the huge building looking for something new and different. We had been doing this for months at every show we worked without finding anything that appealed to us. Now, finally, we came across an item that looked like a winner.

It was a do-it-yourself jewelry kit consisting of matched, tumble-polished gemstones, metal parts (findings) for earrings, necklaces and bracelets, a bottle of glue and a sheet of instructions for putting it all together. There was also some made-up jewelry for those who preferred not to make their own. The man was doing a brisk business; in fact, he was having trouble keeping up with the demand.

"That's it!" Pete was enthusiastic. "It's just what we've been looking for. Let's come back tonight when the show closes and talk to him. Maybe he'll tell us where he gets all that stuff, and how we can go about getting into the business."

As soon as the doors closed that night we went to see him. When we arrived he was covering his counter with a strip of cloth, stopping now and then to wipe perspiration from his almost bald head. He was a heavy set, middle-aged man, jovial and friendly.

"I'm all tuckered out." he said. "This is the first show I've worked with this jewelry thing and I had no idea it would go over with such a bang. Sure wish I knew where I could hire some help."

"Our business is on the skids," Pete told him, "and we're looking for a new item. This is the only thing we've seen that looks good. Would you have any objection to giving us a few tips on how to get started?"

"No objection at all, only you can't work the California shows. I've got them all booked up. You'd have to find other territory."

"That's no problem," I said. "We'll work the shows in the Midwest and in Florida."

"Well, I'll tell you what you do. When this Fair is over you come out to my house in L.A. and I'll sell you enough supplies to get you started, and give you the names of some wholesale houses where you can order more stones and findings. And by the way, since you're not doing too well anyway, how about one of you helping me out for the rest of the time here? I'll pay you four dollars an hour, and it will give you a chance to learn something about the business."

I was elected to take the job because I was stronger and there would be a lot of standing and walking up and down the long counter. It made no difference as far as the money was concerned, as we had long ago given up on the tedious task of trying to keep track of our separate expenses. Now we just pooled all of our resources and everything we owned belonged to both of us.

When the Fair was over we went to Los Angeles and invested most of our money in gem stones, findings, glue, bottles, lumber for a new counter, blue satin to cover it, and some 150 watt light bulbs. Then we took everything to Helen's house in Glendale, and while Pete sat at the dining room table making up jewelry, filling bottles with glue, and putting together the kits, I worked in the backyard building a counter with uprights to hold overhead lights. It had to be made so that it could be taken apart and folded up, and due to my lack of experience as a carpenter it took me about a week to get it right.

It was too late now to get spots in the big summer fairs in the Midwest, but we were able to book spaces at four county fairs in North Dakota, Montana and Wyoming. We sent in deposits, and started for Minot, North Dakota with just about enough money to make it, providing we had no serious car trouble.

It was a fun trip. We slept in the open every night, and the good old Gremlin got us there with no trouble at all, not even a flat tire. The fact that we arrived practically broke caused us a little concern. We gave the manager a rubber check for the balance on the booth space and I put up the counter. When we spread out the jewelry on that blue satin it looked so beautiful, sparkling under the bright lights, that we felt sure we would at least make enough to pay the debt and get to the next place.

By the end of the first day we knew that we had indeed picked a winner. We sent money to the bank in Laguna to keep the rubber check from bouncing, and a couple of days later ordered a large supply of stones and findings to be shipped to the next spot in Great Falls, Montana. We sold a lot of kits, but the demand for ready to wear jewelry was even greater, and when the Fair ended we had a nice little hoard stashed away in our "bank" in the bottom of the corn flakes box.

On the way to Montana Pete came up with a suggestion. "Why don't we forget about those kits and just sell jewelry? That's where the money is, I'm sure."

"You're right, it is the way to go. The only trouble is we don't have a lot made up."

"The Fair doesn't start until Friday. We can get a motel and spend all day tomorrow making jewelry."

"And we can go in a couple of hours early every morning before the doors open and do quite a bit."

It sounded plausible. Fortunately, we had no idea what was in store for us or we would have waited until later to make the switch, when we had more time. Although we worked all day Thursday and far into the night making jewelry in that little motel room, by Saturday, the second day of the Fair, we were almost sold out.

It was a mob scene. All day long people were six-deep at our counter, all clamoring to be waited on. Our only recourse was to let them select their stones and findings, put them in paper bags and promise the finished product could be picked up the next day.

Each night when everyone else went home we stayed in our booth and tackled that mountain of paper bags. That done, we made up jewelry for the next day. Each morning at six o'clock the guard would unlock the door and let us out. I'm sure he thought we were crazy.

"Don't you gals ever go to bed?" he asked us one morning.

"Bed?" Pete grinned at him. "What's that, huh? We never heard of it."

We had given up the motel room and there was no shower in the rest room so we took spit baths, then slept for a couple of hours sitting in the front seat of the car. Soon after eight o'clock we were back in the booth making jewelry. But we could never make enough; the demand always exceeded the supply, and each night we were faced with another pile of paper bags. Thank goodness it was a seven-day fair; I doubt whether we could have survived ten.

During the entire seven days we never went to bed and never left the Fairgrounds. We made a lot of money, but we were exhausted, and when it was over we went to a motel, took long blissful showers and slept around the clock.

Since we had a little time before the next show we spent three days in the motel making jewelry, then went on to Billings, Montana. After picking up a shipment of supplies we drove to the Fairgrounds, only to discover that some one in the office had made a mistake. Another person had the "ex" on jewelry, and since they had booked their space ahead of us, it meant we could not sell our jewelry at that fair, even though it was an entirely different kind. We could only dig out the Runproof and hope that Bing Crosby's product had not yet reached the small towns.

If we had believed in guardian angels we would have been convinced now that we had one following us around. Of all the hundreds of shows we had worked, this was the only time we had a booth with a door in the back wall leading to an unused store room. There was even an old table there, badly beat up but usable. We took turns selling Runproof in the front and making jewelry in the back.

Then Harold came along, a fellow we hadn't seen in more than a year. He was a stocky man of medium height, with a ruddy complexion and a shock of iron-grey hair. He was not overly endowed in the brains department, used terrible grammar and had a slight speech impediment, but he always managed to make a living, sometimes working on the carnival lot, but often selling his "Flucom," as he called it. This was a mixture he made up himself for cleaning windows and mirrors.

"Well, hello, Harold," I greeted him. "Imagine running into you up here in the North Country. The last time we saw you was in Florida."

"Hello Dorothy and Marguerite." He always used our full names. "I been wondering what happened to you."

"Did you get a booth in the building?" Pete asked.

"No, I got here too late. I'm working on the carney lot, in one of them there shootin' galleries."

"Well, where have you been and what have you been doing since we saw you last?"

"I done what you told me to, Dorothy, I got married to a woman in Pueblo, Colorado."

"Where is she?" Pete asked. "Bring her around, we'd like to meet her."

"She's not here. It didn't work out too good. She was real religious, and was always wantin' me to go to church with her, and she kept naggin' me to get a job and settle down. So one day I just took off. You ought not to of told me to get married, Dorothy. It was a lousy idea."

"But Harold, I told you to find some gal who would enjoy traveling and working the shows with you. No wonder it didn't work out. You are definitely not the church-going, job-holding type."

We showed him our jewelry and explained why we couldn't sell it at this Fair. "It sure is pretty," he said, "I know a lot of folks on the carney lot who'd be crazy about it. They could come in one or two at a time, and no one would know what's goin' on."

"That's a great idea, Harold, so send them along," Pete said.

Pete and I never had any qualms about breaking rules, so long as no one was hurt, and in this case no one would be. The people who bought from us would not be interested in factory-made jewelry even if they knew it was there, which is doubtful. The carnies, having already seen it all, seldom came into the building.

Our "under the table" jewelry business was a great success. No one seemed to notice that there was an unusual amount of traffic in and out of our back room. Sales at the front counter were extremely poor, but it no longer mattered; thanks to Harold, Runproof was now just a "front" for the real business that was going on in the back.

At that Fair there was only one fly in the ointment. In the booth next to ours some people were selling accordions, and to attract attention a young girl was playing one of the instruments. That would have been fine, except that she apparently knew only one tune. All day long and on into the night, ad nauseam, she played "The Yellow Rose of Texas" and she made up in loudness what she lacked in talent. After listening to that tune for ten days we hoped never to hear it again.

The life of a vagabond may have been a bit rugged at times but it was never boring. Every show was a new experience and there was always at least one unusual character to make it memorable. At the small county fair in Wyoming it was the cowboy.

Tall and rangy, a real Gary Cooper type, and dressed the part including the ten-gallon hat, he came ambling up to our booth one day and stood there, solemn and silent, surveying our jewelry. Thinking this might be her chance to get some of the elk's teeth she had been wanting, Pete gave him her best smile. And Pete's best smile was famous for breaking up glaciers.

"Hi there," she said. "Do y'all ever catch any elk?"

For what seemed a full minute he stared at her, then his face broke into a grin, "We don't catch 'em, Ma'am, we shoot 'em."

"Oh, well." Pete was flustered, but not for long. "I've been just dying to get some elk's teeth, and I was hoping you might have some."

He thought about it for awhile. "There might be some knockin" around the ranch house. "I'll look, Ma'am," and he strode off down the aisle.

The next day he came back bringing a small box filled with elk's teeth. There's about a hundred there," he said. "That's all I could find."

He refused to take any money. "They didn't cost me anything and I don't have no use for 'em," he said. "They oughta make right handsome jewelry."

We gave him a turquoise bracelet and earrings to match the stone on his bolo tie. "This is gonna make my girlfriend real happy," he grinned. "Thank you kindly, Ma'am."

Chapter 23

When we had worked the San Diego Fair the previous year, 1954, we had both had chest x-rays, mainly because they were free given by a County Mobile Unit, and had thought no more about it. Then, just before we left Wyoming for the West Coast, I received a card advising me to see my doctor as my x-ray showed that I had spots on my lungs. I was really scared, and didn't smoke a cigarette all the way to Seattle. As soon as we arrived I had an x-ray at a clinic and was told that the spots were old, healed-over T.B. scars. Apparently I had had T.B. at some time without knowing it. I told Pete, who was waiting in the car, lit a cigarette and drove to Vancouver, where we worked a Flower Show.

It was November now, and there were no more fairs. We booked a spot in a department store, rented a cheap motel with weekly rates and invested in a small cutting and polishing machine. Now we could grind rough spots on the stones to make the glue hold better. We remade every piece of jewelry, using better glue, called epoxy resin.

One night we were looking over the Billboard, when we came across a full-page ad about a World's Fair in the Dominican Republic. The booth space was free and the Fair would run for three months, December, January and February. It sounded wonderful.

"I think the Dominican Republic is somewhere in the Caribbean, isn't it?" I asked Pete.

"Yes, it is," she said. "We'd have to go to Florida and take a plane."

"In a way it sounds like a crazy thing to do, but we haven't done anything really nutty since we gave up uranium hunting. Do you realize that we've been almost a month in one place? We're getting in a rut, and this sounds like fun, so let's do it."

We wrote to reserve space and as soon as a letter came confirming it, we packed up and went to Los Angeles, where we stayed with my sister in Glendale. We drove out to Orange County to see Ann's new baby boy, Greg, my first grandchild. We replenished our supplies of gemstones and findings at the wholesale houses, and tried to talk Bunny out of marrying a black man she had met in college. No one in the family had an ounce of prejudice, not even Pete who was a Southerner, but we knew that a mixed marriage was bound to create a lot of problems. Having had no success, we suggested that she go with us to the Dominican Republic. She was all for it, so we took her along hoping that in this instance absence would make her heart grow less fond. Also, it would give us a lot of time to try reasoning with her. We had yet to learn that trying to reason with a young person is usually an exercise in futility.

We arrived in Ciudad Trujillo to discover that the only means of transportation for our supplies and equipment was a small two-wheeled cart pulled by a donkey and driven by an old man who appeared to be fast approaching ninety. We gave him the number of our booth, told him to wait there for us, and took a bus to the Fairgrounds.

It was a beautiful place covering many acres of ground. The City Fathers had certainly gone all-out to make it attractive. All of the buildings looked new and someone had done a great job of landscaping; there was a profusion of flowers, lots of grass and scads of trees. An enormous archway at the main entrance proclaimed "World's Fair" in lights.

Although it would be several days before the Fair was officially open, the loud-speakers were already blaring out Bing Crosby's "White Christmas." We learned later that the natives were very partial to "Beeng Crowsby", as they called him, and consequently his songs, especially the ones pertaining to Christmas, were played almost exclusively.

We had told the old man to wait for us; instead we had to wait for him. When at last he showed up in his comical rig I helped him unload. We piled everything in the booth and went back to the airport to collect our luggage. We took a room with three beds in the only large hotel in town, and while we unpacked we congratulated ourselves on having come. We were going to make a killing here, or so we optimistically thought.

We rode the bus, or "Gua-Gua" as it was called, to and from the Fairgrounds every day and it was quite an experience. The bus was always loaded to the rafters, there were never enough seats, and always there were men sitting on the floor in the aisle. No one was allowed to stand up, and the reason was soon apparent. The driver had an alarm clock tied to the dashboard with a piece of rope, and he drove as if he were trying to meet a deadline and was fearful of not making it. If there was a speed limit he blithely ignored it and he never slowed down appreciably when he took a corner. Anyone standing up would have been hurled through a window. One day some chickens a man was carrying in a cage got loose and the place became a madhouse, with everyone jabbering excitedly in Spanish while trying to help catch the chickens. The driver paid no attention; he didn't even slow down.

The trip in the mornings was not too bad, in fact it was exciting and we rather enjoyed it, but coming home in the dark at night was sometimes a hair-raising experience. The driver made no allowance for the fact that it was dark, but traveled at the same dare-devil speed and since the bus had no dimmer switch, when he met another car he simply turned off his lights until he had passed it. Day or night, life on a Gua-Gua was never dull!

At the main intersections downtown there were no traffic signals. Instead, a policeman stood in the center directing traffic with two flashlights, one red and one green. There was a lot of horn-honking when cars going in one direction backed up and the drivers decided it was time for a change. The man in the middle, who was obviously risking his life and the possibility of a nervous breakdown, seemed to take it all very calmly. He ignored the racket and turned when he felt like it.

Most of the people in Ciudad Trujillo spoke a little English, especially in the hotel and in the restaurants and other public places, and we knew a few words of Spanish, so we had no trouble communicating. Everyone was friendly. One day when we were looking for the post office we asked a young, well-dressed man on the street for directions, and instead of telling us how to get there he led us to the very door of the place, which was several blocks away. When we offered to pay him for his trouble he smilingly refused, tipped his hat politely, and went back the way we had come.

On almost every street corner there was a vendor selling oranges, and we concluded that that must be the main crop grown on the island. Many of the small shops displayed their wares on tables on the sidewalk. Shoeshine boys were everywhere busily shining shoes at a dime a throw. In the small park in the center of town a band played Spanish music with great enthusiasm and considerable talent. To us it was a new and exciting atmosphere, completely different from anything we had seen in the States, and we enjoyed all of it—except the Fair.

There we were having nothing but trouble. There was no lack of people, but the majority of them skipped the building and made straight for the rides and games on the midway. Most of those who did come by our booth were discouraged from buying because no sooner had they taken out their wallets ready to make a purchase, than one of the Aduanas (customs collectors), three of whom were stationed directly across from us, would appear and demand an additional fifty-percent as duty. This turned most people off, and consequently, we were making very few sales. After a couple of weeks of this, what with the hotel bill and meals in restaurants, our financial situation was fast worsening.

Then Pete came up with a bright idea. "Let's give our room number at the hotel to the people who renege on account of the duty, and tell them they can come up there any morning before ten o'clock and buy the jewelry duty-free." So now we had another black market going for us. We didn't get rich, but did make a few extra sales, and at that point every little bit helped. Then we learned that what we were doing might turn out to be dangerous and we got scared.

A man who knew about our illicit operation told us, "I've heard that Trujillo, the dictator of this country, is a bad man to fool around with. You do something that displeases him and he'll very likely have you boiled in oil."

We asked several people about Trujillo and the consensus of opinion was that he had a short fuse, an unforgiving nature and an insatiable desire for revenge against anyone who dared to cross him. We gave up the black market.

Pete and I talked it over. "At this rate," I said, we'll be flat broke in a few days. Don't you think we should go home while we still have enough money to get the car out of hock in Miami?"

"Yes," Pete agreed. "Let's go home. It's been an interesting trip and fun in a lot of ways, and I wouldn't have missed it for the world. But now I think its time for us to fold our tent and silently steal away."

We told the head man in the office that we had decided to leave, packed all of our stuff in boxes, and the old man with the donkey cart came and hauled it all to the airport. There was a plane leaving in three hours, which gave us ample time to check out of the hotel and get back to the airport. We were naive enough to think that all we had to do was present our return tickets, board the plane and be on our way.

But it was not to be that easy. A minor official, a woman named Rosita, arrived and informed us that we would have to have clearance papers and a permit, which could only be obtained, in a certain office uptown. I called Bunny and Pete at the hotel, explained the situation and told them to continue packing, that I would let them know as soon as it was definite that we could make that day's flight.

The man in the office was dressed in a military uniform decorated with many ribbons and medals. He could speak no English. He and Rosita held a long discussion, of which I could not understand a word, and finally she informed me that the El Capitaine had decided that the matter was out of his jurisdiction. We would have to go to another office and explain the situation to someone with more authority.

The next man was also wearing a military uniform. I never did learn his rank, but he was obviously higher up in the hierarchy as he had a larger office, a larger desk, and more ribbons and medals. He too could speak no English. Apparently, the V.I.P.'s in Ciudad Trujillo felt it was beneath their dignity to speak any language but Spanish. After another lengthy discussion Rosita told me that having reviewed the case, the man had decided that it was not for him to make the decision. We must go to yet another office. I don't know what they called it there, but in the U.S. it's called "passing the buck".

By this time it was four o'clock, we had missed the plane and there was nothing more we could do that day so Rosita took me back to the hotel. I was beginning to wonder why they were all making such a big thing out of giving us a permit. Rosita told me that both men had insisted that she try to talk us into staying, but I had already told her that since we were not making any money, that in fact we were not even making expenses, we had to go home.

Obviously, the city officials did not want us to leave, probably because they felt it would cause them to lose face. Also, it just might encourage some of the others to get out while they still had plane fare. I wondered how high I would have to go before they finally realized that we were not going to change our minds and let us go.

Rosita picked me up at the hotel the next day and we spent the morning being shunted through two more offices, each larger and more imposing than the last. In the afternoon we arrived at an office where the sign on the door said, "El Presidente."

"Oh, my," I thought, "this guy must be the biggest shot of all, next to Trujillo himself."

El Presidente had what he thought was a wonderful idea. He told me, through Rosita, that the government had decided to lend us enough money to build a booth on the approach to the midway. There, he assured me, we would get lots of customers and make lots of money. I turned him down. Not only did I have no faith in the proposition whatsoever, but after what I had heard about Trujillo, I had no desire to be in his debt.

"Look," I told Rosita, "you tell him that unless he gives me this so-called clearance paper and a permit right now, I'm going to call a senator

I know in Washington, D.C. When I tell him that we're being held here against our will, he'll take drastic action, and heads will roll and his may be among them."

The closest I have ever been to a Senator was when we drove through Washington on one of our trips, but the bluff worked.

"He says okay, he'll give you the papers," Rosita translated. "But we'll have to go to the airport and check off everything you're taking out against what you brought in."

I called Pete with the good news and Rosita and I went to the airport, taking along a young fellow named Jose'. I wondered why he was there and could only assume that he was supposed to double check everything and keep Rosita honest. If that was the purpose it failed miserably. The larger things such as the counter, the cutting machine, the lights, etc., were no problem. Then Rosita came to an item marked on the invoice as one thousand caps. She looked puzzled and pointed to her head, "caps?" she asked.

I picked up a large plastic box and handed it to her. "Those are caps," I said.

She opened the lid, took one look at the assortment of tiny metal findings, and handed the box to me. "You count," she said.

"No way!" I handed it back to her. "You count."

She hesitated only a moment, then put a check mark after the word "caps" on the invoice and placed the box with the other things that had been checked off. She did the same thing with a box containing a couple of thousand jump rings, and from then on nothing was counted. When she came to the boxes containing a dozen or more different kinds of gemstones she barely glanced at them before checking them off the invoice. Meanwhile Jose' just stood there and said not a word. Both of them realized what an impossible job it was. Had they counted everything they would have been there for days.

She gave me the papers that had been so hard to come by and took me back to the hotel. Although she had remained friendly throughout the ordeal, I had no doubt that she was thankful to see the last of me, and was fervently hoping that I would never come her way again.

The next afternoon we were on the plane flying over the Atlantic and we arrived in Miami that evening. Thanks to those two extra nights in the hotel we lacked enough money to pay the man in the trailer park where we had left the car, but he was very nice about it and let us sleep in one of his trailers that night.

Pete called her sister Mary and she sent a little money, and I borrowed some on my insurance policy. We paid the man in the trailer park and drove out to the airport, loaded everything in the car, and were once more ready to travel. But the problem now was what to do with Bunny.

Pete and I had always felt that we could cope with any situation that arose and we had pretty well proved it over the years, but with a nineteen-year-old girl along it was a different story. We decided that it would be best if she went home. She was in favor of the idea, so I called Ann collect and she wired money for bus fare. It would be a long hard trip, but Bunny was young and healthy and she would survive.

Chapter 24

It was February, 1956, now, which was rather late for the Florida season, and when we made inquiries at the various fairs that were still coming up we learned that they were all booked solid. We tried department stores but were unable to get a spot at any of them. By the time we reached Bradenton, a small town in Northern Florida, our finances were in bad shape and we were very discouraged. A County Fair was to open there the next day but it was the same story. The manager told us that every space in the building was taken.

"I'll tell you what I can do though," he said, "there's a vacant space on the midway and you can have that if you want it."

The very idea was a shocker. We had never worked on a carnival lot. Pete looked at me. "I think we'd better take it, Dot. There isn't anything else, and we might make enough to get to Virginia. We can stay with Mary until we can book a show someplace."

I had to agree. "You're right, we really don't have much choice."

It was a typical carnival lot booth. On one side of us people could throw darts and try to break balloons to win a kewpie doll, a gaudy lamp or a stuffed animal. On the other side was one of "them shootin' galleries" as Harold called them. When we spread our jewelry out on the counter that first morning we were feeling decidedly out of place and a little uncomfortable. That didn't last long, however. Some of the carnies came by to say hello and several of them bought jewelry. A short, tubby young fellow named Mike, who ran the Ferris wheel, told us his short but interesting life history, bragged about his girlfriend and bought a necklace. We had a very good day, and although we probably didn't sell as much as we would have in the building, at least we were coming out ahead.

Pete looked at me and laughed. "How does it feel to be a carnie?"

"All I can say is that it's got the World's Fair beat by a country-mile!"

That night when the last customer had left the grounds, the rides and the music had stopped and quiet descended on the carnival lot, we were tired but happy. We had more than made the nut and with six days to go our financial worries were over, at least for the immediate future.

However, we were now faced with a problem we had never before encountered, since the buildings were always locked and a guard was on duty all night. Here we had an open booth, with no way to lock it to prevent thievery. To make matters worse, we had learned that most of the carnival men slept on the lot, rolled up in a blanket wherever they happened to be working. Since we had the pitchmen's natural distrust of carnies we could visualize them helping themselves to our jewelry during the night.

"We could pack everything on top of the car and tie the canvas over it," I suggested, "but I must say, I'm not too enthusiastic about the idea of going through that every night."

There was only one alternative. We put everything in boxes, which we stored in back under the Counter. Then I brought the car, parked it in front of the booth and we slept there, hoping to prevent thievery.

The next morning Mike stopped by looking a little worried. "I've been doing some thinking," he said, "and it seems to me that before this thing is over you ladies might have some of your jewelry stolen. You can't trust these carnies, you know, and even if you are sleeping in your car in front of the booth someone could sneak up here after you're asleep, grab a couple of boxes and you wouldn't know it was happening."

"You're probably right," Pete agreed, "but it's the best we can do, and we'll just have to take our chances."

"I'll tell you what I'll do, if it's all right with you. I'll bring my blanket and sleep here behind the counter. They'd have to step on me to get at the stuff, and besides they'll all know I'm here so they won't try anything."

"Well, that's just wonderful of you," Pete said, "and we certainly do appreciate it."

While it mayor may not have been true that carnies could not be trusted, we did for some reason trust Mike implicitly and from then on we had no worries about being robbed. When the Fair was over we gave him a bracelet and earrings to match the necklace he had bought for his girlfriend.

We met several "characters" at that Fair. There was an ex-cowboy from Wyoming who ran a "snake pit" where he amazed and horrified people by allowing rattlesnakes, copperheads and other poisonous reptiles to crawl all over him. But, apparently he missed the wide-open spaces. He suggested that I marry him and we would go back out west together, but I declined the offer. Then there was the man we called the educated bum. From his manner and speech it was obvious that he had seen better days. He told us that he was an alcoholic and had once owned a successful business, but had lost it because of drinking. Now he was reduced to running one of the games on the midway. He thought the signs we had on our displays were somewhat crude and insisted on making new ones. They were beautiful and quite professional looking; the man was really talented.

By the time the Fair was over we were both glad that there had been no space in the building, as this had certainly been a new and different experience, one we would not have wanted to miss. And we had more than enough money now to get to Virginia and to book spaces at two Home Shows that were coming up in May, one in a small town in Illinois and the other in Denver.

As we drove along through Georgia and the Carolinas I enjoyed the scenery for awhile, but as usual, after a couple of hundred miles it became monotonous.

"These Eastern states are very beautiful, but one thing I noticed is that you never see any bare ground. Everything is absolutely covered with trees and grass. You can't see the mountains you can only see the trees on the mountains. If I had to live back here I'd sure miss those huge, bare rugged mountains with no two of them ever alike. In the West you can see the skeletons of mountains."

"I'm with you," Pete laughed. "Give me the wide open spaces where the deer and the antelope play, as the song says."

We spent a week in Virginia visiting Mary, Dixie and Fred. We didn't see Bob; he was, as usual, out on the ocean. Then one early morning, at what Pete called "the bust of dawn," we told everyone goodbye and headed west, hoping to make enough money to recover from our disastrous winter. We had decided to go first to Toledo, Ohio, where a woman at one of the shows had told us there was a department store that specialized in spaces for pitchmen, for thirty-five percent of the gross. She said it was well worth it, and that you could always get a spot there.

On the way to Toledo we got lost once and went fifty miles out of our way before we discovered our mistake and had to backtrack, but we finally made it. We spent two very profitable weeks at that department store and would have stayed longer, but it seemed that two weeks once a year was the limit. The management liked a big turnover and a lot of variety.

The Home Show at Decatur, Illinois, was a big bust. At the end of the seven days we had barely made the booth space and I was glad when it was over. I loaded the last of the boxes on top of the car and began tying down the canvas cover.

"You know, Pete, next to the World's Fair in the Dominican Republic, this has got to be the lousiest show we've ever worked with the jewelry."

"Well, you can't sell stuff unless you have people to sell it to and at this show they sure stayed away in droves. You could have driven a car up and down the aisles most of the time without hitting anybody."

As usual, it was almost midnight when we got away. We drove for about an hour, then started looking for an over-night trailer park. None of the towns we went through seemed to have any, so finally we pulled into an all night service station. I guess we looked fairly harmless; they let us park for the night behind the station. In the morning we filled the tank, checked the tires and were again on our way.

As we drove along through the flat uninteresting Mid-West plains, I brought up a subject I had been thinking about for some time.

"How would you feel about renting a shop in some town and settling down in one spot, at least for awhile?"

"I think it's a super idea. I've often wondered how you hold up under this constant loading and unloading."

"Well, my muscles are holding out just fine, there's no problem there. But my disposition is getting a bit frazzled. It would be nice to stay put for awhile, if we can find the right location."

We rode in silence for several miles. I examined an imaginary map in mind's eye, discarded several towns for various reasons, and was about to suggest Reno, Nevada, when Pete suddenly burst out, "How about Reno, Nevada?"

"Now isn't that the limit, you took the thought right out of my mind, or vice versa."

Pete laughed. "Yeah, how about that? Two minds with but a single thought."

"A lot of pretty well-loaded people go to Reno to get divorces so business should be great if we find a good spot with a lot of foot traffic."

"Okay, so it's Reno, here we come, as soon as this next show is over." Ten days later the Denver Home Show ended and I hoisted the boxes for what I hoped was the next to the last time. As we drove through downtown Denver we were stopped at a red signal when an expensive looking convertible pulled alongside. It was full of boys in their late teens, who seemed to be fascinated at the sight of us. They looked our car over from stem to stern, and one of them shouted, "Now if that ain't a hell of a looking thing."

"Isn't it though!" I retorted. "But we like it, and it's paid for. Is yours?"

We didn't hear their answer as just then the signal changed and they took off with a roar, laughing and waving. They had probably never seen anything like that car, unless they happened to see the movie, "Grapes of Wrath."

We slept on the desert south of Cheyenne that night and the next day started on the long trek across Wyoming. During the night I had spent some time thinking about the state of our finances, and I wasn't at all sure that we had enough money to swing the deal in Reno. We'd probably have to lease a place and pay the first and last month's rent, and no doubt we'd have to get a business license. I had no idea how much that would cost. I couldn't sleep for thinking about it, and I finally came up with what I felt was a novel, not to say brilliant idea.

"I've thought of a way we might make some money as we go along, Pete."

"If it's a way to make money I'm all for it, as long as it isn't illegal or immoral. Tell me about it."

"I thought we could spread out a lot of jewelry on a blanket in the back of the station wagon, then stop at service stations and buy just a dollar's worth of gas, so the tank won't get too full. While I'm getting the gas you can open the back door and let the guys look at the jewelry. I'll bet we'll make some sales."

"Don't we have to have a peddler's license or something to do that?"

"I don't really know, but to be on the safe side we'll skip the stations in towns and just hit the ones on the edges. We don't want to tangle with the law."

It worked. We sold some jewelry at every place we stopped in Wyoming, Utah and Nevada. It slowed us down a lot. It took us longer to cross those three states than it ever had before, but we didn't mind that. We had plenty of time, and it was fun.

Three days in Reno was all it took to shatter our dreams of a permanent shop. The only places for rent were too far off the main drag, and even those poor locations were quite expensive. Feeling discouraged, we went into a small cafe, ordered hamburgers, with coffee for Pete and a coke for me and discussed the situation.

"It seemed like such a good idea at the time," Pete said, "but it's an idea that's definitely gone down the drain. It just makes me sick to think of the scads of jewelry we could sell to those rich people who are cruising up and down the street, if we just had a place to display it. But let's face it, we're not going to find a good spot in this town. So what do we do now?"

"We don't seem to have any choice. We'd better buy a Billboard and book some Fairs and Home Shows for the summer."

A young man sitting at the counter had overheard our conversation. "Why don't you gals try Virginia City?" he suggested.

"Virginia City!" I looked surprised. "Isn't that the site of the famous Comstock Lode? I've heard of it, but I thought it was an abandoned ghost town."

"It's a ghost town all right, but it's sure not abandoned. About a million tourists go through there every summer and it's loaded with gift shops. You might be able to sell your jewelry wholesale to one of them. Pete was instantly enthusiastic. She smiled at the young man, and when Pete smiled, which she did most of the time, she was a joy to behold. "It sounds absolutely wonderful, and I just can't tell you how much we appreciate your telling us about it. Now, just tell us one more thing, how do we get there?"

"There's nothing to it," he grinned. "You'll see a sign about half way between here and Carson City. Turn left there and just follow the Geiger Grade up the mountain. It'll land you smack in the middle of Virginia City."

We hurriedly finished our hamburgers, and as we were leaving he gave us a bit of parting advice. "You might try Mr. McBride first, at the Bucket of Blood Saloon and Gift Shop. He's a square shooter and will treat you right. But whatever you do, don't have any dealings with a man named Vern Larsen. He's the most hated man in town and they say he's as crooked as a pig's tail."

Chapter 25

Virginia City was built on the side of the mountaintop, so its six streets resembled giant stair steps. The business district on C Street was three blocks long and consisted of twenty-five saloons, fifteen gift shops, five small cafes and one hotel. There was also a large building housing the Territorial Enterprise, a newspaper which had been published in that same building for almost a hundred years, and where Mark Twain had once worked as a reporter.

On the next street up the hill there was a small courthouse, the sheriff's office, and the old opera house where many famous people, including Jenny Lind, had once performed. Down below C Street was a public school, the beautiful century-old Catholic Church, St. Mary's in the Mountains, and the much newer Episcopal Church.

When we arrived the season was just starting, but already there were quite a few tourists wandering up and down the old board sidewalks. We found a place to park and taking along our display case of jewelry, we went into the "Bucket of Blood", only to learn that Mr. McBride was in Reno and would not be back until late evening.

"Let's look the place over. Maybe we can find a spot to set up in," As usual Pete's optimism knew no bounds. "It would sure beat selling the stuff wholesale."

I couldn't see much hope. "From the looks of it, I'm afraid everything is pretty well filled up. By the way, do you remember the name of the man we're supposed to avoid?"

"Oh gosh, no! It's gone completely out of my mind."

"Well, we won't worry about it. If we hear the name or see it on a sign we'll probably recognize it."

Most of the business places were on the other side of the street, so we crossed over and with Pete holding my arm in order to navigate over the rickety, uneven boards, we started our tour of inspection. We went into several of the saloons, which were a far cry from the modern cocktail bars. They were real old-time saloons, large and well-lighted with high ceilings and the original old mahogany bars. Some had roulette wheels and blackjack tables, and all of them had slot machines. In a couple of them piano players were pounding out gay nineties tunes. It was a noisy, blatant and altogether fascinating town, and before we had covered the first block we had literally fallen in love with it.

None of the gift shops had handmade gemstone jewelry like ours. It was all factory-made stuff, what we called "junk jewelry" and we wondered how they managed to sell any of it, especially since they displayed it in glass showcases. If a customer wanted to see a particular item she had to point to it, whereupon the clerk would bring it out for inspection.

"That is not the way to sell jewelry," Pete commented. "They don't realize what they're missing by not showing it properly."

We were nearing the end of the street now, and there was only one place left to try. The sign said, "Mark Twain Gift Shop" and next to it was the "Mark Twain Saloon", in front of which was a life size wooden Indian.

"Let's go in here and rest a minute and have a cold drink before we tackle this last place," I said.

It was a long narrow place with just a bar running the full length, from front to back. There were no slot machines or gaming tables. The only added attraction was a piano player, a woman who looked to be in her seventies, wearing a turn of the century costume. She was sitting on a raised platform at the front end of the bar, playing "Bird in a Gilded Cage" on an ancient upright piano. When she finished the tune she climbed down off her perch and started down the long aisle toward the back.

One of the men sitting at the bar called out, "Hey, Hattie, where you going?" Hattie picked up her long skirts, did a little impromptu dance and said, "Well, after all, you know, a girl has to tend to the plumbing now and then." It brought down the house.

I had a bourbon and coke, Pete had a glass of orange juice, and thus fortified we went into the gift shop. It was quite large, with the usual assortment of glass showcases. Three women were wandering around looking at the various items on display, and the owner was behind the counter near the front.

"We have some handmade gemstone jewelry we'd like you to look at," I said. We can sell it to you wholesale, or if you have space, we'd like to set up our counter and sell it on a percentage basis." I put the sample case on the counter and opened it, hoping he would be dazzled by the sight of all that gorgeous jewelry. He was not impressed.

He shook his head. "People don't want that stuff. I've got some of it there in the case. Had it for months and no one ever buys any of it." On a bottom shelf were a half dozen key rings adorned with colorless chunks of petrified wood, three agate bracelets that no woman in her right mind would wear to a dog fight, and a few pairs of sad looking earrings. Next to them were some Indian moccasins and a few factory-made Indian baskets. I looked at him in amazement. "Did you really expect anybody to buy them? To begin with they're ugly, and you have them hidden down there with a bunch of Indian stuff! If you want to sell jewelry you have to spread it out and flash it up with lights and satin and velvet."

In the meantime, the three women had gathered around the sample case, like bees around a pot of honey. One woman picked up a dangle bracelet with fifty assorted stones just as another lady reached for it. "This is mine," she said, "I saw it first." Another woman held up a long necklace made of alternating Apache Tears and clear quartz crystal. "Oh, I love this," she exclaimed. "How much is it, and do you have matching earrings?"

"I'm sorry," Pete told her, "but I can't sell you anything. We're just showing it to the owner."

Said owner may not have been impressed with the jewelry, but he was certainly impressed with the women's reaction to it. "I'll tell you what I'll do." He pointed to the rear of the store. "I'll move all that junk out of there and give you the whole back-end of the place. You can set up your counter and show me how to sell jewelry. How would twenty-five percent of the gross strike you?"

It struck us just fine! We didn't even have to talk it over. We both recognized a bargain when we saw one. I helped him move his "junk", set up the counter and put up the four 150 watt light bulbs, while Pete put the jewelry out on the counter. In about an hour we were ready for business.

He stood there watching us. "Aren't you afraid people will steal things?" he asked.

"No doubt we'll lose things now and then, but if we get enough volume we can absorb the loss," Pete assured him. "And believe me, this is the only way to go. You know what it says in the Bible. 'Don't hide your light under a bushel', or in this case maybe I should say Indian baskets."

"You've got me there!" he laughed. "By the way, what are your names? What with all these goings-on, I forgot to ask you."

I told him our names. "What is yours?" I asked.

"Vern Larsen," he said, as he left to wait on a customer.

"Ye Gods!" Pete looked horrified. "That's the one! That's the man we were supposed to steer clear of!"

"And wouldn't you know, we'd end up in his store! Still, you can't believe everything you hear and he seems a nice enough guy. Besides, we get first count, so he'll have to trust us, not the other way around."

We didn't want to rent an apartment until we were sure we had a good spot, so that night we drove out to the edge of town and parked in a sort of dell with huge boulders all around. It was a lovely place, and Pete indulged in one of her fantasies.

"Just think, we might become famous some day, and they'll put up a sign saying, 'Dot and Pete slept here.'"

The next day was a super success, so we rented an apartment on the second floor of an old building that in the old days had been a hardware store and was now a saloon. There was a living room, bedroom, kitchen and bath. I insisted that Pete take the bedroom, as I knew it would be more comfortable for her partially paralyzed muscles, and I slept on the couch in the living room.

On our second night there when I removed the sofa cushions preparatory to making up my bed, I stared in utter amazement. "Hey, Pete, come look at this. Virginia City really is a ghost town, and I think: we've been visited by one of the ghosts."

There on the couch, where it had been hidden by one of the pillows, lay a foot-long piece of heavy, rusty chain with a broken padlock on one end. "That certainly wasn't there when we left this morning," I said. "I wonder where it could have come from." I looked at the ceiling. There was no hook from which the chain could have fallen.

"Well, it does fit," Pete said. "After all, you know, this building used to be a hardware store."

We put the chain on the corner of the sideboard and left it there with a note!

> Dear Ghost:
>   We enjoy having you visit us and we do wish we could see you. How about leaving us something useful, like a screw-driver or a hammer?
>
>   Much love,
>   Pete and Dot

When we came home the next night the chain and note were still there, and we never saw another sign of our "ghost!" We decided that perhaps we had hurt his feelings. We discounted the idea that one of the townspeople had played a joke on us because we had locked the door and besides we had so far met no one except Vern Larsen, and he was definitely not the practical joker type.

He did, however, turn out to be a very nice guy. We got along fine with him and all of us made a lot of money. His fourth of the proceeds came to around five hundred dollars a month, which was a lot of money in those days. It was a hectic summer. The tourists began arriving at about eight in the morning and didn't quit until after ten at night. We worked fourteen hours a day, seven days a week, so we had no time for socializing, but we did meet some of the town "characters" when curiosity brought them to our counter.

Naughty Lola, so called because she neither drank, smoked nor ran around with men, was a woman about our age. She was thin, almost to the point of emaciation, and wore her grey hair pulled straight back in a bun. She worked as a waitress in one of the cafes, and her main goal in life was collecting rare coins that she kept carefully stashed away in a safe deposit box in Reno.

Big Annie was a Scandinavian woman in her late forties. She was almost six feet tall, well proportioned, and was always meticulously dressed. Her straight blond hair was braided and wound coronet style on top of her head, and as she waited on customers in one of the gift shops she looked positively regal. But that was during the summer. She and her husband, who was called "The Finn," were alcoholics, and when the season ended after Labor Day they fell off the wagon with a vengeance, and spent the winter reeling from bar to bar. Annie became slovenly, ill-tempered and belligerent, and heaven help anyone who dared to cross her. We were told that once in a bar a man made a remark Big Annie didn't like, whereupon she grabbed him by his collar and the seat of his pants and threw him into the street.

One little roly-poly man came into the store about twice a week. He worked at the Silver Queen Saloon as a shill, operating one of the slot machines that had been set to pay off frequently so as to entice people to try their luck. He had fallen for Pete and every time he came in he brought her a long string of plastic encased lollipops. He didn't much like me, because I disagreed with him on politics, but he was a true gentleman. He always gave me a couple of lollipops. I don't remember his name. We called him Lollipop.

One of the most interesting characters in Virginia City was Bad Water Bill, who had acquired the nickname through having spent quite some time in a place called Badwater, in Death Valley. He was a chunky man of medium height and always wore patched blue jeans, a faded plaid shirt and a wide-brimmed, decrepit felt hat. With his ruddy complexion and white beard he looked like Santa Claus in prospector's clothes. He had a burro named Gravel Gertie laden with a pick, a shovel, a gold pan and a desert water bag. He stood on a vacant lot on C Street, where tourists eagerly paid him for the privilege of taking pictures of their children astride Gravel Gertie. He entertained them with stories of his prospecting trips, and proudly displayed a small worn leather bag full of "gold nuggets" which he claimed to have found in the Klondike. Actually, he was born in Chicago, had never done any prospecting in his life and didn't know one end of a mountain from another. But he certainly added a lot to the local "color" and the tourists loved him.

When we mentioned to Bad Water Bill that we were hoping to find a spot in Las Vegas for the winter he told us he had a ranch there on the outskirts of town. It consisted of several acres of county land and he had been "squatting" there for years along with several of his friends, with no objection from the county.

"You're welcome to park there all winter if you like. It beats paying for a motel. Just follow Charleston Avenue south into the desert and you'll see a sign that says, 'Bad Water Bill's Renegade Ranch'. Turn right there on the dirt road and in a couple of miles you'll come to it. I'll be there off and on during the winter so maybe I'll see you there."

When the season ended most the of the gift shops closed, including Vern Larsen's, but he assured us that we could have the same spot in his store the following summer, so we went to Las Vegas in a happy mood. We drove straight through town, found Charleston Avenue and following Bad Water Bill's directions had no trouble finding Renegade Ranch.

Chapter 26

Renegade Ranch was a new and fascinating experience. In all of our travels we had never seen anything to compare with it. There in the middle of the desert, scattered at random over a couple of acres, were a two room shack, four goats wandering about in the yard, a tiny building which we assumed was a store-room, a travel trailer, a broken down black sedan with no tires and a covered wagon. There was also a small building which was apparently a rest room. A sign over the door said "Opera House".

The two-room shack was occupied by a small, balding man who acted as a sort of caretaker. He tended the goats, fed the chickens and made periodic trips to town to haul out barrels of water. Once upon a time he had been a banker in San Francisco until an insatiable craving for beer had brought about his downfall. He was called Bed-Bug Ray, because he had once spent three nights in a flop-house that was infected with bed bugs and had made the mistake of describing the ordeal to friends.

The little building we had taken for a store room was actually the home of a tall, spare Scotsman in his sixties who was, naturally, called Scotty. He had built the place himself with boards scrounged from the city dump, which was only about a mile away. It was about eight by ten, with room only for a narrow cot, a small table and one chair. A profusion of books and magazines were piled on and under the chair. Scotty spent the long evenings reading by the light of his kerosene lamp.

Nick the Greek, who lived in the trailer, was a short man, not much over five feet tall with dark, swarthy skin. He had a patio in front of his trailer, furnished with things brought from the dump. There was a carpet, a sofa, an overstuffed chair and a table. Every morning he would come out of the trailer wearing swimming trunks, lie down on the sofa and take a sun-bath while reading yesterday's paper. At noon he would get dressed and drive downtown, where he worked as a shill in one of the gambling places.

Even the dilapidated car was someone's home. Keith was a very tall, slender young man in his early thirties who aspired to be a writer. He had removed the back seat of the car, installed a stool and a table for his typewriter, and slept on the floor in a sleeping bag. Two of his short stories had been published and spurred on by this success; he spent his days and most of his nights hunched over his typewriter. Now and then his girlfriend came out bringing supplies, mostly paper and typewriter ribbons and also food, which he often forgot to eat, engrossed as he was in turning out the novel which he felt sure would bring him fame and riches. His only complaint was that he was getting hunch-backed from living in such close quarters. "This is one situation," he told us, "when it would be a blessing to be short."

The covered wagon belonged to an old man named Diamond Jim. He was over six feet tall, had a lot of grey hair and a beard, and looked to be in his seventies. He had a small butane stove, a transistor radio, and a lot of rock specimens he had picked up on his prospecting trips into the hills around Boulder Dam. His three burros were named Nettie, Betty and Hal.

"I really only need one burro," he said, "but I've gotten attached to them. They're like family to me and I can't give any of them up. I let them take turns going with me, and believe it or not, when they see me getting ready to head out, they seem to know whose turn it is."

Several years back on one of his trips into the hills he had found some crystals that he felt sure were diamonds. He brought some back in a coffee can, showed them to several people, and was planning to take them into town to have an expert look at them, when they disappeared, being either lost or stolen. He went back to get some more but was unable to find the place, and ever since then he had been searching without success for his fabulous "diamond" mine

Renegade Ranch was a favorite stopover for many desert wanderers. It was a haven where they could rest and recuperate before going on their next trek. Steve, the desert painter, who had desert scenes painted on all four doors of his old car, stayed there a week and spent the time painting. He had a lot of enthusiasm but no talent. His pictures were gaudy and unreal looking, but somehow he managed to eke out a living, more or less, by parking on the highways and displaying them to passing tourists.

One day a family of Indians, a father, mother and several children, came by and stayed a couple of days. They were riding in a wagon drawn by two tired looking horses, and were on their way to the Hopi reservation in Arizona.

We had been there about two weeks when Bad Water Bill showed up with his Indian girl friend, who was called Princess. She was young and slender, wore her black hair in two long braids, and had quite a lot of Indian jewelry, including a turquoise studded headband.

We all sat around the table in Bed Bug Ray's little house, enjoying cold drinks, discussing show business and telling stories while Bad Water Bill rejuvenated his wardrobe, as he called it. He cut jagged holes in the sleeves of two old shirts he had picked up at a Salvation Army store, then filled the holes with patches of different colored material.

"I have to keep up appearances," he laughed. "Princess and I are going to be in a parade next week."

Often, when there was a parade in Nevada or one of the neighboring states, he and the Princess rode on one of the floats representing the state of Nevada.

Since it was a warm day, the door was left open and now and then one of the goats would wander in, cruise around the room looking for something to eat and wander out again. To Pete and me it was simply hilarious, but none of the others paid any attention. To them it was a way of life.

We were so fascinated with Renegade Ranch and its collection of unusual people that we hoped to stay all winter providing we could find a spot in Las Vegas. It was a comfortable, easy-going life. A couple of times a week we went to a trailer park, where for a small fee we could take showers and do our laundry. Most of the time we lived on sandwiches and fruit, but occasionally we had a regular meal at a cafeteria.

We looked all over town for a good location, but it was slim pickings. All of the gift shops turned us down for lack of space, and most of the vacant buildings were too large and all of them required a year's lease. We finally found a small place that we could get on a month-to-month basis. It wasn't the best location, but we decided to give it a try. We dug into the bottom of the box of cornflakes where we kept our money, paid a month's rent and we were in business.

It was certainly a far cry from Virginia City. There was very little foot traffic. But after the first month when the news got around by word of mouth, more people began to come in and we began to show a little profit. We had no regrets about not making that long trip to Florida for the winter fairs.

One afternoon we closed the shop early and took a sight-seeing trip to the Sunset Strip where the Flamingo, Caesar's Palace and many other famous gambling clubs were located.

We were crossing the street when Pete stepped on a pebble or something and started to fall. With her weak legs it didn't take much to put her down.

I tried to hold her up, but her knee banged into back of my knee and we both went down. And there we sat in the middle of the street, with horns honking and cars going by. No one offered to help, probably because they all thought we were just a couple of drunken broads.

I got up and hoisted Pete's hundred and thirty pounds of dead weight. Whenever she fell, which was infrequently, she could not get up under her own power and had to be lifted. (Not without reason Ann had once remarked that I was a tough old broad, which I took as a compliment.) We staggered back to the curb and sat there a few minutes to recuperate. My knee was swelling and was quite painful.

"We'd better get going while I can still walk," I said. "I'll be lucky if I can make it the two blocks to the car."

Driving home was a problem because I could not use my right leg at all and had to operate the clutch and the brake with my left foot. It was a bit awkward to say the least, and I didn't dare drive very fast, but we made it. I parked by Bed Bug Ray's place, hopped in, heated a pot of water on his butane stove, added a lot of Epsom salts, and soaked my knee for about an hour. By morning the swelling had gone down, there was no pain, and my knee was a good as new. And we had a good laugh over that embarrassing episode.

A week or so later Pete woke in the middle of the night, crying and calling, "Mary! Mary!" Thinking she had just had a bad dream, we thought no more about it, but the next morning when we were on our way to the shop two cops pulled us over. "Are you Marguerite Williams?" one of them asked.

"No, I'm not." I pointed to Pete. "She is. Why, what's the trouble?"

"You're to call your sister Mary Crossen right away," he told Pete. "She didn't have your address or phone number, so she called us and described your car and we've been looking for you. Call her as soon as you can get to a phone. It sounds like an emergency."

Somehow, I knew instantly that it was bad news about Mary's son, Fred, and although I reminded myself that it could be Dixie or Bob, or one of her grandchildren, I just knew it wasn't. I felt positive that something had happened to Fred. We stopped at the first phone booth we could find, called Mary and learned that while painting the outside of a ship Fred had fallen into the James River and drowned. Pete burst out crying, and was so nervous and upset she couldn't talk, so I took over the telephone and talked to Mary, who in her grief was barely understandable. "Marguerite will be there on the first available plane," I assured her.

I packed a suitcase, drove to the airport and was lucky to get a seat on a plane leaving in two hours. Pete's already unstable nervous system had collapsed completely, and during that two hours, which seemed more like a hundred, she never stopped crying and trembling. I took her to the plane in a wheel chair, and explained the situation to the stewardess, who promised to look after her and give her special attention.

With a heavy heart I watched the plane take off, called Dixie to give her the flight number and arrival time, then went back to Renegade Ranch, where I spent the rest of the day just sitting in the car grieving for Fred. He was a wonderful young man, only twenty-four years old, with a wife and two children and another on the way. It was a terrible tragedy.

For lack of anything better to do, I opened the shop every day, but without Pete it was no fun and my heart wasn't in it. Then Bad Water Bill showed up at the Ranch with bad news.

"The last time I was in Virginia City, about a month ago, Vern Larsen told me to let you gals know that he's converting his gift shop into a cafe, so he's sorry, but he won't have a spot for you next summer."

This was a bitter blow. We simply had to spend the coming season in Virginia City, as no other place could compare with it. There was only one thing to do. Knowing that Pete would agree, I closed the shop, which was nothing to rave about anyway, loaded everything on the car and drove to Virginia City, taking Bad Water Bill along as a passenger.

I made arrangements for space at the Silver Queen Saloon, which was owned by Carrol Eaton and his wife, Jerry. It was the largest saloon in town, and was quite famous for its twelve-foot high picture of the Silver Queen, made entirely with three thousand four hundred and three silver dollars.

When I called Pete to tell her all the news, she said she was planning to come back in a week. "I'll meet you in Kansas City," I told her. "I've booked space in a Home Show there, and after that we can go on to Chicago. There's a really enormous Home Show being held there in April."

When I met Pete in Kansas City I was glad to see that she had recovered somewhat, but she had lost weight and didn't look too well. It was good for her to be occupied again, making jewelry and waiting on customers. We stayed with my sister Orva, who took us on several sightseeing tours, mostly to look at houses. She was crazy about houses, and I'm sure we must have seen every single home in the better sections of town.

The Home Show in Chicago was by far the largest one we had ever worked. The building covered literally acres, and the manager rode around from place to place on an electric cart. There must have been hundreds of pitchmen, besides the many booths that were occupied by local advertisers. Bad Water Bill was there with Gravel Gertie representing the state of Nevada.

I was just starting to put up the counter when two men walked up to our booth. One was a tall, sharply dressed man, with a swarthy skin and a black bowler hat. The other was older, shorter and dressed in workmen's clothes.

"My name is Louis Cordoza," the younger man said, "and I represent the Union. This is my friend, Tony. He'll put up your counter and do all the heavy work for ten dollars an hour."

I shook my head. "I'm sorry, but we always do it ourselves. We really don't need anyone."

"Well, the rule here is that you have to hire Union labor. The men need the work."

"I'm sorry if the men need work, but I don't feel that it's our responsibility. The answer is still no."

"Okay, then, but if you don't hire Union labor, you're required to make a twenty-five dollar contribution to the Union fund."

"Now that's got to be the most ridiculous thing I ever heard of." I was indignant. "In fact I think you're a gangster, and you're running a racket. I'll have you know we hang 'em in Nevada for less than that!"

Without saying another word, he took a notebook out of his pocket, glanced at our sign, which read "Tierra Gems—Virginia City", Nevada, carefully wrote it down, and they went away.

The business with the notebook left us feeling uneasy. "What if he really is a gangster?" Pete wondered. "After all, this is Chicago. Maybe we don't realize what we've gotten ourselves into."

"I'll go talk to the manager and see if I can find out what this is all about." The manager seemed reluctant to discuss the matter. "It's just one of those things," he said. "They do it every year and people mark it up as a business expense."

"What do they do about the ones who refuse to pay?"

"I really can't say because so far as I know, no one has ever refused before. You're the first."

I talked to several of the pitchmen and all of them admitted that they either hired workmen or made a contribution, simply because they didn't want to make waves, especially in Chicago. A fat man who made a living cutting silhouettes was more specific.

"I've been working this show for six years," he said, "and I always give them the money. I sure don't need to hire any workmen; I don't even have a counter. All I use is a pair of scissors and some paper. But I always pay, and if you are smart you will too. How would you like it if some guy coming down the aisle 'accidentally' bumps into your counter and knocks it over? It would cost you quite a bit just to replace the broken light bulbs, besides the sales you'd miss while you're setting it up again. Or what if you go out to your car some night and find all your tires slashed? Don't argue with those guys. Just pay and forget it."

Now we really were frightened. We were not up to fighting Chicago gangsters. We decided that principles would have to go by the board, and that if and when the man came back we would give him the money.

"I'm going to throw the money on the floor," Pete said, "rub my foot on it and say, 'There you are, you so-and-so, pick up your dirty money,'"

She never got the chance to carry out her threat. Three anxiety-filled days passed and the man did not come back. Whenever I saw a man who even remotely resembled a gangster I tensed, ready to push against the counter in case he tried to "accidentally" knock it over. Every night when we went to the parking lot we were surprised to find that our tires were not slashed to ribbons. It was not a happy time, even though business was good and we were making money.

"Something's got to be done," I said. "We can't go on like this or we'll both be nervous wrecks. I'll go see the manager and have him call that guy and tell him to come and get the money."

On the way to the office I met the manager, who was wheeling down the aisle in his electric cart. I stopped him.

"Mr. Graves," I said, "will you please call that Mr. Cardoza and tell him to come and get the money? We can't fight Chicago gangsters, so we've decided to pay rather than have our booth wrecked or our tires cut up."

"Have you girls been worrying about that?" He gave me a straight, knowing look that seemed to convey an unspoken message. "Well, you don't have to give them any money and nothing is going to happen so don't give it another thought. Take my word for it."

We wondered what had happened to get us off the hook. "Maybe they just didn't want to tangle with the state of Nevada," Pete suggested with a grin.

The rest of the show was uneventful, except for one rather wild episode. It happened because of my chronic absentmindedness, and also because for the first time in history there was an empty booth next to ours.

Pete was an inveterate coffee drinker, and since I could walk faster I had been making several trips every day to refill her thermos at the nearest refreshment stand, which was six aisles away. It took a lot of time and at that show time was money.

Since our motto had always been to use whatever the gods provided, I installed a hot plate on a small table in the empty booth, put up a screen and we saved a lot of time by making instant coffee right next door. And that was the only thing we used the hot plate for until I got the bright idea of hard-boiling some eggs.

Early the next morning before the doors opened I put four eggs in a small pan, covered them with water, set the pan on the hot plate and went back to work. Ten minutes later the doors opened, the public began pouring in and soon people were crowded around our counter. I was so busy waiting on customers that I forgot about the eggs that were boiling merrily away behind the screen. Suddenly there were four loud "bangs" that sounded exactly like gunshots. Thinking that a gang war had broken out some people froze where they were. Others hit the floor. We realized instantly that the eggs had boiled dry and exploded, and I wasted no time getting back to that hot plate.

One woman, watching me stride past in my blue jeans, cowboy shirt and hat, said to Pete, "I don't know what that was, but whatever it was I'm sure she can take care of it." We laughed a lot over that little episode, and remembering that famous movie, "The Egg and I", we decided to dub it "The Eggs and Us."

That was the most profitable show we had ever worked. As we packed up on that last night we agreed that it was also one of the most interesting mainly because of our little fracas with Mr. Cardoza, who to us was better known as "that Chicago gangster."

Chapter 27

Now it was time to go to Virginia City and we were looking forward to it. We made good time going through the Midwest since there was nothing to see, but when we reached the Rocky Mountains we slowed down and enjoyed the scenery. We took a couple of side trips for some rock hunting, slept four nights on the desert under the stars, and by the time we reached Virginia City we were rested and refreshed and ready to tackle a "million" tourists. We had ordered supplies, which were waiting for us there, and we spent the month making jewelry before the season got into full swing after Memorial Day.

The Silver Queen was somewhat of a disappointment for us. Business wasn't nearly as good as it had been at Vern Larsen's because most of the people who came in were more interested in drinking and gambling than they were in jewelry. We tried all of the gift shops but none of them had space for us, they said. Actually they probably did not want the competition.

One day a young geologist, attracted by our specimens and fossils, stopped and stayed quite awhile discussing rocks. His name was Barney. He was Jewish, over six feet tall and was built like a Greek god. Just looking at him was enough to make us regret our lost youth. He was most interesting and gave us what might be called a quickie course in geology. After that he stopped to see us whenever he made one of his infrequent trips through Virginia City and became one of our best friends.

We had resigned ourselves to making the best of things at the Silver Queen when we heard about a small building that was for rent. It was a tiny, narrow place on the wrong side of the street with no other shops nearby so we would be alone in the middle of the block. It didn't look too promising, but we were always ready to take a gamble. We put a big sign over the door, christened it the "Hole in the Wall", and moved in.

The floor was a problem; it slanted considerably toward the front. Since it was the middle of the season and there was no time to have a new floor put in, I made a trip to Reno, bought several sheets of heavy plywood and a lot of bricks, and built up the floor behind the counter to make it level. It worked fine and we no longer wore ourselves out walking up and down hill all day. Our gamble paid off. A surprising number of people crossed the street to look at our jewelry and rock specimens and we did almost as well as we had the previous summer.

Half a block up the street there was a huge two-story building where a young couple operated a combination ice cream parlor and gift shop. They were leasing the place with an option to buy, but apparently their business was not too great and after the season ended they moved to a place on the busy side of the street. The building belonged to Chuck Clegg, a young man who was a friend and partner of Lucius Beebe, who published the Territorial Enterprise. The asking price was $14,000, with a down payment of $3,500.

"Let's buy it and stay here year round and stop this traipsing around all over the country." As usual, Pete was filled with enthusiasm for a new venture.

"It's a wonderful idea and I'm all for it, but the down payment will leave us broke with no way to get through the winter and make the payments. Do you suppose he'll come down any on his price?"

"He probably will. People always ask more than they expect to get. And Naughty Lola says that quite a few of the divorce seekers in Reno come up here during the fall and winter. We'll figure out some way to get by. Don't we always?"

Chuck settled for $12,000 with $2,500 down, so now we had ourselves a building. And what a building it was! During the past hundred years it had been everything from a general store to a funeral parlor. There were two left over coffins on the second floor, along with a lot of discarded junk. There were three basements, the bottom two being pitch dark and accessible through trap doors. It was said that two Chinamen were buried down there, but although Barney, thinking he might find buried treasure, went down with a flashlight and did some digging, he found neither skeletons nor treasure.

For almost a hundred years the place had been called the Black Building, but Chuck Clegg had a feud going with the McBrides, who owned the famous "Bucket of Blood", and had put up a huge sign that said, "The Bloody Bucket." Not only did this infuriate the McBrides; it also confused the tourists. Then, "just for the hell of it," he said, he painted a girl's name on each of the six second floor windows, thus making it into one of the most popular picture-taking spots in town. Thousands of snapshots were taken by people who naturally assumed that the building had once been a house of ill-repute. We left everything as it was; being on the wrong side of the street we needed all the attention we could get.

The shop area was forty by sixteen feet. A stairway led to a big, carpeted balcony with a large window that overlooked a vast expanse of mountains and desert. The living quarters in the rear consisted of a kitchen, a bedroom and a bath, plus a back porch that was seemingly suspended in mid-air. It was about thirty feet above the ground, which sloped steeply down the hill to where the two churches stood side by side. Fortunately, the place was furnished so all we had to do was move in, which we did soon after Labor Day.

Our counter looked very tiny in that big room. It would never do. So off we went to Reno where we bought lumber and nails, then went to our favorite shopping place, the Goodwill store, and bought a hammer, a saw, a few dishes, pots and pans, all at bargain prices. They had a small glass showcase that would be perfect for displaying our especially beautiful and unusual mineral specimens, things we did not want to sell. We could not resist it, so they loaded it in the car for us and we hauled it up Geiger Grade.

Buffalo Bill, seeing me struggling with the showcase, came across the street and helped me unload it. He was six feet two, had white shoulder-length hair and a white mustache and goatee. He wore boots and a ten gallon hat. His real name was Roy Shetler, but everyone called him Buffalo Bill, and he certainly looked the part.

I went to work at once, building more counter, and when I was finished we had twenty feet for jewelry and ten feet for rocks. We covered the whole thing with blue satin, spread out the jewelry and it really looked great with the light from the 150 watt bulbs making everything sparkle. Now all we needed was a few customers.

They came, and in greater numbers than we had expected! Not as many as during summer, of course, but the winter tourists had more money and bought more expensive items. Most of the people from back East had never before seen gemstone jewelry, and many of them did their Christmas shopping in our store. On Christmas day we closed the shop, fixed a picnic lunch and drove out into the hills where we sat in the car all day reading and talking. It was a perfect way to spend Christmas.

During January, February and March business fell off considerably. I used the spare time to set up a workshop in a small room off the front of the store. After installing the lapidary machine for cutting and hand-polishing,

Tierra Gems, Virginia City, Nevada

I built some tumblers and thereafter we saved a lot of money by doing our own tumble polishing. We bought gemstones in the rough, some in quite large chunks, and I found out what it was like to "work on the rock pile", as I transformed big stones into little ones with a hammer and chisel. The workshop turned out to be quite an attention-getter as people passing by on the street could look in the window and watch the tumblers rolling.

By the end of February we were running dangerously low on money. "I could go to a bank in Reno," I suggested, "and try to borrow a thousand dollars. That would be enough to make the building payments and get us through until all that lovely money comes pouring in this summer. Shall I try it?"

"Sure, go ahead, if you have the nerve. They can't do any worse than say no."

I had no "dress-up" clothes so I just wore my Levi's and plaid shirt, and I felt decidedly out of place and ill at ease as I sat down in front of the loan officer's desk. I told him about our business in Virginia City, and said that I would like to borrow a thousand dollars to be paid back in six months.

"We don't loan money on buildings up there," he said. "They're all fire-traps. What kind of credit rating do you have?"

"The records are in California where I lived for twenty five years, and raised my three children. It was during the depression, and I'm afraid I was late making my payments a few times."

He shook his head. "Banks take a pretty dim view of that sort of thing," he said. "However, I'll look into it. Come back next Monday and I'll let you know."

When I returned the following Monday he greeted me with a grin. "You weren't late a few times, you were late a lot of times. But you always called in, and because you did it seems you have what we call a triple A credit rating."

He loaned me the thousand dollars for six months with no collateral, just my signature. It seemed like a miracle.

That summer was a real bonanza. We did even better than we had at Vern Larsen's, and we began to believe that the boy in Reno had not exaggerated all that much when he said that a million tourists came through Virginia City. It seemed to us that at least that many came into our store. Many were attracted by the portrait of a woman that was painted on the floor, and was supposed to have been done by the man about whom Robert Service had written his poem, "The Face on the Bar-room Floor."

Bad Water Bill gave us a fairly authentic looking sluice box he had built for us, and we kept it filled with fist-sized rocks scrounged from the old mine dumps. Tourists bought hundreds of them for souvenirs at twenty-five cents each.

Since we had no newspaper, radio or television we had no idea what was going on in the outside world, and little time to wonder. One day Big Annie came in and said something about "Sputnik." We had never heard of it and had no idea what she was talking about until she explained that several weeks before the Russians had sent up the first space ship.

Every Sunday morning Pete took off to attend Mass. She had been raised as a Presbyterian, but had turned Catholic several years before we met. Religion was the only thing we disagreed on and we never discussed it. She did not try to convert me, and I made no effort to de-convert her. All over the country I had sat in front of churches reading "who-done-its" while she went to Mass. Now she had a Catholic church practically next door. It was very convenient.

Over the years there had been a succession of priests at St. Mary's in the Mountains. None stayed very long for various reasons. One of them ran over and killed a woman in a parking lot outside a bar in Reno. Of course, the word leaked out over the grapevine in Virginia City, but the matter was hushed up and never reached the newspapers. The priest was shortly removed to parts unknown. Another became too fond of the sacramental wine, and many devout church-goers complained to the Bishop in Reno that all too frequently Mass had become a "Mess". He too, was soon removed. One priest was definitely a psycho; he had a dog he claimed could talk. Another stole money from the poor box and disappeared.

Lucius Beebe frequently made caustic remarks in the Territorial Enterprise concerning the poor quality of the priests sent to Virginia City. In one editorial he said, "Apparently this is the last stopping off place for discarded priests before being sent on to Siberia." This did nothing to endear him to the city fathers, all of whom happened to be Catholic.

The new priest, Father Robert, had been there only a few months when we arrived in town. He was in his thirties, somewhat less than average height, with curly brown hair, a round face and a round body. He wasn't fat at all, just round. He reminded us of an animated kewpie doll.

Soon after he arrived, Father Robert had imported four young boys in their early twenties, whom he called Brothers. They wore long, full-skirted black habits, with black hoods. Their names were Bernard, Timothy, Richard and Mark, and they formed the nucleus of a proposed Monastery.

Father Robert seemed to be a nice, friendly fellow, and we became good friends. Now and then he stopped by to talk, and sometimes we gave him a few gemstones to use in his art shop in the basement of the church, where he and the Brothers made vases, picture frames, crucifixes and various items which he sold to other churches throughout Nevada.

During the winter when business was slack the Brothers also came in occasionally. We all sat in the kitchen drinking coffee and cokes while Brother Timothy, who missed his calling when he did not become a professional comedian, kept us laughing with his impersonations of various local "characters." He was short and fat, and when he did a takeoff on what he called the "Zulu Nuns" it was screamingly funny.

Two years passed more or less uneventfully. The door to the back porch fell apart and we had to have a new one installed. The carpenter had to cut the new door on the bias to fit the frame as the building had subsided on one side. This was a common occurrence in Virginia City because the town was built on top of the old mine shafts.

It was the "in" thing then to be married in Virginia City, so there were several weddings that year. One couple was married on horseback in front of one of the saloons. Another young pair had the knot tied while cuddled together in a wheelbarrow, then were trundled at a rapid pace down the length of C Street.

The Justice of the Peace who performed the ceremonies was a woman who had taken over the job when her husband died. She was called Marryin' Matilda. She was a small woman but she had a loud commanding voice and when she performed a marriage ceremony she pulled out all the stops and spoke words with heart-rending pathos, emotion and dramatic fervor.

We were invited to a conventional wedding that was held at Matilda's house. About thirty people were there, waiting anxiously for Marryin' Matilda to appear, but she kept us waiting ten to fifteen minutes, no doubt to build suspense for the big event. When she finally appeared she beamed upon the assembled crowd.

"DEAR FRIENDS," she began, "WE are GATHered HERE—in the SIGHT of GOD—to JOIN this MAN—and this WOMAN—in HOLY MATRIMONY!" It took quite awhile to complete the ceremony, because of Matilda's long pauses between words, but at last she was nearing the end. "WHO GIVETH—this WOMAN—to this MAN?"

The bride's father was drunk. He was leaning against the wall and seemed totally oblivious to what was going on.

Again Matilda asked, "WHO GIVETH—this WOMAN—to this MAN?"

Again there was no reply, until someone jabbed the man in the ribs, whereupon he suddenly straightened up, gazed blearily around the room and shouted, "Uh, ME!"

The audience tittered, but the photographers in the back of the room waiting to take pictures were not so polite, they burst into shouts of laughter. Matilda, shocked at such unseemly noise at a wedding announced sternly, "THIS is SACRED! There will be no more LAUGHING! The laughter stopped instantly, and all was quiet as she pronounced the final words. "I NOW—proNOUNCE you—MAN and WIFE."

Barney always stayed at our place now whenever he was in town. He had become like a son to us. One day in March he came back from a long and unsuccessful prospecting trip. Tired, unshaven and very discouraged, he flopped into a chair in the kitchen.

"Barney," Pete suggested, "why don't you go take a shower? It'll make you feel so much better."

Barney said nothing, just kept on sitting there looking dejected.

A few minutes later Pete said, "Barney! I do wish you'd take a shower."

He looked at her then and shook his head. "Pete, why are you so all-fired anxious for me to take a shower? And why should I anyway, if don't feel like it?"

"Because you're a dirty Jew!"

Barney's shouts of laughter could probably be heard out on the street. "No one has ever called me that," he said. "No one else could get away with it." Still laughing, he got up and took a shower.

A man from Reno, named Dean, fell in love with Pete and wanted to marry her. When she turned him down he went off to Mexico, but returned a month later bringing her some Chanel #5 perfume, an electric skillet, and for each of us a gaudy Mexican skirt with spangles, which we doubted we would ever have occasion to wear. Being very persistent, he showed up frequently and took Pete out to dinner and to see the shows at the Casinos in Reno and Carson City.

They were on the way to Carson City one night when they noticed a huge glow in the distance, and being curious to find out what it was they followed a dirt road across the desert and arrived at the city dump, which was burning merrily. A brawny, roughly dressed woman, a regular Marjorie Main type, came striding up to the car and announced, "I'm the caretaker fer this here dump, but don't mind me. I know what you're here fer. I weren't bawn yestidey. Stick around awhile and you'll hear the cans start poppin'." They stuck around for awhile and listened to the cans pop. It sounded like fireworks. When the fire died down Dean gave the woman a dollar. "It was a darned good show," he told her, "probably better than the one we'll see tonight at the Gold Nugget."

Unable to persuade Pete to marry him, Dean finally gave up and we didn't see him again for almost two years when he came in the shop with a girlfriend, bought some jewelry and gave us a check for twenty-five dollars, which turned out to be no good.

We had accepted hundreds of checks, to the consternation and amazement of the other business people. Several of them warned us against such a foolhardy practice. "You just don't take checks in Nevada," they said. But we did and the only bad one we ever had was the one given us by Pete's ex-boyfriend.

A week or two after the season ended that year Jerry Eaton called us. She was giving a going-away party at the Silver Queen for Bouncing Buster, the piano player, and wanted us to come.

"Everybody is giving him a shirt so each of you bring one. And for God's sake, Dot, wear a dress."

"But I don't have a dress, Jerry. I suppose we could wear those Mexican skirts that Dean gave us, but we don't have any tops to wear with them. You wouldn't want us to come topless, would you?"

"Oh, hell." Jerry was a very rough talking gal. "What color are the skirts?"

"Mine's red and Pete's is blue. Why?"

"I'll make you some blouses today. Come down and pick them up around six o'clock."

Dot and Pete Dressing Up in Virginia City—1958

They were beautiful, off-the-shoulder blouses made of satin. We were all dressed ready to go and feeling quite elegant, when we suddenly realized that we had no pockets. And no purses. Neither of us had carried a purse for years, as I could keep everything we needed in the pockets of my jeans. We solved the problem very cleverly, we thought. We put a few necessary items, including cigarettes and matches, in a small brown paper bag and went to the party.

Jerry saw us come in, took one look at the paper bag and cried, "For Christ's sake, what the hell is that? Did you bring your lunch?"

"Believe it or not," I laughed, "this is our purse. After all, you know, they never do put pockets in these damn women's clothes!" It was a fun party and we had a good time. At one point in the festivities we all filed past the piano and gave Bouncing Buster "the shirts off our backs". He received forty-two shirts.

Don Bovea, an artist who specialized in painting horses, was sitting at the bar and I went over to say hello. Since he had never seen me in a dress he didn't recognize me at first, then he looked surprised and said, "Why Dot, this is the first time I've ever seen you without your pants." The man sitting next to him overheard the remark, passed it down the line and soon it was all over the place. It became the joke of the evening.

A man named Mel, who worked as a dealer at the crap table, asked me to go out with him the next night. "We can see the show at the Nugget and do some dancing," he said. "How about it?"

If he hadn't mentioned dancing I would probably have turned him down, since I had long ago decided that while men were just great as friends, as boyfriends or husbands they were more trouble than they were worth. But I could tell by the way Mel walked that he was a good dancer, and I was tempted. Dancing had always been the love of my life, but it had been a long. time since I done any dancing and I couldn't pass up the opportunity. "Had I but known!" as they say in mystery stories.

Mel had no car so we went in mine. On the way he confessed that he was an alcoholic. "But I'm on the wagon," he said. "I haven't had a drink in two years and I don't want to spoil my record, so I'll stick to cokes and let you do the drinking for both of us."

We had reached the outskirts of town when Mel suggested that we forget about the show and dancing and go to a motel. When I turned thumbs down on that he became sullen and moody, but I drove on anyway thinking that once we were in the Gold Nugget he would get over his sulks. As soon as I parked he got out of the car, went to a liquor store and came back with a fifth of whiskey. I tried to reason with him, using every argument I could think of but he ignored me, opened the bottle and proceeded to take a healthy slug, then another and another.

"Ye gods," I thought, "This is turning into a sticky situation. I'd better get him home as fast as this old crate will take us!"

All the way up the mountain he continued to drink and when I asked him where he lived he wouldn't answer, so I parked in front of our building wondering what to do with him. He solved the problem by getting out of the car and staggering across the street toward the Mark Twain Saloon, carrying his bottle which was now only about half full.

Mel stayed drunk for days and, of course, lost his job. Several people knew I had gone out with him that night, and the word quickly spread over the grapevine that Dot had taken Mel out and ruined him! I didn't suppose I would ever live it down. That was my first date in years, and my last for a lifetime!

One summer Jerry and Carrol Eaton hired a group of actors from San Francisco to come to Virginia City and put on some old-time melodramas. They built a stage and put in seats for about a hundred people in a vacant building next door to the Silver Queen. Admission was two dollars and they did a smashing business. They had a full house every day. The night we went they had little Nell with her baby, being cast out in the snow. The villain was a short, overweight man with black hair and a handle-bar mustache. On cue the audience applauded the heroine and booed the villain, and the whole thing was riotously funny. We had no regrets about having closed the shop for a couple of hours to see it.

Three of the actors decided to spend the winter in Virginia City. One got a job as a bartender, one as a waitress, and Vern Larsen hired the villain to help remodel an apartment over his saloon. Having been an actor most of his life, it is doubtful that the villain had ever handled a saw or hammer, but life in Virginia City was highly informal, and it was not usually necessary to have experience in order to get a job.

The old warped floorboards had been removed and a new floor was to be put in. The workers had to step carefully, for they were walking on the century-old boards that served as a ceiling for the saloon below. The man in charge handed the villain a long board. "Here," he said, "saw this in two where it's marked."

The villain laid the board between two saw-horses, then straddled it and began sawing, not realizing that he was reenacting the old story about the man who cut off the tree limb he was sitting on. When the saw neared the end of the cut, the board collapsed, the villain went crashing through the old ceiling, and landed in one of the liquor cabinets behind the bar.

The cabinet was completely demolished and several bottles of whiskey were broken, but except for a few cuts and bruises the villain was unharmed. Several of the boozehounds at the bar, thinking they were hallucinating, swore off drinking for several days. And the villain, deciding that San Francisco was a safer place to live, left town unmindful of the fact that he had become a legend in Virginia City.

There was no doctor or hospital in town, only a county nurse, who was there to help in case of emergency. There was a fifteen-year-old vehicle, which could only charitably be called an ambulance. The police department consisted of one man, who naturally called himself the Chief of Police since he was the only cop in town. The locals called him "Sputnik," after the Russian space ship, because he orbited around town giving out tickets. He had a lucrative speed trap going for awhile until the City Fathers, all of whom owned stores, made him cut it out as they felt it was hurting business. There was also a volunteer fire department, a district attorney and a sheriff, who was fat and lazy, and whom Pete and I privately named "Fat-ass Morrison."

The only time any of these guardians of the law did anything exciting was the night they burned the bawdy house. This house of prostitution was located in a large trailer out on the desert at a spot where three counties converged. When word reached the Madam via the grapevine that a raid was planned all she had to do was wheel the trailer across the line to another county. So far, all efforts to catch them in Storey County had been unsuccessful.

One night Sputnik, Morrison, District Attorney Moore and Bill Marks, one of the city councilmen, descended on the place without warning, and before the trailer could be moved set fire to it. It burned to the ground. Fortunately everyone got out and no one was injured. Telling clients to get lost, the Sheriff arrested the Madam and her four girls. Irate protests were made by the woman in San Francisco who owned the trailer and who had been renting it to the Madam. She immediately sued Storey County and the four men involved, and the last we heard the case was still dragging its slow way through the courts.

Thus was another legend added to the long list of strange and almost unbelievable events that the locals were fond of saying, "could only happen in Virginia City."

Chapter 28

St. Mary's in the Mountains was a truly beautiful church, reminiscent of the cathedrals in Europe. Large and imposing, it had stained glass windows, lots of "gingerbread", and a tall spire reaching toward what all good Catholics fondly believed was "Heaven." It was good for our business, because in order to go down the hill and take close-up pictures, the tourists had to cross C Street and pass our shop. I jokingly remarked to Pete that at last I had found something good about the Catholic Church.

Suddenly Father Robert went on a modernizing binge, and decided to remodel the church. Full of enthusiasm for the project, he put the Brothers to work ripping out the ornate balcony and removing all the bricks from the inside walls. He took out the old pews, demolished an antique organ and had the remains hauled to the dump, "Because," as he later explained to a reporter, "I discovered that a mouse had built a nest in it." Also to the dump went several old vases, some pictures whose nineteenth century frames would be out of place in the proposed modern decor, an elaborate red velvet priest's robe, and a solid ebony crucifix. The latter item was rescued by Betty Staab, a good friend of ours, who with her husband ran a bar at Gold Hill, a town about half-way down the mountain with a population of six. Betty gave the crucifix to Pete because she felt that a Catholic should have it.

"I'm getting rid of all that horrible 'gingerbread'," Father Robert told us, "and when I get through the church will be a thing of beauty."

"That's if it doesn't fall down first," I said to Pete after he left.

It seemed that the tall spire on top of the church no longer pointed straight to Heaven; it was now listing a bit to the south. Every day local people could be seen standing at a certain spot up the hill at the end of C Street, looking to see if the spire had moved since they had last checked. It was feared that eventually the spire would fall and crush the school building next door to the church. Several people wrote letters of protest to the Bishop in Reno, but the letters were ignored. Apparently the Bishop was in agreement with what Father Robert was doing.

Said one disgruntled parishioner, "He's not going to be satisfied until he has the church looking like a Safeway store."

We hadn't seen the Brothers Richard and Mark for some time, so the next time Timothy and Bernard came in we asked about them, thinking they might be sick.

"No, they're gone." Timothy looked unhappy. "They weren't getting along very well with Father Robert, and they didn't like what he is doing to the church so they left."

"Where are they?" Pete asked. "Did they go home?"

"No, they didn't have any money for bus fare. Mark got a job in Carson City and Richard is working in Reno, but he is still in town. He's living in a little house up on D Street. Father wants him to leave town but he won't go."

"How do you boys feel about the remodeling job?" I asked.

"Well, we liked the church better the way it was, but we were taught that we must always obey the Priest so if he tells us to tear it down, we'll tear it down."

Pete could sympathize with the boys, but she felt they were right about obeying the priest. She was an avid Catholic. Whatever she did, she always did with her whole heart and soul; with her there were no half-way measures. She went to Mass every Sunday morning, which now was held in the basement of the church and one night a week during the winter she attended a religious instruction class at the Rectory.

Then almost overnight, it seemed, Pete was no longer a Catholic. In fact, she threw out the whole bit and no longer had any use for any religion. In a way it was my fault, because I had brought home a book on evolution from the library and another book called, "Ingersol's Forty Lectures." I had heard of Robert Ingersol; as a child I had gained the impression that he was close kin to the devil. Naturally, I was eager to see what he had to say on the subject of religion. I had finished both books and was planning to return them when I discovered that Pete had read the book on evolution and was deeply engrossed in "Ingersol's Forty Lectures."

"You shouldn't be reading those books," I reminded her.

"But they're very interesting, and they're making me think."

"As a Christian you're not supposed to think. That's why you're not allowed to read them."

"Who say's so?"

"The Pope says so! Didn't you know that the Church has a 'verboten' list, I forget what they call it, but I'm sure any book about Ingersol would head the list and, of course, all books on evolution would be banned."

"I don't believe it!" Pete looked incredulous. "You're making it up!"

"Okay, next time you see Father Robert, ask him. He'll tell you I'm right."

When Pete came home from the meeting a few nights later she was angry and upset. "Father Robert told me that there is a list of books that Catholics are not allowed to read, but he gave me permission to read these books. I assured him that no one, not even the Pope, was going to dictate to me what I could or could not read, and that I intended to read a lot more similar books because they made a lot of sense."

Soon after that we heard that attendance at the church had fallen off sharply, and that many of the parishioners were driving to Carson City for Sunday services. It was also said that most people were not permitting their young boys to go near the church because Father Robert was molesting them. We simply could not believe that and put it down as just idle gossip. Then one day a fourteen-year-old boy named David came in the shop to buy a bracelet for his girlfriend. Noticing that his left ear was horribly bruised and swollen, I asked what had happened.

Looking shame-faced and embarrassed, he said, "Father Robert hit me because I wouldn't do what he wanted me to do."

One evening in March, when there was no business, we were sitting on our back porch admiring the sunset when we saw a woman climbing the steps of the rectory. She rang the bell, waited awhile, and when no one answered she opened the door and looked in. Just then Father Robert appeared and, apparently furious at her for daring to open the door, he gave her a push and she went backwards down the steps, only keeping herself from falling by grabbing the railing. She must have sprained her ankle because she was limping as she walked away.

"That's terrible," Pete cried. "He must be crazy. Why doesn't someone do something about him?"

"No one can anything to a priest except the Bishop, and from what I've heard he's not about to do anything to his precious Father Robert."

Another month went by. It was now the end of April, 1958, and we were beginning to get a few early tourists. Timothy and Bernard came in about once a week and sat in the kitchen with us for awhile, drinking coffee and talking about inconsequential things. Both of us had the feeling that they wanted to tell us something, but whatever it was they held it back and we didn't press them.

Then late one evening they came in looking and acting like candidates for nervous breakdowns. Timothy was almost in tears. "We have to talk to someone and you two are the only ones in town we feel we can really trust."

"You can tell us anything," Pete said, "and no matter what it is, you can rest assured it won't go out over the grapevine."

Fortunately there were no customers in the shop. I turned the sign to "Closed," turned the key in the lock and we all went back to the kitchen. I made coffee and after they had calmed down a bit suggested that they go ahead and tell us what was troubling them.

"Actually, we're afraid of Father Robert," Bernard said. "He's sick and should be sent away somewhere for a long rest. Besides destroying the church, until it's about ready to fall down, he's beat up two young boys, pushed a woman down the rectory steps, and yesterday he tried to drown Brother Timothy."

"Yes, he really did." Timothy took up the tale. "We took a bunch of little kids to the public pool in Reno. One little six-year old boy was afraid of the water and refused to go in. Father Robert grabbed him and began dunking him. The kid was screaming with fright so I tried to get Father Robert to stop, but he insisted that this was the best way to get him over his fear and he dunked him again. I took the boy and sat him on the side of the pool, but Father Robert was so furious he shoved me under the water and tried to hold me there. I managed to get away from him, but I'm positive he was planning to drown me and claim it was an accident. And because he is a priest everyone would believe him."

"He has a terrible temper," Bernard said. "Sometimes when he gets mad he hits us, and we're afraid that sooner or later he'll kill one of us."

"Why in the world don't you fight back?" I asked.

Bernard looked shocked. "Oh, no! We would never hit a priest no matter what he did."

This seemed to me the height of the ridiculous, but then I had never been a Catholic. Obviously, these boys were suffering from a most thorough job of brain washing.

"Well, then why don't you just leave the way Richard and Mark did?"

"They were a lot older and more experienced. We've never lived in the outside world, and we wouldn't know where to go or what to do, and we don't want to give up the religious life."

Now Pete remembered something. "Didn't you tell us once that Father Robert promised all of you that if you wanted to go home he'd give you the bus fare?"

"Yes, he did promise that," Timothy replied, "but he wouldn't give Richard and Mark any money when they wanted to leave. We asked him, anyway, just on the chance, but we should have known better. He flew into a rage, slapped us around and screamed, 'you're not going to leave here! Do you understand that.' He knows we don't have nerve enough to go out on our own."

I thought of another possible solution. "Write your folks in Boston and ask them to send you the money to go home. Surely they'll send it when they know how miserable you are."

"We thought of that, too, but we know it won't work," Bernard shook his head. "Oh, sure, they'd send the money all right, but we'd never see it. Father Robert opens all the mail first. He cashed a check for $1,500 that came for Richard, and refused to give him the money. He said that when we became Brothers we gave up all worldly possessions, and that any money we got belonged to the Church. That's the real reason Brother Richard left."

"Do you kids have any money at all?" Pete asked.

"We have thirty dollars that we stole, may God forgive us." Timothy crossed himself. "Father Daniels in Carson City knows what is going on and he sympathizes with us. He told us to take a little from the poor box now and then until we had enough to get to Snowmass, Colorado. We could stay there at the monastery until our folks sent us money. But even that won't work, because if we got on the bus in Reno in these clothes, and we don't have any other kind, we'd be too easy to spot. Father Robert would call the Bishop in Reno, tell him we stole something and ran away, and he'd have us picked up and brought back. No, there isn't anything that we or anybody else can do about it. As the saying goes, we're stuck between a rock and a hard place." Timothy managed a grin. "But it helps a lot just to be able to talk about it."

"Give us a day or two to think about this," I said. "Over the years Pete and I have acquired a knack for solving problems and getting around people, and we may think of something. It would give us a lot of pleasure to 'foil the villain' as they say in the old melodramas."

After they had gone we sat in the kitchen discussing the situation. "You know what we could do, Dot? We could take the boys to Salt Lake City and put them on a bus to Snowmass."

"I thought of that while they were here, but I didn't want to say anything until we talked it over. We can't do it anywhere in Nevada because they're afraid Father Robert will catch them, but its only six hundred miles to Salt Lake City. We can make it in about 10 hours."

"The biggest problem will be getting them out when Father Robert isn't looking. He's there most of the time, but he does go to Reno now and then to see the Bishop, and that would be the time to do it, if we had some way of knowing when he leaves."

"The boys would know. They could give us a call the minute he leaves and we'd snatch them out of there and be on our way long before he'd find out they were gone."

I was looking forward to this escapade, and so was Pete.

"We'd have to have some sort of code. They can't just call up and say, 'Father Robert is gone, come down and get us.' Within ten minutes everyone in town would know about it."

The telephones in Virginia City were antiques, with a handle on the side, which you wound to get the operator. Everyone was on the same line so anyone in town could listen in and many did, a fact that helped a lot to keep the grapevine active.

It was decided that at the crucial moment one of the boys would call and say, "Pete, I just wanted to remind you that there will be a meeting Tuesday night. Hope you can make it."

So it was all settled, and when the boys came by a couple of days later we outlined the plan to them. They were overjoyed to realize that they might actually get away, and were very grateful that we were willing to make that long trip for them. Our motives were mixed. Not only did we feel sorry for the boys and wanted to get them home, but it would be such fun to outwit Father Robert.

"When the time comes," I told them, "pile your stuff by the back gate of the rectory and I'll pick it up. We can't drive through town with you in the car, that would be a dead give-away. After I leave walk down A Street to the edge of town, where it joins Rattlesnake Canyon and we'll pick you up there. It's a rough dirt road and hardly anyone takes it, and it's a short-cut to Carson City. You can see Father Daniel and tell him goodbye, and then we'll be on our way."

"We should leave a note for Father Robert and send a copy to the Bishop. It would look a lot better for us than if we just left without saying anything."

"Okay, I'll type it for you. What do you want to say?" "Tell him that we realize he's sick and can't help what he's been doing, and that we hope the Bishop will send him away somewhere for a rest."

"How about adding 'and some psychiatric treatments,'" Pete suggested.

Timothy and Bernard grinned at each other. "It'll make him mad, but he's going to be awfully mad anyway, so go ahead and put it in,"

Timothy said. "Tell him we know we're leaving against his wishes, but that he's been keeping us here like prisoners, that we're very unhappy and just want to go home, and have finally found a way, so goodbye and God Bless you."

After adding a "Hail Mary" and some other garbage, the boys approved the letter. I made five copies, they signed them, and I put each copy in a separate envelope. I gave them three, and reminded them to be sure and put one in Father Robert's room when they left. "We'll mail one to the Bishop when we get back."

Now all we had to do was wait. For several days nothing happened, then one evening at about five o'clock the boys came in carrying a jug of wine they had bought for Father Robert at the Crystal Bar across the street. They were obviously excited and anxious to tell us something, but there was a customer in the shop. They waited impatiently until she had made her purchase and left, then Bernard burst out, "Father Robert is going to Reno this afternoon, and he's about ready to leave, so be expecting that phone call."

We immediately turned the sign to "Closed" and watched from the back porch as they hurried down the hill. They didn't run; such indecorous behavior was forbidden. But they would have won going away in a fast walking contest. While waiting for the phone to ring, we made sandwiches, filled two thermos bottles with hot coffee, put six cokes in a small ice chest for me, and parked it all just inside the front door along with a couple of blankets and some pillows. Even though we no longer lived in the car we kept the mattress in the back for occasional rock-hunting trips. The boys could sleep there during the all-night ride.

The phone rang and Pete answered. Timothy said, "Hello Pete, I just called to remind you that we're having a meeting Tuesday night. I hope you can make it."

"Oh sure, I'll be there," Pete said.

I dashed out to the car and drove down the hill. As I neared the rectory I saw Timothy in the middle of the road motioning me to go behind the Episcopal Church. "Oh Lord," I thought, "Already something has gone wrong!" Not knowing what to expect, I followed directions and parked behind the church where a half-dozen boxes, two small satchels and two large duffel bags were piled by the side of the road.

Bernard was standing there looking frightened. "Father Robert is in the rectory. He must have forgotten some papers and came back for them. He's in the study."

The study window was almost directly across from where we were. It would have been much better had the boys left their things by the back gate, but I suppose their first instinct was to get as far away as possible. It was a wrong move. Now, if Father Robert happened to glance out of the window he couldn't fail to see us. But it was too late to go back. We did the only thing we could do. Frantically, we threw the boxes and duffel bags into the car expecting any minute to see Father Robert come out screaming. But he didn't see us! He must have been totally engrossed in whatever he was doing.

I got out of there fast. What a relief it was to be out of sight of that menacing window! I had supposed the boys would walk on down the road, but in the rear view mirror I could see them going through the gate. I wondered if they would be able to get out again. I drove back to the shop, picked up Pete and we went down to Rattlesnake Canyon.

"I don't know whether the boys will get there or not." I described the wild scene at the rectory. "The boys went back inside, and if Father Robert has decided not to go to Reno, they probably won't be able to get out."

"And we have all their stuff in the car! What a ghastly mess that would be! What could we do?"

"I don't know. We'd just have to think of something. So start thinking in case they don't show up."

We had waited almost half an hour with every minute adding to our feeling of panic, when here they came down the road, running now that bushes screened them. Timothy got in the front seat with us and Bernard, being smaller, climbed in the back and sat on the mattress. They had barely gotten in when I had the car moving.

"What happened back there? How come you didn't just walk on down the road after I left?"

"We thought we'd better go back." Timothy explained, "Father Robert was sure to find out very soon that we were gone, and he'd have had Sputnik after us before we could get out of town. He practically runs the town, you know. Sputnik, Morrison, all of them do whatever he tells them to."

"If he had decided not to go to Reno," Bernard said, "we intended to ask permission to take a walk. He usually allows us to do that figuring we need the exercise." But he came to the study and told us he was going to Reno and would be back in a couple of hours." Timothy went on, "he said we'd have a late supper when he got back and wanted to know what we were having tonight. I couldn't think of anything else, so I said, ch-ch-cheeseburgers. He said that would be fine, then looked at us sort of suspiciously, and asked why we were both so out of breath. We told him we had been taking some strenuous exercises. And that was no lie! We certainly had!"

"After he left," Bernard said, "we waited about ten minutes, then started sauntering slowly down the road."

Timothy turned around and clapped Bernard on the shoulder. "And here we are, Brother, with two women and a mattress." Even in a time of crisis Timothy could be depended upon to come up with a one-liner.

It was dark when we got to Carson City. We went to the church, where the housekeeper told the boys that Father Daniels had gone to the Church in Reno. It was a forty mile trip, but since it was right on our way it didn't matter. When we arrived at the church in Reno we learned that Father Daniels had gone back to Carson City. Back we went. We were covering a lot of miles without getting any farther forward. However, this time Father Daniels was there, and Pete and I waited in the car about thirty minutes while the boys talked to him. It was nine o'clock when we finally got started on that six hundred mile trip to Salt Lake City.

We no longer had the old Gremlin. At the age of seventeen it had finally begun to fall apart and we had been forced, reluctantly, to get rid of it. Now we had a Ford station wagon only six years old with very good tires. When we had left Reno behind and were out on the open road I kept the speedometer at around eighty, and we made good time.

Suddenly Bernard cried, "There's a police car behind!"

"Well, we tried," Timothy said, "but I guess it's all over. We might have known Father Robert would figure we'd be in a car somewhere on this road, because it's the only highway going east out of Reno. He and the Bishop have sent the cops to arrest us."

"Maybe they're just going to give us a ticket for speeding." I didn't really think so since there was no speed limit in Nevada, but the boys probably wouldn't know that. I slowed to sixty ready to pull over and stop. Much to our surprise and relief the police car passed us and disappeared in the distance.

"Okay, heart," Timothy thumped his chest, "you can start beating again. The cops are gone."

Soon after we crossed into Utah I stopped at a rest area.

"You can relax now guys, you're out of Nevada."

Pete passed out sandwiches and poured coffee into plastic cups. "Congratulations, boys," she raised her cup, "on escaping from what was literally a concentration camp."

"We're so thankful that we got away," Timothy said, "but Father isn't really a bad man. He's sick and can't help what he does."

"I'll drink to that." I raised my bottle of coke. "We all do what we have to do, according to the equipment we're born with, and over which we have no control. That old idea that we have free will is pure fallacy. You should read George Bernard Shaw's books. He said, 'You can choose what you will do, but you cannot choose what you will choose.' He was a very wise man."

"But the Bible teaches that we have free will."

"The Bible is wrong, about that and a lot of other things." Any attempt to get past their well-entrenched mental blocks with a shot of logic was useless, as I had known it would be. I changed the subject.

"How did you two like living in the West?"

"Oh, we both like it out here," Bernard said. "We love Virginia City and most of the people there, and we hope to come back sometime, if they ever get a new priest."

"In order to get a new priest, you first have to get rid of the old one," Timothy laughed. Then he looked at me. "Hey, I just had an idea. Why don't you and Pete get out a petition to have him removed? Lots of people would sign it, even some of the Catholics. A lot of them don't want him there. You could send it to the Archbishop, and maybe he'd do something."

"What do you think Pete, should we do it?"

"Sure, why not?" Pete was packing away the cups. It was time to move on. "I really don't care to live in a town where a priest is practically a dictator."

Timothy looked at Bernard. "Shall I tell them Brother?" Receiving a nod of assent, he went on. "It's so terrible that we weren't going to tell you, but it should be in the petition. It would carry a lot of weight. Father Robert has been breaking the seal of confession. Often at supper, when he was in a good mood, he would tell us things about the local people that he had heard during confession and he would make jokes about it."

"Do you think the archbishop will believe any of this stuff? He may think we're just making it up."

"As soon as we get home we'll send you notarized depositions testifying to everything we've told you and you can send copies along with the petition."

I suggested that Timothy get in the back with Bernard. "Push everything to the back and along the sides, so you'll have room to stretch out and get some sleep. We'll wake you up when we get to Salt Lake City."

Pete stayed awake for awhile, enjoying the ride through the desert, but before long she gave in to drowsiness, curled up in the front seat and went to sleep. There are times when it's convenient to be short.

I didn't feel the least bit sleepy and I enjoyed driving. I always felt more at home behind the wheel of a car than any place else. I passed the Salt Flats and if I hadn't known it was salt, would have sworn that the ground was covered with snow as far as the eye could see. The illusion was enhanced by the light of a three-quarter moon. It was an awe-inspiring sight.

None of the passengers awoke as I pulled into an all night station in a small town, and asked the attendant to fill the tank. As he went toward the back of the car he saw the two sleeping Brothers, side by side in their black habits and cowls, and did a double take. Wearing a puzzled expression he filled the tank, and on the way back took another quick look as if he hadn't really believed what he saw the first time.

As I paid for the gas, I knew he was dying to know what it was all about, but lacked the nerve to ask. "We stole them from a priest in Nevada, who was abusing them," I said, and drove away thinking, that'll be something to tell his grandchildren.

It was 7 a.m. when we arrived in Salt Lake City. I pulled into a deserted parking lot at a supermarket, and we discussed our next move.

"First," Timothy said, "we have to go through all our stuff and pick out what we'll take with us. In the excitement of getting away we just threw everything in helter-skelter."

We emptied the contents of the duffel bags and satchels on the tailgate and they began sorting. They were still at it when the store opened and customers began driving in, and we got a lot of puzzled glances from curious onlookers. It was certainly a most unusual sight; two bedraggled looking middle-aged women and two monks in full regalia, pawing through a mountain of assorted items on the tailgate of a car! But we were way beyond caring what people thought.

In the pocket in one of the satchels was the letter to Father Robert; they had forgotten to leave it for him. "Well, don't worry about it." Pete reassured them. "We'll give it to him when we get back. Maybe it's for the best. He might try to claim you didn't leave a letter, which would look bad for you. Now we can swear that you did."

When the boys had everything they would need in the two satchels, they stuffed everything else back in the duffel bags. Those and the boxes we would take back with us, to be shipped to them when they got home. Then we drove to a service station, filled the tank, and used the rest rooms to freshen up. The cold water on our faces and arms felt wonderful, and after combing our hair and putting on a little lipstick, we felt decidedly more presentable.

I called the bus station and learned that the next bus going to Snowmass would leave at ten o'clock. It was now eight-thirty, so with time to spare we went to a restaurant, had a substantial breakfast, then on to the bus station. We bought the tickets, because the fares would have taken all of the thirty dollars the boys had "liberated" from the poor box and left them broke. With hugs and a farewell we saw them off. We would miss them and our talk fests in the kitchen.

We left at once for the trip back, and drove non-stop all the way to Virginia City, arriving there at nine o'clock that night. The first thing we did was go to the rectory to get rid of that letter. We had planned to slide it under the door, but as we drove up Father Robert was crossing the road and he came over to the car.

"We just got back from a rock hunting trip," Pete told him, "and we found this letter under the door. It's addressed to you and we thought it might be important, so we brought it right down."

"Maybe it's from the Brothers," he said. "They left last night, and I have no idea where they are. And they didn't take anything with them, just the clothes they were wearing."

I was tempted to throw back the blanket that covered the boxes and duffel bags, and call him a liar, but we were a little bit afraid of him alone there in the dark. If he knew that we had taken the boys away, he might fly into a rage and turn violent, so we just went home, fell into bed and slept for twelve hours.

Chapter 29

If we had known what we were getting into when we put out that petition we might have backed off, but we never had any regrets. It was the most exciting adventure we ever had.

We told two local people that we had taken the Brothers away, and before the day was over everyone in town knew about it. Barney came back from a prospecting trip, and when we told him the story he was shocked.

"Is there anything you gals won't do?" We had told him about some of our experiences over the years. "You fought the Chicago gangsters, and now you're taking on the Catholic Church. You can't win, you know. No one ever has."

"Maybe not, but we're going to have a shot at it. The worst that can happen is that the Archbishop will ignore the petition. He can't do anything to us for taking the Brothers away. After all, they're free, white and twenty-one, well, almost twenty-one, and they have a right to leave if they want to."

"We're going to church Sunday." Pete's "Irish was up" and as usual, she was undaunted. "Timothy said that when the other boys left, Father Robert made a lot of derogatory remarks about them from the pulpit. He accused them of stealing, lying and being disobedient, among other things, so we plan to be there, and if he says one word against Timothy and Bernard we're going to stand up and call him a liar, right there in front of God and everybody. Would you like to go with us, Barney?"

"I sure would, I wouldn't miss it!"

When Father Robert saw the three of us; a Jew, an atheist and an agnostic, sitting there in the congregation, he became obviously nervous and frustrated. He hurried through the various rituals as if anxious only to get out of there, and he did not mention Timothy and Bernard. Pete said it was the shortest service she had ever attended. I think she was a little disappointed; she had primed herself for a confrontation. But at least we had the satisfaction of throwing him temporarily off stride.

We had no trouble getting signatures on the petition. Pete covered the business district and I went up and down the hills canvassing the residential areas. Many of the store owners and saloon keepers declined for business reasons, but Vern Larsen (that so-called "bad guy") did not hesitate. "I hope you get rid of that son-of-a-bitch," he said. Quite a few people came in the shop eager to sign the petition.

A few Catholics were still loyal to "Dear Father Robert" as they called him, and one of these was a woman named Angelina. She was skinny and thin-faced, with an enormous nose and a pointed chin. She looked amazingly like a witch. Angelina got out a petition to keep Father Robert, and Big Annie reported to us that at last count she had sixteen names. She tried, without success, to call the Pope in Rome. Since we were giving everyone nicknames, she became to us, the "Brain-washed Witch."

We had over a hundred names on the petition when one of Father Robert's devotees, a big Italian woman named Angela, brought the petition business to a screeching halt. She was almost six feet tall, and would have been a fairly attractive woman except that she was more than a little bowlegged. Naturally, after what she did to us we dubbed her the "Bow-legged Bitch."

She came in the shop one day and asked to read the petition. Since everyone, friend or foe alike, was welcome to read it, we sat her in the kitchen and gave her a cup of tea. When she finished reading, she got up and started toward the front door carrying the petition with her.

"I don't believe a word of this," she announced. "It's all lies."

"You have a right to your opinion, of course." I reached for the petition.

She held it high above her head. "I want my husband to read it."

"Your husband is welcome to read it, but he'll have to come in here to do it."

"He's not very well, I'll take it to him. I'll bring it back."

"I think you intend to give it to Father Robert."

"Oh, No!" she crossed herself. "I swear on my mother's grave I won't give it to Father Robert."

There was no way I could get the petition since she was holding it about eight feet in the air. I stood in front of the door in a vain attempt to block her exit, but with little effort she pushed me aside and marched out. She went across the street to the Crystal Bar and had a drink, because as she said later "I have a bad heart." She then went down the hill toward the rectory and from the back porch we watched her hand the petition to Father Robert. So much for swearing on her mother's grave. But she needn't worry, she could go to confession and Father Robert would forgive her for lying and she could still go to Heaven!

"Well, what shall we do now?" Pete wondered. "Shall we type another petition and start allover again?"

"He must realize we'd do that, so it wouldn't do him any good to keep it or destroy it. He may just read it and send it back. Let's wait awhile and see what happens."

"Do you suppose if we talked to Father Robert quietly and tried to reason with him, that we could possibly persuade him to leave of his own accord before some kind of scandal erupts?"

All my life I've had the ridiculous idea that people can be reasoned with. It very seldom works, but like a fool, I keep on trying.

"We'd have to go to the rectory," I said. "I'm sure he'll never come in here again."

"Well, let's think about it overnight," Pete said. "It's probably a dumb idea."

Early the next morning, much to our amazement, Father Robert came in carrying the petition. He handed it to Pete. "All the things you said in there are lies."

"We're convinced they are true, otherwise we wouldn't have said them." I kept my voice calm, with no hint of anger. "We saw a couple of things ourselves."

Pete and I looked at each other. We were both thinking, "If we're going to try this crazy thing now is the time."

Pete smiled at Father Robert. "Let's go back and sit in the kitchen. I'll make us a cup of tea and we can discuss this quietly. Maybe we can work something out."

He seemed to like the idea. He followed Pete to the kitchen while I turned the sign to "Closed" and turned the key in the lock. We wanted no interruptions at this crucial time.

When I got back to the kitchen Pete was making the tea, and Father Robert was saying, "If the boys had only come to me I would have given them the bus fare."

Making a supreme effort, I kept my voice quiet and said, "They did ask you and you turned them down, just as you did the other boys when they left. That's why we had to take them to Salt Lake City. They were afraid to get on a bus in Reno for fear you'd have them picked up and brought back."

"Father Robert," Pete said, "you must realize that most of the local people, even a lot of Catholics, have turned against you for various reasons. We think you're having a nervous breakdown, and we sympathize with you, but surely you won't be happy in a place where you're not wanted. Why don't you ask the Bishop to send you someplace for a nice long rest? Don't you honestly think that would be the best solution to this problem?"

Father Robert got up and walked over to stand in front of Pete, who was sitting in a large over-stuffed chair.

"I have no intention of leaving Virginia City, and don't think for a minute that you can drive me out. You two women are nothing but trouble makers, and I'm warning you right now that you'd better not send in that petition, or you'll regret it."

Now Pete was angry. She stood up, pointed her finger at him and said, "Father Robert, you know what you've done and you that we know what you've done so why don't you take off that Roman collar you're desecrating?"

He raised both arms and pushed her into the chair with such force that the chair went over backward and she landed on the floor with the chair on top of her. I rushed to her at once and moved the chair. "I don't think I'm hurt," she said, "just leave me and call the police and have him arrested."

Father Robert was still standing there, apparently shocked by the enormity of what he had done, but when I ran to the phone and told the operator to send the county nurse and the Chief of Police, he unfroze and took off down the long aisle toward the front door. I went after him and, because he was delayed by having to turn the key in the door, I caught him on the front porch. Grabbing him by his sleeves I held on with grim determination, knowing that if he got away I would never be able to prove what he had done.

Across the way, Buffalo Bill saw us struggling, strode across the street and shouted at Father Robert, "Take your hands off her!"

"It's the other way around," I told him. "He's trying to get my hands off of him. He knocked Pete down and she's lying on the floor in the kitchen."

By that time a dozen or more people had converged on the scene and more were arriving. There was an audible gasp from the crowd as Father Robert spoke the words that were destined to become headlines.

"I didn't hit her, I pushed her."

The county nurse arrived and went back to attend to Pete. Fat-Ass Morrison drove up and stopped, but when someone told him the priest had knocked down a crippled woman, he said, "Well, it's out of my jurisdiction," and drove on. The Chief of Police never showed up; I hadn't really expected him to.

Now that Father Robert had admitted his guilt in front of a lot of witnesses, I saw no point on holding on to him so I let him go. He got in his car and drove off, after shouting, "I am responsible only to the Bishop!"

Pete was still lying on the floor. Her only visible injury was her right arm, which was swollen enormously from elbow to shoulder and had turned red, purple and black. The nurse advised that she be taken to the hospital in case of internal injuries, so the ambulance came, they carried Pete out on a stretcher and away we went.

On the way to Carson City the ambulance broke down, but after about twenty minutes the driver got it running again, and we finally arrived at the hospital. Meanwhile Pete's arm kept on getting bigger and more colorful, but she insisted that it was not the least bit painful.

When the doctor saw Pete's arm, He said, "Good Lord, what happened to you?"

"A priest knocked me down." Pete told him.

"You've got to be kidding. A priest wouldn't do a thing like that."

"Well, this one did." Pete assured him. "Father Robert in Virginia City pushed me down and a big chair fell on top of me."

The doctor was truly astonished. "No doubt he said a bunch of 'Hail Marys' and told his beads afterward."

Except for her arm the doctor found nothing wrong with Pete, so back we went up the mountain in the decrepit old ambulance. On the way we made plans to sign a complaint against Father Robert the next day and have him arrested for assault and battery.

However, that old saying that "trouble comes in bunches," certainly proved to be true. For the past month Pete had been bothered by a pain in her left side. She had gone to a doctor who examined her and told her it was probably just gas pains, nothing to worry about. But that night the pain became so intense that we decided the doctor must have been wrong, as they so often are. The next morning we went to another doctor in Reno who told her she had an ovarian tumor the size of a grapefruit, and immediately had her admitted to the hospital. She was operated on the next day.

They had a lot of silly rules in that hospital, rules that were just begging to be broken. When I told the nurse that I intended to stay with Pete that first night, she said, "Oh no, you can't do that. It's against the rules." Knowing that Pete would wake up several times during the night and feel frightened, I had no intention of leaving her alone. I stayed, and short of having me forcibly removed, there was nothing they could do about it. I sat by her bed all night holding her hand and calming her when she woke up calling for me, as I had known she would.

We wanted to get some pictures of Pete's arm while it was still at the height of its glory, as we would need them as evidence against Father Robert. But taking pictures of the patients was also against the rules. I brought my camera wrapped to look like a box of candy and while the nurse was out of the room I got several good color shots.

Pete couldn't have had a more interesting roommate. She was a fat woman named Marjorie, and was a real snuff-dipping hillbilly from West Virginia. She kept Pete entertained with stories about the revenuers and the stills that were hidden in the hills.

"When my dad would see the revenuers coming he'd hide the bottles of whiskey in the wash tub under a lot of dirty clothes, and that was one place they never thought to look."

A Catholic priest came in one day, stopped by Marjorie's bed and asked if she'd like to talk to him. "Hell, no," Marjorie shouted. "I ain't no Catholic, thank God. Look what one of your damn priests did to my friend Marguerite!"

The priest took one look at Pete's arm and departed hastily, never to return, at least while Pete was there.

When she had recovered from the operation I took Pete home. A couple of days later we went up to District Attorney Moore's office to sign a complaint against Father Robert.

"This sort of thing is not part of my job," Mr. Moore said. "You have to go to the Justice of the Peace for this."

As little as we knew about the law, this didn't seem right to us, but we went to see the Justice of the Peace. He was a skinny little man named Ed Colleti, who had taken over the job when Marryin' Matilda married a Jehovah's Witness preacher and moved to Reno.

"I don't have anything to do with signing complaints," he said. "Only the District Attorney can do that."

Back we went to Moore's office. He seemed surprised to see us again. No doubt he was hoping we'd forget about it. He didn't ask us to sit down.

"Mrs. Williams," he said, "I can't allow you to sign a complaint against Father Robert. It would cause a terrible scandal."

"But he knocked me down. He even admitted it in front of witnesses. Do you mean to say that you want to let him get by with it just because he's a priest?"

"Let's just say that I think it would be better for all concerned if you just forget about it. After all, you were not seriously injured."

"But I was injured." Pete rolled up her sleeve, "Look at my arm!"

"Nevertheless, I refuse to allow you to sign a complaint."

Unable to think of any way to force him we went home, but we still felt there must be away, if we could think of it. But all we could do at the moment was to give him a nickname, and we felt that since he was afraid of a priest, the name "Milquetoast Moore" would be appropriate.

We made inquiries in Reno and Carson City and were told that they were in a different county and that the matter could only be handled by the District Attorney in Virginia City. We were stymied. In our anger and frustration we followed the advice of a friend, who was a lawyer, and filed a civil suit against the Church, but our hearts were not in it. Our only desire was to get rid of Father Robert, and in that we seemed to have failed.

Father Robert, confident that he had won the battle, but now bereft of his Brothers, came up with an idea. An old man with a long white beard, who was known as Hard Rock Peter, had been sitting on C Street surrounded by boxes of rocks containing specks of pyrite, otherwise known as fool's gold. Pointing to these specks he would tell the tourists it was gold, and had been doing a brisk business selling the rocks for whatever the traffic would bear. Occasionally some wiser person, geologically speaking, would challenge him and insist that the specks were pyrite, whereupon Hard Rock Peter would let go with a string of very colorful profanity, undeterred by the presence of women and children. The shocked City Fathers had given him three days to get out of town.

Enter Father Robert. That misguided entrepreneur took Hard Rock Peter, dressed him in a black habit and cowl, and Presto! he had himself a Monk, who was henceforth known as Brother Peter.

None of the city officials made any objection, nor did the Bishop. Father Robert was now a very big frog in a very little pond and could do as he pleased.

Hard Rock Peter had fallen into a very cushy spot. He was getting free room and board, plus all the wine he could drink. All he had to do was walk around in front of the church looking pious, while tourists snapped his picture. With that long white beard he looked like Moses and many people were spiritually inspired to drop money in the poor box, which they might not otherwise have done. When people asked him how long he had been a Monk he would intone soulfully, "I've been in the Holy Orders for nigh onto thirty years."

It was late June now, the tourist season was in full swing, and we were working the usual fourteen hours a day so we had little time to worry about the complaint. We had discussed it with several people, but so far no one had come up with a solution to the problem.

We mailed a copy of the petition to the Archbishop, along with a letter describing Father Robert's latest act of violence, plus a picture of Pete's arm and copies of the depositions from Bernard and Timothy. We received no answer.

"He probably threw the whole thing in the waste basket," Pete said. "Apparently a Catholic priest can get by with murder, rape, theft, any crime in the book, and as long as there's no publicity the Church just sweeps it under the rug and does nothing."

Then one evening Naughty Lola came in. She had just returned from a month-long trip to California.

"Are you going to let that priest get by with knocking you down?" she asked Pete. "How come you haven't signed a complaint against him?"

"We tried, but Moore wouldn't let me, and we haven't been able to think of any way to force him."

"Oh, is that so?" Lola was indignant. "Well, that panty-waist character is breaking the law. Every citizen has a legal right to sign a complaint. Call the Circuit Judge." She wrote down his name and phone number. "Nobody pushes him around, and I'll bet you get some action fast."

When I described what had happened to the Circuit Judge, and told him that Mr. Moore wouldn't let Mrs. Williams sign a complaint he seemed surprised.

"But he has no legal right to refuse." he said. "We'll see about that."

Early the next morning Moore's secretary called and said, "Mrs. Williams, would you like to come up and sign a complaint?"

We immediately turned the sign around and as soon as all the customers had gone, drove up the hill to Moore's office, Pete signed the complaint. Then two days passed while nothing happened. Apparently Moore had just filed the complaint away with no intention of serving it. I called the Circuit Judge again, and now he was really angry.

"What does that so-and-so think he's doing? Never mind, I'll take care of it."

Father Robert was arrested that day, and released on his own recognizance. Up to that point the only public mention that had been made about the fracas was an amusing article on the front page of the Territorial Enterprise, titled, "PRIEST AND PARISHIONER IN WALTZ AROUND."

Now that Father Robert was actually under arrest, well, there is a very vulgar expression to describe what happened next, but I will simply say that all hell broke loose!

Reporters from all over the country converged on Virginia City. Even "Newsweek" sent a man. They interviewed people and took pictures of everyone involved.

Father Robert told the reporters that he had been framed, that Lucius Beebe had connived with us to ruin him. Beebe was in Europe at the time, and knew nothing about what had happened until he returned later in July. He was a wealthy man and fairly well known, and also because he had lashed out frequently against Father Robert, it made a good story that the reporters latched onto with fervor.

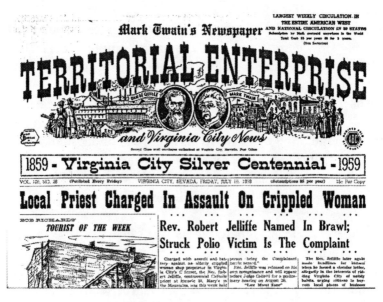

Territorial Enterprise, July 10, 1959

The San Francisco Chronicle ran a continuing front page series every day for a week, called "THE PRIEST AND THE PLUTOCRAT". Many of Beebe's remarks were quoted, among them the comment, "Those women seem to be running an underground railroad for dissatisfied Monks."

Letters began pouring in from allover the country. Some were quite abusive. One woman ended her vitriolic letter by saying, "I hope you rot in your's and Beebe's slime." Many praised us for having the courage to get rid of the no-good priest.

One girl wrote that a priest had gotten her pregnant after getting her drunk: on sacramental wine, and offered to testify in court if it would help. We enjoyed those letters, both the good and the bad.

Several Catholic boys in their early teens decided to get even with us for having Father Robert arrested. First they threw stones breaking a couple of windows, then lobbed lighted firecrackers into the building. This was not only hard on our nerves and dangerous; it was also bad for business. People tend to lose interest in jewelry when firecrackers are exploding around them. The boys always came at night when it was too dark for us to see who they were, and we knew there was no point in calling Sputnik or Fat-Ass Morrison. Had they known about it, they would no doubt have been tempted to join in the fun.

This went on for three nights and there seemed to be no way to put a stop to it. We could only hope that the boys would either tire of the project or run out of firecrackers. But we had learned that invariably, when we had a seemingly unsolvable problem something would happen to resolve it. This time it was one of the disenchanted Catholics. She told us that she had driven up the hill past our building the night before, and had caught one of the boys in her headlights, in the act of throwing a firecracker. She gave us his name and directions for finding his house.

After telling the boy's father what had been happening, I said, "We have a witness who recognized your son as one of the firecracker brigade, and we are warning you that if one more firecracker is thrown into our building, we'll sign a complaint against your son and have him arrested." That was all the man needed to hear; there were no more firecrackers.

The date of the trial had been set for August 20, 1959, and the time was fast approaching, but it was hard to find a Judge who was willing to try a case where a Priest was the accused. Finally, a Judge agreed to serve providing it was a trial by jury, thus letting him off the hook. Paul Laxalt, who later became Governor of Nevada, defended Father Robert. We, of course, had no choice. The District Attorney, Milquetoast Moore, acted as prosecutor representing the people. It was probably the only trial in history with two defense attorneys and no prosecutor.

Father Robert told several lies on the stand, thus adding perjury to his other crimes. He claimed that Pete had tried to tear off his collar, that he had to push her away to defend himself, when in fact she never touched him. He said we had locked him in and Moore did not allow us to explain that the key was in the door and that he had only to turn it in order to get out, which he had done. He was outside on the porch when I caught up with him. The jury never saw the picture of Pete's bruised arm that I had taken in the hospital; Moore refused to show it to them. He did everything possible to make us appear guilty.

As his reason for getting involved in the town politics, Father Robert said that Virginia City had become a cesspool of evil, that certain people were trying to bring back the whore houses and that bartenders were selling drugs to young people. It was pure fabrication, of course, but the jury and the spectators loved it.

We were not surprised by the "not guilty" verdict, and perhaps it was for the best. Had Father Robert been found guilty, some of the more rabid Catholics might have killed us or at least burned down our building. As it was, we had accomplished what we set out to do. As Pete said, "we ran him off the ridge."

Catholic Priests can get by with anything, of course, so long as it doesn't hit the newspapers. When it does, as this little fracas did, the Church has only one solution. The Bishop removed Father Robert and sent him to an obscure little church in Sacramento, California.

St. Mary's in the Mountains did not collapse because the Church officials spent $40,000, which would be the equivalent of about $200,000 in today's money, to shore it up and stabilize it.

While he was in Sacramento Father Robert was paid to make stained glass windows for a church, kept the money but did not make the windows, which may have been one of the reasons he was shunted off to a small town in North Dakota. We have often wondered how the folks there were faring with a psycho priest in their midst.

Now that Father Robert was no longer there to keep Virginia City pure, one would have expected that crime would be rampant, that a red light district would be going full blast, and that scores of young people would become dope addicts, yet none of these things happened. The juiciest items now going out over the grapevine were reports that a husband was stepping out on his wife, or vice versa, that Big Annie and the Finn had fallen off the wagon again, and that two boys had been caught trying to play the slot machines with lead slugs.

Virginia City was once more a quiet peaceful little ghost town—and no doubt even the ghosts were happier.

Chapter 30

During the next two years Pete's condition gradually worsened. Her good muscles seemed to be deteriorating and she now had to use two canes for walking. She tired easily, and wasn't sleeping very well. Feeling that the daily grind was too much for her, I suggested that we sell the business and take a nice long vacation, for at least a year.

At first Pete was shocked at the thought of selling out when we were doing so well, but the more she thought about it the better she liked the idea. Parked in the little dell where we had spent our first night in Virginia City, we talked it over.

"It would be sort of nice," Pete said, "to just travel around the country with no deadlines to meet. And we could visit all the interesting spots that we had to pass up for lack of time when we were working the shows."

"We could sell the car and get a camper shell on a pickup truck. It would beat sleeping in the car. And since the building is paid for, we'd have a nice chunk of money to go on with. The expenses we'd have would be gas, food, and an occasional tire."

"Some smart guy once said that the way to stay young is to live dangerously. So let's do it!"

We had no trouble finding a buyer. Less than a month later two young couples in their forties, planning to go into partnership, offered to buy the building, the business, and the goodwill, for an amount large enough to leave us with a substantial profit. We spent two weeks showing them how to tumble the stones and make the jewelry, and warned them to have nothing to do with factory made jewelry.

"Every gift shop in town sells that stuff," I told them, "and if you want to make a lot of money you have to be different. The secret of our success is that every piece of jewelry we sell is handmade, much of it made to order while the customer waits."

"And don't put in slot machines," Pete said, "They'll ruin your business."

When we left town in our camper we took along our little lapidary machine, two boxes of stones and findings, and a cocker spaniel that we had acquired several months earlier. We didn't need a dog, in fact we really didn't want one, but he had decided he wanted us, so what could we do? He had belonged to a man named Glen who lived in Gold Hill, and worked as a shill at the Gold Nugget from early afternoon until midnight. Every day when Glen left for work the dog would trot three miles up the mountain to our place and stay, and every night when we closed the shop we took him home and put him in Glen's house. He was probably the only dog in the world with a private chauffeur. Glen, who had a very bad heart, worried about what would happen to his dog if he died, and tender-hearted Pete promised that we would look after him. Glen did die of a heart attack and we had ourselves a dog. We named him Rocky, and he was with us for nine years.

The thing we wanted most when we left Virginia City was peace and quiet, and lots of it. We drove out into the desert about ten miles beyond the nearest small town, parked at the foot of a mountain near an interesting looking canyon, and spent the days doing absolutely nothing useful or productive. It was early September, the weather was perfect, and we spent a lot of time just lying in the sun, talking. We read a great many books, and did some rock hunting. The alarm clock ran down and we didn't bother to wind it. Time no longer mattered. After awhile we even lost track of the days, and when we left there and drove back to the little town we really didn't know whether it was still September, or if October had arrived.

We pulled into a service station and when I paid for the gas I asked the man, "What day is this?"

"It's Friday."

"What's the date?" I asked.

"This is the 17th."

I knew my next question would throw him, but we had to know. "What month is it?"

He gave us a strange look. "This is Friday, October 17, 1960."

"Oh, we knew the year," I assured him, as we drove away leaving him looking decidedly flabbergasted.

Our next stop was Southern California to see my children. Ann had two boys and a girl now, plus the twin boys her husband Orris had when they were married. Bunny had married her black boyfriend, Jack, and now had three boys. Dick had worked his way through college, earned an engineering degree, and was working for an electronics firm in San Diego. He was married for the second time and had a boy and a girl, besides a girl from his first marriage. That made eleven grandchildren for "Gramma Dot", as they called me.

We had a wonderful time visiting everyone and getting acquainted with the grandchildren. I'd play outdoor rough and tumble games with them, but when it came to entertaining them quietly I simply had no knack for it, whereas Pete was a natural in that department. She knew a thousand stories and could keep them happy and laughing for hours. They called her Aunt Pete. One little five year old was puzzled, "Pete is a boy's name," he said, "so how come we don't call you Uncle Pete?"

Then, on our way to Virginia to see Pete's folks, we took our time and did a little sightseeing, spending the nights on the desert until we reached the populated areas, where we were forced to stay at trailer parks. It was a pleasant, leisurely trip and although we knew that eventually we would have to get back to business, right now we were free as the birds, and like them we were taking no thought for the morrow. Sometimes we wondered if we both had a little Gypsy blood inherited from long-gone ancestors.

Both of our families seemed to be following that old adage to "be fruitful and multiply." Pete now had seven great-nieces and nephews. Our two-week visit was enjoyable, despite Pete's sister Mary who had a jealous streak, which over the years was becoming more and more pronounced. She had never liked me simply because she felt I had taken Pete away from her, not realizing that it is possible to love more than one person. She was also jealous of Pete and Dixie, and consistently made every effort to keep them from getting close. While we were there, however, she kept her feelings fairly well hidden and we had a good time with Dixie and the children.

While we were on the East Coast we went to New Jersey to see Pete's other sister, Pauline. We then took a trip to Niagara Falls. Heading West, we stopped to see the Petrified Forest, the Painted Desert and the Grand Canyon, all the places that we had passed many times, but had never seen for lack of time.

Back on the West Coast again, we visited Fern and Ralph, from the home show days, and we also saw Jerry who had his own beauty shop now in Pasadena and was making lots of money. He had a plush mobile home with a swimming pool and had taken flying lessons. He now had his own plane and a fresh supply of stories to keep us laughing.

We had always wanted to see the geysers at Yellowstone Park. On the way there we went through Virginia City, being curious to know how the people at Tierra Gems were doing. Much to our dismay we saw that more than half the counter was taken up with factory jewelry, and that two of those "one armed bandits" were holding forth near the front door. It seemed they had found that it was too much work tumbling stones and making all that jewelry. It should have been easy since there were four of them. We learned later that the business had failed. Too bad! But we had warned them!

After making the rounds to see our many good friends in Virginia City, we went on to Yellowstone Park. We rented a space in a trailer park in the little town of West Yellowstone and made the grand tour of the park to see the dozens of geysers, including Old Faithful. One night we went to the dump on the edge of town to see the grizzly bears. There were about a dozen cars there, and since everyone left their headlights on, we had a good view of those enormous animals as they rooted among the cans and other trash. They used their long claws to tear open sacks looking for edibles.

For about a year and a half we had been wandering around the country visiting and sightseeing. It was early May now, and in another month the tourist season would be getting under way. The thought of all those well-heeled people who would be cruising around town somehow got to us, and we decided that if we could find a good spot we'd go back into the jewelry business for the summer.

At the only large hotel in town, the owner, John Bayless showed us the lobby, half of which was occupied by a travel agency. He would rent us the other half for $200 a month. There was a long glass showcase were no bottom shelves in the lobby, and knowing we would need extra display space, we spent almost a hundred dollars to have glass shelves installed, and bought a couple of stools. Then we ordered stones and findings from the wholesale houses, rented a small cabin and set to work making jewelry. We planned to open for business on the first of June.

The man at the travel agency never talked to us much; in fact he seemed almost unfriendly. Now and then we caught him looking at us with a puzzled expression.

"What's with him, I wonder?" Pete whispered to me.

"I can't imagine," I whispered back, "but I get the definite impression that he doesn't approve of our being here."

Finally one day he could no longer contain his curiosity. "You know, that space belongs to the travel agency. Did they give you permission to use it?"

"No, Mr. Bayless rented it to us."

"I don't see how he would dare to do that, when he's already rented it," he said.

I immediately called the headquarters of the travel agency and was assured that they had indeed rented the entire counter, whereupon we confronted Bayless and demanded our money back. Apparently reluctant to let go of money once he had his hands on it, he offered us space, at the same rent, in a downtown restaurant that he owned. However, he flatly refused to refund the money we had spent for improvements, thereby earning for himself the nickname "Payless Bayless."

We made up a lot of jewelry in our little cabin. I built a counter and we set up in the restaurant. The chef-manager loved our gemstones, and almost every night we had a steak dinner in exchange for a few stones or a couple of pieces of jewelry. Business was nothing to get excited about but we were making a little money, and it was fun, especially since I had thought of a way to get back the money we had spent needlessly at the hotel.

"I know how we can get even with Payless Bayless," I told Pete. "All we have to do is just not pay the last month's rent. One dirty trick deserves another."

"You certainly have changed, Dot. When I first met you, you were shy and sort of afraid of people. Now you don't take nothin' off nobody."

"Well, you've been a good influence on me. Besides, working the shows will either kill or cure you."

When Payless Bayless came by soon after the first of August to collect the third month's rent we told him business had been very poor, and we just didn't have it yet, and that we'd appreciate his giving us a little more time. He came back a couple of weeks later and again we put him off. We never saw him again. No doubt he was very busy at the hotel, and he may have thought we planned to stay through September. On the last day of August we loaded everything on top of the camper and took off.

"We'd better get out of town in a hurry, Pete. He might try to have us arrested for skipping out."

"I don't believe he would. He knows we'd tell what he did and that we can prove it by the travel agency; I'm sure he wouldn't want that story made public. And boy, would we publicize it!"

Having no immediate plan in mind for the future, but anxious to get out of West Yellowstone, we drove East through Yellowstone Park and on into Cody, Wyoming, where we spent the night. The next day we looked the town over, liked what we saw, and noticing a small shop for rent on the main drag, I asked Pete what she thought of the idea of setting up a shop there.

"Sounds like a good idea. I just love Wyoming, and if we do well we could stay here a long time, and have a cowboy on our license plate."

While we were moving in, the man who owned the shoe repair shop next door came in to see us. He was small, not much over five feet, but would have been a couple of inches taller except that his shoulders were stooped with age. He was 86 years old, and had lots of wrinkles and a surprising amount of grey hair. He had no family and lived alone in a small three-room house two blocks from his shop.

The old man, whose name was Jake, seemed to "take a liking" to us, as the saying goes, and at least once every day he would come in to say hello. Often in the evenings we would go to his house where over a can of beer he would tell us stories of his experiences as a prospector. Once he had made quite a bit of money from a gold mine he had discovered. He had enough to live on without working, he told us, but he enjoyed repairing shoes and talking to the people who came in his shop, and it gave him something to do.

"Keeps me young," he laughed. "People get old in a hurry when they stop doing things and start sitting."

One night Jake said, "You've noticed that car sitting in my driveway? Well, it hasn't been driven for six months. I used to drive it around town once in awhile just to keep in practice, but now I just go out about once a week and start it up so it won't forget how. I'm not going any place where I'd need a car, and I'd like to give it to you girls if you want it." (We were in our fifties, but to him we were "girls. ")

The last thing we needed was another car, but we couldn't very well turn it down, not only because it was free and we couldn't look a gift horse in the mouth, but because we could sense that the old man would be disappointed if we didn't take it. So we accepted it with many thanks, and thereafter drove it to work every day and parked it in front of the shop.

Fortunately, it was a station wagon. It was ten years old and could have used a paint job, but we had never been much concerned about the outside appearance of a car. To us, the important thing was the stuff under the hood, and everything in that department seemed to be working well. Pete dearly loved that car, mainly I think, because it had a cowboy on the license plate!

We told Jake to pick out anything he wanted and he selected a bolo tie with a large piece of polished jade. We noticed that he was admiring a pair of petrified wood bookends and we tried to insist that he take those, too. But he would take nothing else. "Maybe with this bolo tie I'll be so handsome I'll get myself a girlfriend." He grinned, "If I do, I'll give her a bracelet or something."

It wasn't too long before we realized that the shop in Cody was a bad deal. We stuck it out for two months, not even making expenses, hoping that business would improve. When it didn't we knew we would have to look for greener pastures.

"How about Palm Springs?" Pete suggested. "Lots of wealthy people spend the winter there, and if we can find a decent location I'm sure we'd make money."

"That's a good idea. Let's try it and if we can't find a spot we'll just think of something else. We could always go back to working shows, but I do hate the idea of moving every ten days."

Since we couldn't take both cars, we made a deal with a man who owned a garage to park the station wagon inside for the winter. We said goodbye to Jake, who in that short time had become like an old friend.

"We'll be back in April or May," Pete told him, "and we'll drop you a card when we get to Palm Springs. You behave yourself now, and we'll be seeing you."

He gave her a peck on the cheek. "Just what the hell else can I do, except behave?" he chuckled. "I'll miss you girls, and I'll look forward to seeing you next spring."

As usual, we were lucky. On our second day in Palm Springs we found a small vacant shop on Palm Canyon Drive, the main business street. We could rent it by the month, no lease required. It was a small narrow place with hideous. mustard colored walls, and the floor was covered with linoleum that had seen better days. There was a large storeroom in the back and a tiny room containing a toilet and washbowl. It wasn't much, but it was the only place available so, of course, we took it. We knew too, that once we spread our jewelry on the counter even the upper crust people would pay no attention to the decor.

"We could put a couple of army cots in the storeroom and sleep there," I said. "It would sure beat driving that long distance from the trailer park every day."

Our first night in Palm Springs we had discovered that all of the trailer parks were full. The only one we could find with a vacancy was in a little place called Palm Desert about ten miles from downtown.

Since it seemed the sensible thing to do, we bought two cots at the Salvation Army store, ran some extension cords for lights over our beds for reading at night, and plugged in a hot plate for making coffee. Then, knowing that we could not endure spending several months with those horrible walls I spent two days painting them off-white and although the mustard still showed through a little here and there it was a big improvement. While I was waxing the linoleum Pete came up with some bad news.

"While I was talking to the man next door I mentioned that we were going to live in the back, and he said we couldn't, that it was against the law."

"Then we'll just keep it a secret, and if they catch us we'll plead ignorance. When you get to be our age, especially if you're a woman, people expect you to be stupid."

We set up the counter and gave it a pleated skirt of new material in an effort to make the place look better, but there was no way we could compete in appearance with the other shops. All of them had wall-to-wall plush carpeting and expensive glass and polished wood show cases. It was like putting a hillbilly fresh from the hills in among a group of fashion models. But it was the best we could do, and we didn't let it bother us.

For the first time in our checkered career, we had to have a business license, so we went to the proper office, filled out papers and gave the man fifty dollars.

"I can't approve this until the place had been inspected," he said.

Pete thought fast, "What day will you be there?"

He checked through one of his books. "Someone will be there on Wednesday."

Early Wednesday morning we folded the cots, took down the extension cords, unplugged the hot plate, and piled everything in a corner and covered it with canvas. When the inspector arrived he looked the place over, announced that everything seemed to be in order and went away. As soon as he had gone we put up the cots, restrung the extension cords and plugged in the hot plate. During the five months we lived there no one bothered us. It was a most convenient and time saving arrangement.

Before we opened for business we doubled and tripled our prices, as we had learned from experience that well-to-do people take a dim view of items with too low a price tag, especially jewelry. It was the right move. People came in dressed to the teeth in furs and diamonds and bought without considering the price. None of them seemed to care that our shop was a long way from meeting the Palm Springs standard of elegance.

"You know Pete, I think they all go home and tell their friends about our place. I can just hear them saying, 'You'll never believe what I saw on Palm Canyon Drive today. You'd have to see it to believe it.'"

"It just goes to prove what we've always said, that it pays to be different."

We had quite a few visitors that winter. Ann and Orris came in a camper with their five children. Bunny spent a weekend in Palm Springs with her three children. Barney came by and stayed around a few days. He had sold cars in Los Angeles to get another grubstake and was on his way to do some more prospecting. So far he had found nothing worthwhile, but he never gave up. While he was there he introduced us to Jewish food, and we found it delicious. There was a Jewish delicatessen just down the street and we became regular customers.

It was a wonderful winter and we enjoyed every minute of it. We would have stayed longer, but we had heard that during Easter vacation hordes of drunk and disorderly teenagers descended on the town, wrecking stores, breaking windows, overturning cars, and creating general havoc. Apparently, the police were unable to control them. Since we wanted no part of that we packed up and headed for Wyoming.

We were looking' forward to seeing our friend Jake again, but when we arrived in Cody we learned that he had died of pneumonia during the winter. Feeling very sad about it, we took some flowers out to his grave, cried a little, and bade him a final farewell. Then we got his station wagon out of storage, drove out and around town and talked about what a fun guy he had been and how much we had enjoyed his company.

We had not yet decided what we would do next. While we were driving around we saw a large cement-block building with a for rent sign. It was about two miles out of town on the highway leading to Yellowstone Park.

"Hey, look at that building, Dot! I've always thought it would be fun to have a roadside rock shop, and that place would be perfect for one. It's right on the highway, and there's a motel across the street, so we should get plenty of tourists."

"Well, we've done just about everything else so why not give it a shot? It might be a good place for summer."

Inside the building there was one very large room and one very small room. The rent was quite reasonable, so we decided to give it a try. We put up a large sign, ordered supplies, and spent the rest of April and May making jewelry in anticipation of the many tourists we optimistically thought we would attract once the season started.

The woman who ran the motel across the street came over to get acquainted. Her name was Grace and she seemed to be a nice, pleasant person, but we soon learned that she was hung up on religion. She was shocked to hear that we did not go to church, and considering us grist for her mill, she launched into a crusade to save our souls. We looked forward to the coming of the tourists, when hopefully she would be too busy to spread the Gospel.

There was another motel about three miles farther up the highway, and between there and Yellowstone Park there was nothing but forty miles of uninhabited wilderness. The couple who ran the motel were interesting people. They often stopped by on their way into town and we were always glad to see them. They, too, were religious and invited us to attend their church, but when we politely declined they didn't press it.

One evening in early May we noticed a young couple walking up the highway. The man was leading a little boy about three years old, and the woman was carrying a baby in her arms. We were amazed when we realized they were hitchhiking. Since there were few cars on the road that early in the year we thought their chance of getting a ride was indeed slim. They stopped in front of the motel, and while the woman waited by the road with the children the man went to the office. He soon came back again and they walked on up the highway.

Both Pete and I had the somewhat lamentable habit of getting involved in other people's troubles, and this seemed to be a real crisis because of the babies. I sprinted up the road and caught up with them. The man told me they were trying to get to Oregon, that his uncle had a job for him there. "I asked the woman at the motel if she'd let me do some work to pay for a room, but she turned me down."

"Well, you simply can't go on up the highway tonight with those babies. It's over forty miles to the Park. It will be dark in an hour and very cold, and if you don't get a ride, for which your chance is about one in a thousand, where will you spend the night?"

"We'll find a gully where we will be out of the wind. We have a couple of blankets."

"And the babies will either die of pneumonia or be eaten by bears. There are lots of them roaming around up there. Wait here, I'll be right back."

Thinking that Grace had not seen the children, I explained the situation. "I don't know how they got themselves into this mess, but that makes no difference. We just can't let those children sleep out in the open as cold as it is. If you'll put them up for the night Pete and I will pay for the room."

"I feel sorry for them, of course," she said, "but after all they are hitchhikers, and I just can't have people like that in my motel. Besides, they might steal something."

Since it was a lost cause anyway, I refrained from reminding her that even the "best" people often stole things from motels, else why did they keep pictures, TV sets and other removables nailed down? I went back and reported to the young couple that I had struck out, then suggested that they come back to the shop where they could sit down and rest while I made another phone call.

When I told Pete what happened she could hardly believe it. "How could anyone turn thumbs down on babies?"

"I don't know, but she did. And that's the woman who had the gall to try to save our souls! It seems to me that her own soul needs a bit of repair work."

I called Bessie at the other motel and explained the problem. "The reason we're so concerned is that they have two babies, and we're trying to find a place for them to sleep. Otherwise, they'll spend the night out in the open somewhere along the highway. If you'll take them in we'll bring them up there and pay for the room."

Bessie went into a buck-passing routine. "It might be all right with me," she said, "but I know my husband would definitely be against it. Wait a minute, I'll ask him." She was back in less than a minute. "He says absolutely not, and says to tell them to go to the Salvation Army."

When I passed along that suggestion they vetoed it at once, because they believed if they did that the children would be taken away from them. We didn't know whether that was true or not. The only dealings we ever had with the Salvation Army was shopping in their thrift stores. But since we couldn't force them to go there we did the only other thing possible. They spent the night with us.

We were sleeping in the camper, but there was a mattress in the station wagon, and the woman could sleep there with the baby. And we could put the two folding cots in the little back room for the man and the little boy. There were quite a few mice scrabbling around there during the night because someone had stored some sacks of grain in a building behind ours, which was why were sleeping in the camper. But they could stand it for one night. Better mice than bears!

We sat on the cots and talked, while the little boy played on the floor with Rocky. The parents' names were Linda and Charley, and they were in their mid-twenties, although they looked a bit older, with good reason. I made sandwiches and coffee and Charley went to the little store about a half mile down the road to get milk for the baby. While he was gone Linda told us that there was no uncle in Oregon and that they lived on the road all the time just going from place to place.

"Charley gets a few days work now and then to get money for food. I hate living like this. I'd like to stay in one place and live like other people, but Charley won't even consider it. He likes this life."

"Why don't you leave him?" Pete asked.

"I don't have any folks. Where would I go, and what would I do? And I'm pregnant. In about six months we'll have another baby to worry about."

"Go to the police, tell them he's abusing you and you want protection."

"He never lets me out of his sight long enough, and he says if I try to leave him I'd regret it, so I'm afraid of what he might do."

"When you start up the road in the morning, if you want us to we'll call the police and have them come out. You can tell them your story and ask them to take you to the Salvation Army. They'll look after you until you get squared away. You can get a job of some kind and put the kids in a day nursery. How about it, do you want to try it?"

"Sure, go ahead. I'm willing to try anything."

They hadn't gone very far the next morning when the police car arrived. We couldn't hear the conversation, of course, but apparently either Linda lost her nerve or the cop believed Charley's story about the uncle in Oregon. He made a u-turn and went back to town leaving Linda and Charley trudging on up the highway. There was nothing more we could do.

By the middle of June we realized that we had made a mistake. The expected hordes of tourists failed to materialize. There was no lack of traffic, but few people stopped, and of those who did many were dedicated rock hounds interested only in talking about rocks and describing their various rock hunting trips.

"Well, I wanted a roadside rock shop, and I got one, but it sure is a bust," Pete said, "So what shall we do now?"

"We could spend another winter in Palm Springs, but I've been thinking about those cases with the revolving glass shelves that we saw in that department store. They would be perfect for the jewelry, and they don't take up much space so we could probably get spots for them in Denver. How does the idea strike you?"

Pete was instantly enthused. "That's a wonderful idea, let's do it."

Chapter 31

With the station wagon hooked to the back of the camper we headed for Denver, stopping off in Cheyenne where we made a deal with the Holiday Inn there to put in one of the cases. As we neared the Colorado border we saw a sign warning that all cars towing vehicles must be stopped for inspection. It had started to rain, and was soon coming down like a cloudburst. Although we watched both sides of the road for the inspection station we never did see one and since nobody stopped us we just kept on going.

Leaving the camper in a trailer park in Denver, we started out to look for spots and made an arrangement to put cases in two motels in Denver, the drug store at the Hilton Hotel and the Holiday Inn in Boulder. Then we located the company that sold the cases, bought five of them and had them delivered to the various spots.

Our jewelry looked beautiful on those revolving glass shelves, and we felt quite optimistic about our new venture, but we waited awhile to make sure it would be profitable before looking for a place to live.

Being hillbillies at heart, we preferred to live in the country. (Bunny had once remarked that we were the original hippies and that we had thought of it long before the kids did.) We found a place that appealed to us about twenty miles south of Denver. It was a little village called Sedalia and had a population of about a hundred. It was situated at the foot of Jarre Canyon, which had a two-lane winding paved road leading up into the mountains.

We were hoping to find a small house on an acre or less, but the only place for sale was a converted old country school house about three miles up the canyon. It had a living room, kitchen, two bedrooms and a bath. The rooms were all quite small, but we didn't mind that. The only drawback was that thirty-seven acres came with the house. We needed thirty-seven acres like we needed some more holes in our heads, but we loved the area and the price was reasonable, so we bought it figuring that we could eventually sell some of the land.

A man named Harold, whose wife had left him, was living there alone, planning to move to Iowa when he sold the place. While the negotiations for the sale were being completed we parked both vehicles in the big yard and lived in the camper. Harold was a religious fanatic, but he was one of those rare people who can argue without getting angry, and in the evenings when he came home from work we had some of the most interesting conversations.

Rocky loved the place. He had thirty-seven acres on which he could roam and chase rabbits. Fortunately, he never caught any. We added on a large room for a work shop, set up our lapidary machine and bought two tumblers of a new type that would turn out polished stones in less than a week. Since we no longer needed the camper we sold it for almost as much as we had paid for it.

Business was not sensational; we hadn't expected it to be. But with five spots going we were making a good living and we were satisfied. Often we took walks up the hill to what we jokingly called the "north forty", and when we saw in the distance the layers of yellow smog hanging over Denver we were thankful we could live out here in the country and let other people sell the jewelry for us. Once a week I made the rounds, tallied up the sales, gave the managers their cut and refilled the cases.

Gradually we became acquainted with the other people in the canyon. There were quite a few of them, but they were scattered. Their houses were a mile or more apart. The road wound on up the canyon for about ten miles ending in a campground where people went for hiking and picnicking in the summer. About half way up the canyon there was a roadhouse where many of the locals gathered on Saturday night to have dinner and dance, and some did a little drinking, although we never saw anyone drunk. Some people brought their children, and it was a get-acquainted fun sort of thing.

I don't remember the name of the place. Pete and I dubbed it "Sin City" because the folks at the two religious camps in the canyon, one hard-shell Baptist and the other Seventh Day Adventist, objected strenuously, and in a hopeless effort to have it closed down, even got out petitions that, needless to say, Pete and I did not sign.

Our New Year's Eve parties became a sort of tradition. That first year we thought it would be fun to have a few friends in to celebrate, but we made it known via the grapevine that anyone who wanted to come was welcome. Well, it certainly is true that when you live in the country everybody is your neighbor. At least twenty people showed up and everyone had a wonderful time. At midnight the older folks went home, but the rest of us continued the festivities until dawn. Then we had a ham and egg breakfast and everybody went home to get some sleep. Every year after that, during the seven years we were there, we threw a New Year's Eve party.

Some of our experiences in the canyon were quite laughable. One day a young couple named Tom and Charlotte offered us twenty dollars a month to let their two horses graze on our land. That was fine with us but after the first month they were unable to come up with the money. We didn't care. We had no use for the stuff that was growing there anyway, and it was sort of nice to have horses—the kind we couldn't bet on—roaming around on our north forty. However, Tom said he didn't feel right about it, and he came up with what he though was a brilliant idea.

"I'll cut the hay, bale it and sell it, and we'll split the profits."

It sounded good, but it didn't work out so well. After getting the hay all baled, Tom found that he couldn't sell it because it had too much cactus mixed in with it, so he took it home, weeded out the cactus and fed it to his horses.

"How's that for funny?" Pete doubled over laughing. "They couldn't afford to have the horses eat the hay here so they took the hay home and fed it to the horses."

We had lots of company when we lived in Sedalia. Jerry, Fern and Ralph spent a week with us, and they were always great fun. Jerry said, "We wanted to bring you some fresh peaches, but you know they won't let you bring fruit across the border." Then, grinning broadly, he added, "I don't know how come they let me across."

Fern fixed a chicken dinner and she wanted to make biscuits. She turned down my offer to get some rolls of frozen biscuits, which really can't be beat. Nothing would do but she must make them from scratch, so Jerry and I had to go to the village and buy Crisco, baking powder, and I don't know what all, things we never kept on hand. Our motto was always, "Don't make if you can get it already made!"

One year Bunny arrived with her husband and three boys. We went on hikes together, and we took them to see Pike's Peak, Manitou Springs and the Garden of the Gods, as we did with everyone who came. Over the years Pete and I became very well acquainted with those places. Dixie and Mary came all the way from Virginia on the train with Dixie's four children and one summer Pete's thirteen-year-old nephew and Ann's son Eric, spent two months with us.

Pete's other sister, Pauline, made a most memorable visit. She arrived just two days before a twenty-foot wall of water came tearing down little Plum Creek. It demolished the bridge, our only access to Sedalia, and took out many houses and trailer parks on its way to join the swollen Platte River in Denver.

We were safe on high ground, but for almost a week the electricity and phone were cut off, and the only water we had was the little we kept stored in jugs for emergencies. After a few days when the creek subsided, the mailman came across on horseback, Pony Express style, to deliver the mail. Since we couldn't cook we lived on cheese and crackers, bread and butter and cold canned food. There was no way to make coffee, but as always I had a good supply of cokes.

It had been a long time since Pete and I had had an adventure, and we thought the emergency exciting, but Pauline was anything but enthused about the situation. She missed her coffee, she didn't enjoy cold food, and she was particularly upset because we would not allow her to use any of the precious supply of water to wash her underpants. She wanted to go home.

To get her to the airport we had to drive almost a hundred miles. First to the campground at the top of the canyon, then across a long stretch of mountain road, and finally over the river into Denver, on the only one of five bridges that was still standing. We saw her off to New Jersey, where she didn't mind telling us she was looking forward to a civilized life. Within a week things were back to normal. Plum Creek had dwindled to a small stream that we could drive across while a new bridge was being built, so we could get into Denver again to service the cases.

What spare time we had was spent in reading. Also, Pete was writing poetry, and I was writing a book, a satire on the Bible. So involved were we in these projects that it never once occurred to us that we should have a radio, a TV or a newspaper to find out what was going on in the world. If someone had asked us who the President was I doubt if we would have known.

Then Ann and Orris came for a visit and made a drastic change in our life style. Orris made no comment about not being able to get any news. He was the strong silent type and never talked much. But every morning he drove the three miles to Sedalia to get a newspaper. Ann wrote us later that on the way home they were talking about it, and Orris shook his head and remarked, "I have never in my life seen anyone so out of communication with the outside world!"

As soon as they got home they sent us a clock radio. Now we could hear all about the political skullduggery, the blood running in the streets and other items of national interest, but mostly we listened to a talk show in Denver. We loved the interesting arguments and we could listen while we worked.

Not long after that some friends up the canyon got a new TV and insisted on giving us their old one. We had never had a TV and really didn't want one, but we couldn't refuse it without seeming ungracious. We never watched it much as we were far too busy with other things, but it was nice to have when company came.

We had been in Sedalia about four years when a blow fell that seemed likely to ruin us. The management of the Holiday Inns made a ruling that henceforth there would be no selling in the lobbies of their motels. Since we were unable to find other spots for the cases we had to sell them and thus were left with only the one spot at the Hilton Hotel. But Pete and I were always so lucky. Good things seemed to come along for us just in the nick of time. A salesman, having seen our jewelry at the Hilton, came out to the house and made us a proposition. He traveled allover the West selling stones and findings to rock shops and gift stores. He wanted to carry samples of the jewelry and take orders. It seemed like a good idea, so we went for it, and it proved to be quite successful.

However, it was seasonal. Most of the orders came in the spring and summer, there being almost no winter business. We went in for retouching negatives at home for a studio in Denver. Pete, having had some experience, taught me, and we learned a lot from a Japanese girl named Amie who lived in the canyon and was an expert. With everything combined we were making almost as much as we had made before with a lot less traveling. The winters were a bit rough financially, but we managed.

A couple of years earlier Dick had started his own company, marketing a machine he had invented for intravenous feeding in hospitals. He had started on the proverbial shoestring, but was hanging in there. He had formed a corporation, and was now selling stock, but only to people who worked for the company since it was a closed corporation.

Pete's faith in Dick was unlimited. "I have a very strong hunch that he's going to make a big success of this," she insisted. "It's our chance to make a lot of money if we could get some stock."

One day she said to Dick on the phone, "Look, how about hiring me to come down there and sweep the floors so I can get some stock?" She was joking, of course, but I believe that given a chance she would have done it.

A few weeks later we were working on negatives when the phone rang. It was Dick. "Hi Dot," he said, "I've fixed it so you and Pete can get some stock. How much do you want?"

I called to Pete and told her the good news. "We have a thousand dollars. Shall we risk five hundred of it?"

"Oh, no." she said, "Lets put in the whole thousand."

"If we do that we won't have much left. How will we get through the winter?"

"We'll think of something, don't we always!"

203

Sure enough, she thought of something. When I came home from town one day she grinned and said, "I got you a job, Dot."

"You've got to be kidding."

"No, it's for real. A man from the school came by and asked me if you'd take the job, and I told him yes."

"What kind of job is it, working in the school cafeteria?"

"No, driving the school bus. You start Monday."

I had never driven anything bigger than the camper, except the time in Utah when I turned the trailer around on the side of a cliff, but I was willing to try anything. It turned out not to be a fun job. Although most of the children were well-behaved, there were a few unruly ones who delighted in breaking the rules by throwing empty soft drink cans and coke bottles out the windows. There were the three teen-aged Smith sisters, who apparently hated each other and who frequently engaged in fist fights on the way down the canyon. I tried making the three girls sit in widely separated seats, but before I had gone any distance they would be in the back of the bus making a concerted effort to kill each other. Sometimes noses would bleed, and I had to wipe blood off the floor at the end of the day.

Reporting the names of miscreants to the school authorities did no good, which explains why there was such a big turnover in drivers, but I stuck it out through the winter and to the end of the school year, then politely bowed out and told them to get someone else next year.

At the end of the seventh year in Sedalia we decided it was time to retire. I was sixty two and Pete was sixty one. Over the years her good muscles had been gradually deteriorating, as usually happens to people who have had polio. Thinking that she would be better off in a warmer climate, I suggested that we move to Arizona.

Although we had sold ten acres, we still had twenty seven acres and the house, and it was all paid for. "We'll have enough money to last us a long time," I said.

"And don't forget," Pete reminded me, "we're going to make a lot of money on Dick's stock."

I was beginning to believe it. Recently there had been a stock split and already our investment had increased twenty fold.

We sold our one display case and all of the jewelry making and retouching equipment and some friends who had a rock shop in Colorado Springs bought most of the gemstones and jewelry.

Rocky was no longer with us. He had gotten old and sick, had lost the sight of one eye and his hearing, and was badly crippled with arthritis.

Although it almost broke our hearts, we had him put to sleep and we buried him high up on the north forty with his favorite rubber rat. We vowed then that never, under any circumstances, would we have another dog. It hurts too much when you lose them.

We planned to leave on a Saturday morning, and since we had decided to take along some of the furniture, I went into Denver early that morning and rented a U-Haul. Some of the neighbors came to see us off and soon there were fifteen or twenty people there. The men set to work loading the U-Haul. Noticing that they were loading the heavier things in front, I suggested, "Don't you think it would be better to put the heavy stuff in the middle?"

They paid no attention to me, and when they were finished both the back of the car and the front of the U-Haul were almost touching the ground. They unloaded everything and reloaded, this time putting the heavy stuff in the center, over the wheels. That was fine and we were ready to leave when someone noticed a large crack in one of the iron bars connecting the U-Haul to the car.

Since our phone had been disconnected, we went to a neighbor's house, called the company and were assured that they would send out another U-Haul right away. The men unloaded the furniture again and unhooked the U-Haul, and then we waited and waited and waited. "Right away" turned out to be about three hours. People were getting hungry; so some of the folks went home and brought back sandwiches, hot coffee and beer. Chris and Rudy, the people who were buying the house, brought a big pot of baked beans. It was like a big picnic, and everyone had a great time.

Finally the man arrived with the U-Haul, hooked it to the car and once more the men loaded the furniture. As he started to get back into his truck the man turned to me and said, "Do you know what to do if you have a flat tire?"

Puzzled as to why he asked me such a stupid question, I said, "Well, of course, you take it off and put on the spare."

He went into paroxysms of laughter, and someone explained that what the man meant was that if we had a flat on the U-Haul we could call the nearest branch office and they would send someone to change it. He was still laughing as he drove away. I didn't think it was that funny.

By now it was getting on toward evening so we spent the night with a neighbor and started out early the next morning. And we did have a flat on the way to Arizona. Unfortunately, it was on the car so I had to change it myself.

Chapter 32

We had no idea where we were going to settle, but we knew that when we came to the right place something would tell us, "This is it." We didn't care much for Flagstaff. It was on Highway 66, the road traveled by the Oakies when they were escaping from the dust bowl in the thirties. It appeared to consist mainly of railroad tracks. We spent the night there and the next day drove down Oak Creek Canyon, which was a smaller version of the Grand Canyon, except that instead of being on top looking down, we were at the bottom looking up at the sheer rock cliffs.

From the canyon we emerged into Sedona, a small town surrounded by the famous towering red rocks. We liked the rocks, but we didn't like the town. Both sides of the main street were lined with expensive looking gift shops, art stores, and restaurants. It looked like what it actually was—a modernized tourist trap.

Dropping down into the valley, we came to Cottonwood. It was a nice enough little town, but failed to send us any particular vibes, and besides, we were told the temperature there during the summer often went as high as a hundred and ten and we didn't care to cope with that.

Now the road wound steeply to the very top of a high mountain, and there perched precariously on the side of that steep mountain was a little ghost town called Jerome, population about fifty. The buildings on the down side of the narrow winding main street looked as if it wouldn't take a very strong wind to tumble them down into the valley far below. It was an interesting place, but having no desire to live there we went on down the south side of the mountain, past scores of abandoned mines, into another valley.

Suddenly, after crossing many miles of flat, almost treeless desert, we came upon a wondrous sight. On both sides of the road, stretching back as far as we could see, were rock cliffs and towering piles of huge, colorful boulders. A few determined little pine trees were eking out a living in some of the crevices.

Noticing a side road that appeared to be well traveled, we followed it for a short distance, crossed a little bridge over a creek and came upon a small settlement. Several houses were scattered at random along the road and up the hillsides. There were plenty of trees including several tall willows growing along the creek.

Pete was enthused. "This is absolutely marvelous, I love it! I hope there's a town somewhere around to go with it."

"Yes, according to the map there's a place called Prescott about five miles on down the road. Let's go have a look at it. And keep your fingers crossed."

The moment we drove into Prescott we knew this was the town we had been looking for. It was surrounded by mountains, and while some of them were covered with trees, many were bare, gaunt and rocky, the kind we loved most. The population was about twelve thousand, the elevation one mile. The place had an Old West look about it. There were no tall buildings, the highest being only two stories, and all of them looked as if they had been there a long time, which they had. There were no one-way streets, and no parking meters. The town fathers had tried that once, but the people rose up in wrath and the meters were quickly removed.

In the center of town was an old-time village square surrounding the Courthouse, and during the summer months all sorts of festivities were held there, including square dancing, art exhibits, band music and political speeches. The block west of the Courthouse was called Whiskey Row because in the old days every building was a saloon where the old-timers used to whoop it up on Saturday nights. Now there were only three saloons, but it was still called Whiskey Row.

We rented a three-room cabin with a garage at a motel, unloaded the U-Haul, turned it in and began looking around for a place to live. We wanted to be in the Dells, that beautiful place we had seen on our way in, but since nothing was available there we bought a mobile home and parked it in a trailer park about a mile from the Dells.

When we had been there only a short time, my sister, Jean, left her husband, hypochondriac Ed, and came to live in Prescott. I must admit that we encouraged her mightily, for which old Ed never forgave us, but we did not regret it, as Jean was now reasonably happy for the first time in her life.

About two years after we went to Prescott, Dick went public with the stock and the value shot up incredibly. We sold our shares for sixty thousand dollars, and built a lovely three-bedroom home high on a hill in The Dells. In those days a lot of house could be had for around thirty thousand dollars.

We had to move in before the house was finished because they failed to complete it on schedule. Since we had sold the mobile home and had to vacate, we had the pleasure of watching Adolph Kunkle build the fireplace. Adolph was a thin, wiry Dutchman in his late sixties and had the reputation of being the best stonemason in Prescott. He used what we called "picture rock", a colorful schist from a quarry east of town. Pete loved to tell people that she had helped build the fireplace because she frequently reminded him to "put the pretty side up, Adolph." When it was finished it was, as Pete said, "A thing of beauty and a joy forever."

Adolph's wife, Mary, a slender attractive woman with white hair, sometimes came along with him, and she and Pete would spend most of the day crocheting and discussing various patterns, a subject about which I knew less than nothing. Adolph and Mary had traveled quite a bit, in most of the western states and had interesting stories to tell about their experiences.

We bought a piano and Pete taught herself to play by ear and note and before long was sounding quite professional playing popular music and some classical. She had a natural talent for it. I spent a lot of time working in the yard building a rock wall and making some effort to landscape the place.

There were a few rabbits and squirrels around and we kept them happy with vegetable scraps. Every night a mama skunk came with her two babies to a spot underneath the balcony to eat the pieces of meat we dropped over the railing. One early morning I opened the front door to find her sitting on the porch as if she belonged there. She seemed to sense that we meant her no harm.

It was a great place to live and we would have been happy to stay there permanently except for two drawbacks, the most immediate one being the water supply. All of the houses in the Dells were supplied from a community well, and during the first year there was no problem. Then the pump began periodically breaking down and sometimes we were without water for three or four days while repairs were made. Twice the main pipe rusted out and had to be dug up and replaced, which took even longer. Often when we did get water it was so muddy as to be unusable.

We stuck it out through the second year and might have stayed, assuming that the situation would be resolved eventually, but there was another problem. When we first moved to The Dells there was only one other house on our hill, but now lots were being sold all over the place and before long we would be hemmed in by houses, some of which would inevitably contain dogs and cats to frighten away our precious wild life. That and the thought of a dozen or so neighbors converging around our little quarter acre was enough to make us decide to move. Adolph kidded us about it. He said to Mary, "When Dot and Pete can see the smoke from someone else's chimney they figure the place is getting too crowded and they move on."

We anticipated some trouble in selling the place because of the water situation, and several lookers did turn it down on that account, but Jim and Barbara Moriarty, a young couple with two small children, were so smitten with the house that they discounted the problem. Jim was on the police force in Prescott and had left New Jersey because he said he couldn't stand the graft and corruption there.

"The people who manage this development are getting a lot of static from the County about that well, and either they get it squared away or they'll be forced to put in a new pump and all new pipes."

The second time they came back to look at the house we were all standing on the patio admiring the view, when Barbara noticed Oscar, our pet spider. She recoiled in horror. He was unusually large, as spiders go, and had built a web just outside the kitchen window. Since he never bothered us we never bothered him, and we found it interesting to watch him sitting in the middle of his web surveying his domain.

"We've decided to buy the house," Barbara said, "but only if you get rid of that awful spider."

"There's no way I could kill Oscar, but I'll move him way off down the hill far away from the house," I promised.

"When you get him down there, turn him around two or three times so he won't know the way back!"

I got Oscar on a stick, took him down the hill and across the road, and deposited him on a bush, hoping he would be able to rebuild and be happy.

Chapter 33

While exploring on the outskirts of Prescott we had come across a place that was made to order for us. It was eleven acres covered with scattered pine trees and many of those gorgeous boulders that we loved so much. It was in the foothills, four miles on a dirt road from the little town of Chino Valley. There were four houses in the area, the nearest about a half mile away, while farther on around the road, on the other side of a hill, were three houses. There was a hundred mile view. On a clear day, which most days were, we could see the snow covered San Francisco Peaks beyond Flagstaff.

Considering the beauty and the privacy of the place, the fact that no electricity was available was only a minor inconvenience, and since the man who sold us the property assured us that electricity would be there within a year, we had a well dug, put in a septic tank, and bought a large double-wide mobile home at a bargain price because it was slightly used. We had it set up flush with the ground above a foundation thus creating an enormous crawl space underneath, which Pete suggested would make a dandy air raid shelter in case we ever needed one.

A large room added on the front of the house, enclosing the well, gave the place an "L" shape, with a twenty-foot long front patio. When this was roofed over with natural log posts as uprights the place no longer resembled a mobile home. It looked like a ranch house.

Pete wanted the patio paved with picture rock, and although I had no experience, I had learned a little from watching Adolph so I undertook the job myself. Before I was half-finished a bird built a nest under the patio roof and in it laid three tiny eggs. Then every time I went to work she flew away and would not come back while I was there. We simply could not bear the thought of those eggs getting cold, so I suspended operations until the eggs hatched and the birds were big enough to fly. Then I went back to work and finished my rock-laying job. It was a long way from being perfect, but it didn't look too bad considering it had been done by a rank amateur.

Although we had talked about giving the place a name, so far we had come up with nothing we really liked. One day Pete said, "Speaking of names, it should be something that means it's a long way from town."

"Where I grew up in Oklahoma they would say, 'It's plumb out of town.'"

"It's not only plumb out of town, as you call it, it's also nearly out of the country."

"That's it! Take those two words, plumb and nearly, shorten them and you've got Plum Nelly. How's that for a name?"

"It's great. I like it. That's what we'll call it."

Pete and Dot at Plum Nelly

Ann brought us a sign with the words "Plum Nelly" carved on a slab of wood and we hung it on a tree near the end of the driveway.

It was November when we moved to Plum Nelly, and for the first two weeks we nearly froze to death trying to keep warm with a small kerosene heater. Every morning I got up early and drove to Prescott to look for a wood stove, but that year there was a rumor going around about a possible shortage of gas for heating so everyone was buying wood stoves. New ones were not to be had at all and even used ones were almost impossible to come by. Finally in a second-hand store I found an old Ben Franklin stove that someone had just brought in that morning and I bought it just ahead of two other people who were looking. Had I been five minutes later I would have missed it.

Had we been able to see into the future we would no doubt have invested in an electric generator in order to get water from the well, but it was an expensive and complicated procedure and we saw no point in it when we confidently expected to have electricity in a year or less. Instead, we had a company in Prescott bring out a large water tank and put it on a small rise behind the house. Then I ran the garden hose from the tank to the back porch where I filled thirty plastic milk jugs at a time and stored them in a large cupboard in the kitchen.

We kept a twenty-gallon can of water in the bathroom, and in order to flush the toilet one needed only to pour in a fast bucket of water. We couldn't take showers, of course, but fortunately Jean was living in Chino Valley then, and once a week we went to her house and took showers. The rest of the time we managed very nicely with "spit" baths.

For cooking and heating water we used a small two-burner stove that ran on butane cartridges. A funny thing happened once when we ran out of cartridges. It was a cold night, and knowing that Pete would enjoy a bowl of hot soup, I came up with what I thought was a great idea. I put a can of vegetable soup on the coals in the fireplace, and when I judged that it was hot enough I carried it with a pair of tongs to the kitchen and applied the can opener. Instantly the can exploded, and with a great hissing and roaring, spewed vegetables all over the walls and ceiling. It was an experience in learning the hard way!

We had no telephone, of course, but Orris rigged up a C.B. at our house and one at Jean's and that worked fine for a couple of years until so many people got them that all we could get on ours was static and other people talking, so we finally gave up on that!

Lights were no problem at all; we did quite well without any. A friend brought us a kerosene lamp, and we had a gasoline lantern, but we never used them except when we had company. Flashlights were all we needed to find our way to bed. Occasionally we would light a candle, but most evenings we spent sitting on the couch facing the two big picture windows looking out at the stars and watching for U.F.O.'s. Often we saw strange looking lights traveling across the sky, but we realized they could probably be explained as satellites, weather balloons or whatever.

However, we did see two things that could in no way be considered man made. The first one was low enough so that we could see it was some sort of craft with lights at both ends. We assumed it was a plane until it stopped in midair for a few seconds, then flew straight back, stopped and went forward again. It did not turn, because the lights were different colors and they never changed position. We knew then it was not a plane because even as I write this in 1991, planes have not yet learned the trick of flying backwards. And there was no way it could be a helicopter since it was completely silent. After making six trips back and forth it went off towards Prescott. We were so disappointed that it didn't land. It could have easily enough, as there was plenty of parking space at Plum Nelly.

Our policeman friend, Jim Moriarty, told us later that a patrolman had called in that night reporting a strange craft in the sky.

Jim said, "Then we lost contact with him for quite awhile, and we thought maybe the little green men from Mars had picked him up. When he finally did call in he said he was so dumfounded watching the weird maneuvers the thing was making that he forgot to push the button."

One night several months later we watched what we again thought was an ordinary plane coming toward us out of the east. It was flying fairly low, and as it got closer we could see that it was enormous, much larger than any jet plane we had ever seen. It was literally covered with lights of several different colors. When it was within a few hundred feet of the house it turned and disappeared behind the mountain.

"Let's go out on the back porch and watch," Pete suggested. "Maybe it will come back."

It came back, all right, and nearly scared us to death. Out from behind the mountain it came, and straight toward us, flying so low that we thought it would surely slam into the house. Fortunately for us, it didn't, but it went directly over the house, just above the treetops, and we realized then that it wasn't making a sound. If we had not been watching it, we wouldn't have known it was there. Our families were not too impressed when we told them about our U.F.O.'s. Although they liked us fine, most of them thought we were a bit nutty. We got the same reaction when we told them about the ghost who lived with us at Plum Nelly.

He was a friendly ghost, never did any harm, and we grew quite fond of him. We named him Casper. We first began to realize he was there when we heard a horse galloping around the house. When we ran outside we found no horse anywhere in sight. This happened frequently. Casper played all kinds of tricks, such as moving things around from one place to another, things that we knew beyond all doubt we had not moved ourselves. Once when the water storage tank was empty, it filled all by itself without the generator being turned on, a quite impossible feat.

But the strangest, most inexplicable event occurred when one night I crawled into bed and discovered the bottom sheet near the foot of the bed was wet. I leaped out of bed and yelled, "I don't believe it!" and Pete and Bunny, who was visiting, came in to see what it was all about. It couldn't have been from a leaking roof, as it hadn't rained for weeks, and anyway, the spread, blanket and top sheet were not wet, only the bottom sheet, in a circle about three feet in diameter. It wasn't water, anyway, because in about five minutes, while we stood there feeling it and wondering how it could have happened, it dried up completely. I don't know what it was, but there was absolutely no logical explanation. It had to have been Casper. If there had ever been any slight doubt in our minds about having a ghost, there was none now.

Because we were close to the mountains there was an abundance of wild life at Plum Nelly. I built a fairly large cement pond and it attracted animals from miles around. There were deer, coyotes, foxes, rabbits, squirrels and at least a dozen kinds of birds. Once a cougar appeared, drank an amazing amount of water, explored around the house, then ambled off toward the mountains. There were lots of roadrunners and quail too. Every June the baby quail appeared strung out in a long line behind the papa and mama. While the papa quail perched on a high rock acting as lookout, the babies lined up on the rim of the pool and drank, their little heads going up and down like piano keys. We never missed TV. We had a much better show just outside the window.

There were skunks at Plum Nelly, too, as we discovered when I woke up once in the middle of the night and felt something nuzzling my ear. Thinking it was a mouse, I jumped up and grabbed the flashlight, but saw nothing on the bed. Then I looked under the bed and there sat a beautiful baby skunk. When I shone the light on him he came out, went down the hall and made a tour of the house paying no attention to me. He went into what we called the jungle room, sniffed at the plants that Pete had growing there and then disappeared down one of the heat vents in the living room. The cover wasn't fastened down and the skunk had pushed it off.

I put some heavy rocks on the vent, but the next night he came in again through a different vent and got in bed with Pete. One night a squirrel got in and ate a hundred vitamin C tablets. There must have been a hole in the pipe that was normally supposed to bring us heat instead of animals. We were quite fond of all the little creatures, but since it was not really a good idea to have them in the house with us, I battened down all the vent-covers and we had no more midnight visitors.

One day we heard knocking at the back door and discovered a road-runner pecking away at his reflection in the glass. No doubt he thought he was looking at another road-runner. For several weeks he showed up every day, spent an hour or more trying to get at the other bird, and was not bothered in the least when he saw us standing there watching him. We named him Narcissus because he loved looking at himself in the glass.

Then one afternoon when I found blood and feathers on the back porch I knew that some animal had killed Narcissus. I was heartsick about it, but I said nothing to Pete. I just let her assume that he had tired of the game and had found other diversions.

Plum Nelly was a great vacation spot, so we had lots of company. One year we counted twelve groups. No one seemed to mind the inconveniences and everyone pitched in and helped haul water and split wood. The hardier ones hiked to the top of the steep hillside to see the bat caves, and everyone went to the Indian ruins which were on top of a steep hill a couple of miles from the house. Because Pete was unable to climb now, she had never seen the Indian ruins until Dave, one of Ann's and Orris' sons, took her in his jeep up a dirt road to the top of a high hill where she could look down on them.

When we had been at Plum Nelly two years and there was still no electricity, and no hope for it in the foreseeable future, we invested in a butane generator to operate the well, had the water tank removed and took the can and bucket out of the bathroom. It was quite a luxury to have running water even though it was cold.

But Pete was after more creature comforts. "Now that we have a generator, what do you think about getting a gas water heater so we can have hot water?"

"I think it is definitely the way to go. It sure would be nice to take showers."

"And we could sell the electric stove and get one that runs on butane."

"Why not? It would just mean running about fifty feet of gas pipe under the house and that's no big deal. And just think, when we get all this done we'll be about three-fourths civilized.

Plum Nelly had everything anyone could want, including an old dead tree. At least fifty feet tall, its branches twisted into weird shapes, it stood all by itself in lonely grandeur not far from the house. Although to most people a dead tree is strictly for burning, to us it was magnificent and we loved it. When a neighbor offered to cut it down and chop it up for firewood, we were horrified.

"No way!" Pete cried. "We would freeze to death before we'd allow anyone to cut down that gorgeous tree!"

Dot Near the Old Dead Tree

Every morning at sunrise two ravens perched on the topmost branch of the old dead tree and sat there for some time surveying their kingdom. We called them Romeo and Juliet. In the spring they used the tree as a launch pad for teaching their babies to fly. The little ones would fly a short distance, then rest for awhile on the mother's back before taking off again. Soon they would become more daring, flying longer distances, and within a short time they would be on their own.

Adolph and Mary came to see us frequently. Mary was a great cook and they usually brought along one of her homemade pies. Having been badly bitten by the horseracing bug, they often went to Turf Paradise in Phoenix. They wanted us to go along but we constantly turned them down, explaining that we were "Horse-Aholics" and dared not go near a racetrack, even once, lest we be hooked again.

Over the years we had dabbled at horse playing now and then with no luck. We never lost much because we never bet much, but I had spent innumerable hours pouring over racing forms trying to come up with a system and had finally come to the sad conclusion that what we had heard all along was true. "You can't beat the ponies." For seven years in Sedalia we had been only fourteen miles from a racetrack and had never been tempted to go. Although there was horse racing in Prescott during the summer, we were barely aware of the fact and had no desire to get involved. We were cured, we thought.

Then one day, in what must have been a very weak moment, we agreed to go to the races with Adolph and Mary. We were like the alcoholic who says, "I'll just have this one drink. It can't do any harm as long as I don't have any more." For the first four races Pete and I made no bets. We had no system, no plan of attack. We couldn't just play a horse because his name appealed to us, or play the top jockey as many people do. I had long ago discovered that on the list of important factors the jockey is near the bottom, but I also knew that the odds changes are near the top of that list. During the fifth race, just for something to do, I began watching the big board where the odds change every minute. I wrote them down on my program.

Noticing that the odds on a horse named Fleet Marie suddenly dropped from 47 to 15, then immediately went back up to 25 and continued to climb. I said to Pete, "Hey, look, here's one of those 'big drops', as you call them. Shall we take a chance on it?

"Sure, let's bet two dollars to win on it."

Fleet Marie placed by a nose in a photo finish so we were out two bucks, but it was close. In the very next race there was another big drop and this time we bet it to win and to place. It won and suddenly we were sixty dollars ahead of the game. Since the last four races had no big drops we made no more bets that day.

Had we gone home losers that day that might have been the end of it, but we went home with a profit so we were off and running. After that we drove the hundred miles to Turf Paradise in Phoenix two or three times a week to try our luck. By the end of the racing season we had barely broken even, but considering the overhead, admission, parking, racing forms, programs and gas, we were in the hole. That bothered us very little. Reminding ourselves that we spent no money in restaurants or movies, and that what few clothes we needed and all of our books we bought at garage sales, thrift shops and the flea market for practically nothing, we marked it up to entertainment with a clear conscience.

The important thing was that we had played the horses all those days without losing any money on bets. It was enough to spur me on to further efforts. "I think the answer is to combine handicapping and odds," I told Pete. "What we should do, I believe, is to pick out the two or three horses in each race that have the best chance on class, speed and distance, then watch the odds to see which horse the "smart money" is on, and play all four or five of them in the exactas. That's where the big money is."

I spent a lot of hours studying the racing forms in preparation for the big killing we expected to make the next winter. In the meantime we were faced with a more immediate problem. We had lived at Plum Nelly for five years and had enjoyed every minute of it, but the possibility of getting a telephone, which was now far more important than electricity, seemed as remote as ever and we realized that we no longer had a choice. We would have to move back to Prescott.

When we first began having trouble with the C.B. I had taught Pete to drive well enough that in case something happened to me she could go, at the breakneck speed of ten or fifteen miles an hour, to the nearest neighbor. Now we had to give up that plan because during the past few months it had become almost impossible for her to lift her foot high enough to step on the brake. Even though I was a "tough old broad", I could still break a leg, have a heart attack or even a stroke, Pete would be unable to go for help and it might be days before anyone came out there.

Although we felt quite sad about leaving the place we loved so much, it was the only sensible thing to do. We sold Plum Nelly for quite a bit more than we had put into it, but we didn't get cash, just a down payment. Now we had two choices. We could spend a lot of money for a nice large place, or we could settle for a small cheap place and have a fair-sized backlog. We opted for a very small, very cheap place in a mobile home park in Prescott. Since we couldn't stay at Plum Nelly, we really didn't care much where we lived.

SEEDS

THE OLD DEAD TREE AT PLUM NELLY
by Marguerite "Pete" Williams

The old dead tree, gaunt and bare,
Her storm raped body, she still defends.
With pallid arms stretched to the air
She rips the gale that still descends.

When twilight falls and evening lingers,
In memory of the "Lost Lenore",
Poe's ravens, on her brittle fingers,
Perch and mumble, "Nevermore".

Stripped of bark and bare of leaf,
Deprived of growth, deprived of bloom,
Robbed of Life by the stormy thief,
She stands a phantom on her tomb.

Chapter 34

When we had been there only a couple of months, Dick, who did not approve of our lifestyle, bought a beautiful house on a hill in an exclusive area called Wildwood Estates. We sold the trailer and moved again. Dick named the place for us suggesting that since so many doctors lived in the area we should call it Pill Hill. We liked the name. It was both humorous and appropriate, and soon everyone in the family was calling it Pill Hill.

Our love affair with the horses was still at fever pitch. The following winter we spent several months in a rented trailer in Phoenix playing the horses five days a week, but it rained a lot that year and the track was muddy more often than not. Since I had not yet learned how to cope with off tracks, we didn't do too well. However, we did come out with a small profit, although it did not cover the overhead. But the important thing was that we had made a profit, however small, and that fact spurred us on. I was convinced that with a few hundred more hours of study I could perfect the system. Also, it gave us something to do.

Pete and I had not lived what, by any stretch of the imagination could be called a "normal" life. During the almost thirty years we had been together we had experienced many strange and exciting adventures and had met a lot of "characters" who, though sometimes a bit weird, were always interesting. Now here we were in Dick's plush house, surrounded by luxury and with nothing to do. Often we were invited to the women's "coffee klatches" but we always politely declined, explaining that Pete was too crippled to climb steps. She wasn't, if there was a railing, but it was a good excuse. Nothing was more boring to us than sitting around listening to a bunch of women yak about recipes, clothes, husbands, and housekeeping, in none of which we had the slightest interest. Fortunately our families approved of our addiction to horse racing. Not that we would have given it up, in any case, but it was nice to have their approval. As Ann once jokingly remarked, "It keeps you off the streets."

The next winter we bought a mobile home in a very nice park in Phoenix, just three miles from the racetrack, and thereafter spent the winters there and the summers at Pill Hill. The park had a large clubhouse where dances were held on Saturday nights and Bingo games once a week. There was also a swimming pool that was heated year round, and that was great for Pete. We bought her a small electric scooter, and every day she would zip up the street to the pool and swim, in an effort to strengthen her muscles.

One day Dick and his friend, Jerry Englert, came driving up to our little place in a long limousine that they had rented at the airport. They wanted us to go down to the stables with them to look at a horse. We wondered why, since we knew absolutely nothing about horses except how to bet them, but we assumed since they already owned several racehorses that this was one they had bought or were planning to buy and they wanted to show him off.

At the stables they showed us a beautiful dark brown four-year-old gelding. "Are you guys thinking of buying him?" I asked.

"We already bought him," Dick said. "What do you think of him?"

"He's gorgeous." Pete was petting the horse. "What's his name?"

"Lotta Fleet."

"How about that!" Pete exclaimed. "Lotta Fleet. It rhymes with Dot and Pete. What a coincidence!"

"It's an especially lucky coincidence," Jerry handed me some papers, "because he belongs to you and Pete. Dick and I bought him for you."

"Jerry and I were sitting in a bar one night," Dick said, "and we got to talking about you two and we decided that since you're so crazy about horses you should have one. He's a good horse, very fast and should win a lot of races for you."

Pete and I were too stunned for words. In our wildest imaginings we had never dreamed of owning a racehorse. Now we actually had one, and he would soon be racing right there at Turf Paradise. What a thrill! We went to see Lotta Fleet almost every day, fed him carrots, which he loved, and before long we felt that he recognized us. We offered him apples, but he didn't like those at all. He would take a piece of apple in his mouth, then drop it on the ground and look at us as if to say, "Hey, how about some carrots?"

Dot and Lotta Fleet

Within a week the trainer entered Lotta Fleet in a $12,500 claiming race. We didn't think he had a chance, as horses seldom win their first race after being moved to a new track, but just as a sentimental gesture, we put twenty to win on him. Much to our amazement and delight, he won by three lengths. We had our pictures taken with him in the winner's circle and sent video tapes to Dick and Jerry so they could watch the running of the race on TV.

Lotta Fleet Winning the Easter Bunny Purse

Lotta Fleet in the Winners Circle
Phoenix, Arizona April 22, 1984

Ten days later Lotta Fleet won a $15,000 claimer, and from then on we wouldn't consider entering him in a claiming race for fear of losing him. Before the season ended a month later, he won an allowance race and placed in a Handicap, losing by only a head. What a horse!

Ann, Bunny, Dot and Dick at the Track

Both Dick and the trainer thought it would be a good idea to take Lotta Fleet to Prescott for the summer and though we felt a bit uneasy about it we went along with the plan. Prescott Downs was a half-mile track with sharp turns and a record of frequent accidents, but since Lotta Fleet was always out in front of the pack it was unlikely that he would become involved in any pile-ups.

Pete often called Prescott Downs a half-ass racetrack, and it was an apt description. It was almost a hundred years old and the enormous barn-like grandstand was in a sad state of repair. The roof leaked more than a little, and whenever it rained, which happened frequently since the races were held during the "monsoon season", people scrambled about trying to find dry places to stand. At our table, which we shared with Adolph and Mary, we used stacks of paper napkins to catch the drips to keep our racing forms from getting wet. When an especially hard rain came, the ramp leading down from the main entrance became a small river and only the other entrance at the far end of the building was usable. But since neither rain, nor hail nor snow will deter the inveterate horse player, there was usually a good crowd.

I had an unforgettable experience one rainy afternoon. Since Pete had not come along that day I decided to park in the infield, which meant I would have to walk quite a distance, then across the track and up two long flights of steps. I needed the exercise. When I drove through the short tunnel and up the incline on the other side the sun was shining and there wasn't a cloud in the sky. The races had been going on for a couple of hours before a few clouds began to gather. Across from the grandstand on the roof of the paddock building, jockeys who were not riding in the next race sat on benches watching the action and enjoying the sunshine.

Then storm clouds came rolling in accompanied by thunder and lightening, and it rained steadily the rest of the afternoon. The track changed from fast to sloppy and after each race jockeys and horses came back plastered with mud. During the last race the rain suddenly came down like a cloudburst and continued for twenty minutes keeping the people trapped in the building unable to leave. Then, just as suddenly, the rain stopped and the sun came out.

Since the track was now a sea of mud no one was permitted to take that route back to the infield. Those who had parked there had to take the long way around through the tunnel, which was discovered, to everyone's dismay, to contain about four feet of water. There was a narrow walkway along one side where the water was only about three inches deep, and there was no other way to get back to our cars, we all took off our shoes and socks, rolled up our pant legs and started across, single file. When I was about halfway across a car came barreling through the tunnel at a fast clip, driven by a young man who mistakenly thought speed would get him through, and we were slapped with a tidal wave of cold, muddy water. Of course, his engine flooded out and he had to sit there, the butt of some pretty foul language until a truck came to push him out.

When we reached the end of the runway we had to wade through quite a stretch of knee-deep water to reach the muddy incline. When I finally arrived back at my car I was wet, cold, and mad. As I drove through another tunnel at the other end of the infield, where the water was only about two feet deep, I was fuming and wild ideas of revenge, including suing the owners of the track, went surging through my mind. I hadn't bothered to put on my shoes and socks since they had gotten wet in the tidal wave. I drove home in my bare feet, took a hot shower and hoped I wouldn't get pneumonia.

By the next day I had calmed down, and Pete and I could laugh about it as just another adventure, but I still felt the management should be called on it. When we went to the track that day I sought out the top man. I had learned long ago that when making a complaint it pays to smile and be pleasant. As the saying goes "You can catch more flies with honey than you can with vinegar." Putting on my best smile, I told him all about my experience in the tunnel.

"I really don't think it's fair to charge people to park in the infield without warning them about what happens when it rains."

"We have a pump that's supposed to remove the water."

"It didn't seem to be doing a lot of good yesterday. There was four feet of water in that tunnel."

"Actually, the pump wasn't there yesterday. It's being repaired."

I laughed. "Fat lot of good it does then to have a pump. Anyway, if you did remove the water people would still plow through the mud to get from the end of the walkway to the incline. It seems to me it would make a lot more sense to let them wade across the muddy track." I grinned at him. "If I had caught a bad cold or gotten pneumonia I'd have filed suit against you and would no doubt have won. That's just a little food for thought that you'd do well to pass along to the big shots who own the track."

He looked worried now. "I didn't realize it was that bad."

"Well, now you know. My friends call this a half-ass track, and after my experience in your tunnel I'd say the name surely does fit!"

We both laughed at that, parted amicably, and lo and behold the very next day when there was another downpour a wooden walkway was placed across the track after the last race and no one had to wade through the tunnel. The threat of a lawsuit sometimes works miracles.

One day in August Dick called. "When is Lotta Fleet scheduled to run again?" he asked.

"He's entered in a race this coming Saturday. Why, are you coming up?"

"Yes, Jerry and I will fly up Saturday morning and you can meet us at the airport. But wait at the house. We'll call you from the plane and let you know what time we're landing."

When I told Pete the news, she said, "I wonder what they'll think of Prescott Downs. They're used to tracks like Santa Anita and Del Mar. I think they're in for a shocker."

We all waited at Pill Hill for Dick's call, but it was almost one o'clock when he finally called from the airport. Something had gone wrong with the phone on his plane and he couldn't get through to us. "It's so late now don't bother picking us up. We'll rent a car and drive to the track," he said. "Meet us at the clubhouse entrance."

"What clubhouse? Prescott Downs doesn't have one."

Dick sounded shocked. "What kind of a race track doesn't have a clubhouse?"

"This kind doesn't. We'll meet you at the main entrance."

I had reserved two tables near ours, since Dick had brought along another friend, and his son, Greg, but much to our surprise people were sitting at those tables and we found that a mistake had been made, that our tables had been reserved for Sunday.

"What in the world am I going to do?" I asked the woman in the office. "I have four guests who have flown in from California just to see our horse run and I have no place for them to sit."

"Don't worry," she said, "we'll think of something."

She put us in a box right on the finish line, just about the best seats in the house. Lotta Fleet won, everyone made some money and we all had a wonderful time. After the races we went back to Pill Hill for a buffet supper.

Dick, in the process of building himself a sandwich, grinned at Jerry. "Pete was certainly right when she called that a half-assed racetrack. But after all, its over a hundred years old and its the site of the world's oldest rodeo, a real historical landmark. It was an interesting experience. And wasn't it great to watch Lotta Fleet come tearing down the stretch four lengths ahead?"

Chapter 35

Lotta Fleet won every race he ran at Prescott Downs, except the last, when he suffered an injury to his left leg. We sent him to a place north of Phoenix, hoping the damage could be repaired, unable to believe he had run his last race. A few weeks later we moved to Phoenix for the winter.

We did quite well at Turf Paradise that winter. My system was improving as I learned to ignore most of the information in the Racing Form and concentrate on looking for the "smart money." Most of my evenings were spent making up charts for the next day's races. While I was thus involved Pete wrote poetry, read or played the piano.

In March Pete's niece, Dixie, came for a two-week visit and we were so happy to see her. She went with us to the races, we took her to see Lotta Fleet, and she and Pete spent hours just talking. She might have stayed longer, but her husband had driven out with her and had to get back to work. We were sorry to see her go.

A few days after Dixie left I was working on my charts late one night. It was almost midnight, Pete had been reading in bed, and was about to turn out her light when she called to me from her room.

"Dot, I suddenly feel awful. I seem to be having a bad case of heartburn."

Since Pete often suffered from indigestion I wasn't really worried. I gave her some alka seltzer, which had solved the problem before, but this time it didn't seem to help. When a short time later her entire body turned cold and clammy and she seemed to be having trouble breathing, I felt helpless and frightened and called 911. In a few minutes the medics arrived, said that she had had a massive heart attack, and took her to the hospital. I paced the corridor, hoping against hope, while the doctor worked on Pete. I'm sure he did everything possible, but he was unable to save her. She died at two o'clock that morning.

If I could have cried it might have helped, but because it happened so suddenly, with no warning, I was in a state of shock. It seemed that one minute Pete was with me, as always and the next, she was gone beyond recall. I was unable to cope with the enormity of it. After awhile I went home and just sat at the kitchen table, smoking and staring into space until it began to get light. Then I forced myself to make the necessary phone calls.

When Ann and Dick arrived early that morning they took over, handled everything, and made all of the arrangements. Like a zombie, I simply did as I was told, and I don't believe I could have managed without them.

Bunny came down from Berkeley and we buried Pete's ashes on the desert not far from Plum Nelly, near the Indian ruins. I feel sure that if by chance there is a consciousness after death, Pete approves of the spot we chose. She would also be happy to know that Ann's daughter, Karen, came all the way from Colorado, bringing a bouquet of Pete's favorite wildflowers.

That evening we held a Memorial gathering at Pill Hill, and Ann and Bunny read some of Pete's poetry. Later they had the best bound into a book and we sent copies to all of Pete's many friends and relatives. That was a real and long lasting memorial.

Epilogue—1990

Lotta Fleet never raced again. I sent him to Karen, who wanted him, but who found that what with doing the bookwork for the restaurant that she and her husband, Rick, own in Durango, Colorado, plus having a baby, she had no time for riding. She gave him to a friend who planned to turn him into a show horse. That failed to work out, and he now belongs to a man with three children, who owns a ranch near Durango. It's a comfort to know that Lotta Fleet has a good home.

Several years ago Ann and Orris retired, he as a scientist-engineer at North American Aviation and she as grammar school principal. Now they have moved to Durango, where they have built a beautiful house high on a cliff with a spectacular view of the town and the surrounding mountains.

Ann, Dot and Bunny in Durango

Dick also retired, but finding himself bored soon started another business and went back to work. He is Chairman of the Board at Scripps

Institute, has homes in La Jolla and Palm Springs, and has an office in San Diego where he oversees various business enterprises.

Bunny, who now prefers to be called by her real name, Martha, lives in Berkeley and works for a firm of lawyers. She started as a legal secretary but was recently promoted and is now supervisor of a department. In spite of two divorces and a bout with breast cancer, she is still bubbly and enthusiastic, laughs a lot and makes friends easily. In that way she reminds me of Pete; everybody loves her.

Dick, Dot and Bunny in Berkeley

Plum Nelly no longer exists. Weeds grow on the spot where our house once stood, our rock garden has been destroyed, the wild animals have fled to the hills, and the old dead tree that we loved so much has been cut down. The dirt road that meandered across three miles of open plains, where the deer and the antelope once were, is now infested with dozens of ugly little houses and trailers. The road leading to the Indian ruins where Pete's ashes are buried is no longer passable. It was a sad trip, and I will not travel that road again. I will wipe it from my mind and will picture Plum Nelly as it used to be when Pete and I were so happy there.

I live alone now in a mobile home in Prescott, and spend my time reading, typing, working jigsaw puzzles and playing the horses. I no longer go to Phoenix during the winter as they now have off-track betting here. I do very little housework, just the barest minimum, and most people would not concede that I do even that much. Once a day I turn on the TV and listen to the evening news in order to keep informed of wars, earthquakes, political skullduggery and other catastrophes.

Every summer I go to Prescott Downs on weekends, sharing a table with my friend Adolph, who is really a remarkable old man. He is almost ninety-one now, and since his wife Mary died he has lived alone in the house that he built himself over twenty years ago. It has a beautiful fireplace, faced with stones that he and Mary collected from various western states. He still drives his car, and his hobby is playing the horses.

Although I am quite happy now, and do not in the least mind living alone, I find myself for the first time in my life with no one to take care of, no one to be responsible for, and it has taken a bit of getting used to. Now my children take care of me, a fact that never ceases to amaze me.

Ann is constantly buying me new clothes, in a valiant effort to keep me from looking like a bag lady. All of them worry because I don't eat right and because I smoke too much. Yet I continue to live, as always, mainly on sandwiches, junk food, cokes and cigarettes. I never did learn to care much for vegetables.

I really have tried to quit smoking, but after going through two packs a day for over sixty years, its not easy. And I'm often reminded of that old lady who, at the age of one hundred and five, while being interviewed by a reporter, took a package of cigarettes from her apron pocket and lit one.

The young man was shocked. "Don't you realize that smoking is bad for you?"

"Sonny", she said between puffs. "I've been smokin' for nigh onto a hundred years and I ain't aimin' to quit now."

One little episode that had a happy ending occurred when Ann, during one of her frequent visits, noticed that my feet were swollen. She got uptight about it, called Dick, he came up, and they insisted that I go to a doctor. Since I had been operating successfully for eighty-three years on the theory that if you leave things alone they'll go away I wasn't too crazy about the idea, but I went. They gave me a complete run-down, and found nothing else wrong except for a slight touch of emphysema, which I already knew about, and which was the only reason I had tried to quit smoking. The nurse asked me how long it had been since my last check-up and I told her that I had never had one.

At first she looked shocked, then she grinned and said, "Well, you should have one every eighty years whether you need it or not."

As doctors go, this one was very nice, and it wasn't his fault that I was allergic to the diuretic pills he gave me, which almost killed me. I went back to smoking as much as ever. I figured that since I was going to die anyway, what difference did it make? Then Dick's wife, Alice, sent me a book on herbs. I discovered that parsley capsules act as a diuretic, and that small problem was solved.

Dick and Dot—1990

In looking back over the years I feel that I have had a good life, having been fortunate more often than not. Besides my three children, all of whom are much too good to me considering the mistakes I made along the way, I now have twelve grandchildren and fifteen great grandchildren. And I may even live long enough to become a great, great grandmother.

As Karen says, "If Gramma Dot would only stop smoking she would probably live to be over a hundred."

But I am still a tough old broad, as Ann says, and I go along with George Burns who, when asked how it felt to be eighty-five, replied, "It feels pretty good considering the alternative."

Dorothy Ramsey Cramer Stillman (1907-1996)

SEEDS

LIFE AND DEATH
by Marguerite "Pete" Williams

Stay, oh dawn of the rosy morn
Tarry, early spring.
The child is the heart and vernal chart,
Future's hopeful fling.

We ask a boon of life's high noon,
A little longer remain.
For youth is bold and sets his goal,
On tomorrow's courageous gain.

The shadows sway on evening's day,
Linger, oh twilight, linger.
The elder one in the fading sun,
The curtains of night shall finger.

Abide, abide, ye ebbing tide,
(Alas, the headless ocean).
We cannot stay Life's waterway
Nor force continued motion.

As on earth before our birth
We knew not we were to be,
So now in peace we gain release,
In death we are set free.

Printed in the United States
98890LV00005B/100-114/A